THE
FILMS
OF
ORSON
WELLES

THE FILMS
OF ORSON WELLES

Charles Higham

UNIVERSITY OF CALIFORNIA PRESS
BERKELEY, LOS ANGELES, LONDON 1971

University of California Press

Berkeley and Los Angeles

University of California Press, Ltd.

London, England

Copyright © 1970 by The Regents of

the University of California

First Printing, 1970

Second Printing, 1971

First Paperback Printing, 1971

ISBN: 0-520-01567-3 cloth

0-520-02048-0 paper

Library of Congress Catalog Card Number: 72-92677

Printed in the United States of America

FOR DAVID BRADLEY AND TOM WEBSTER

ACKNOWLEDGMENTS

I am grateful, first of all, to the chancellor and faculty of the University of California, Santa Cruz, and to the Regents of the University, whose offer of a Regents' Professorship made the writing of this book possible; to David Bradley, who lent me his guesthouse and, most indispensably, his telephone during much of my stay in Hollywood; to Bill Collins, who provided me with opportunities to examine Welles's films frame by frame; to Richard Wilson, who filled in many fascinating details and gave me access to his incomparable vault of Wellesiana, devotedly preserved for thirty years, including the complete set of Mercury files; to Joseph Cotten, who lent me his marvelous scrapbooks; to Arthur Knight, who showed me *The Fountain of Youth;* to Nathan Scheinwald for *The Trial,* Philip Jones for *Chimes at Midnight,* Max Nosseck and Altura and Pacific Films for *The Immortal Story;* to Vernon Harbin of RKO-Radio Pictures, for help with musical copyright titles in the *Kane* newsreel. I also owe a debt of a kind to Bernard Herrmann who, after telling me that any interest in *Kane* today was an absurdity, reluctantly informed me that the libretto of his fake opera *Salammbô* sprang from an "obscure work of Racine," thus involving me in days of searching until I found it in Racine's most famous play. I am more properly grateful to Mr. Herrmann (and RKO) for permission to reproduce pages of his scores. It is to Hazel Marshall and Charles West of Paramount that I owe my most extraordinary moment in half a lifetime of film-going: the unreeling on a squeaky Moviola of the fabulous lost footage of *It's All True,* the cinematic equivalent of the treasure of King Solomon's mines or the lost city of the Incas. Others who helped are far too numerous to list, for seemingly half the civilized world has an interest in, and special stories about, Orson Welles. I must, though, thank the following for much that was invaluable: Anne Baxter, Joseph Biroc, William Castle, John Collier, Stanley Cortez, Floyd Crosby, Brainerd Duffield, Alexander Golitzen, Bill Harmon, Viola Lawrence, Milton and Gitta Lubowiski, Russell Metty, Agnes Moorehead, Mark Robson, Karl Struss, Howard Suber, Lurene Tuttle, Harold Wellman, Robert Wise, and Colin Young. I am also particularly indebted to *The New York Times* for much indispensable factual material, and to Herbert Lightman for background on *Lady from Shanghai.*

For illustrations, I am grateful for the cooperation of Altura Films, Joseph Biroc, David Bradley, Brandon Films, Sheila Whitaker and the National Film Archive, Columbia Pictures, Joseph Cotten, Floyd Crosby, George Fanto, Al Gilks, Shifra Haran, Robert Hughes, Arthur Knight, Paramount Pictures, Republic Pictures, Willard Morrison, the Museum of Modern Art, Alex Phillips, RKO, Universal Pictures, and Richard Wilson.

ILLUSTRATIONS

In most instances the content of illustrations will be self-evident by reference to the adjoining text. The following guide covers those few uncaptioned stills where identification may present a problem, or where particular details would seem useful.

AUTHOR'S NOTE

This book is not intended to be a biography of Orson Welles — though a good one is long overdue. Nor does it cover his multifarious activities in theater, radio, television, magic, ballet, and vaudeville, and as an actor in the films of other directors. It concentrates wholly on Welles's films themselves and is intended as a descriptive and critical study of these works, breaking with the format only to provide information about the circumstances of their production. Accounts of events in the films are not intended to be all-inclusive, but rather to illuminate the most dramatically significant scenes. The exception is the treatment of *Citizen Kane;* here, in order to examine the very complex and beautiful structure of the work, I have separated considerations of its narrative patterns and its visual construction.

Accurate credits for Welles films are hard to achieve; those appearing on prints of the films are frequently inadequate. It is a curious part of the Welles puzzle that many significant contributors to a work have gone unacknowledged — Welles's own name appears nowhere on the credits of *Journey into Fear,* at his own wish. The credits as given in this volume result from my attempt to fill such gaps. I apologize to any craftsman whose name may be omitted.

Since the first edition of this book appeared, supposed inaccuracies in the text have been alleged by Peter Bogdanovich in the *New York Times* and by Richard Wilson in *Sight and Sound.* (Bogdanovich is the co-author, with Welles, of a forthcoming book, and Wilson was Welles's assistant for many years.) I have carefully considered their charges, and have rejected them; this new edition contains no significant alterations. As for their implication that I have injured Orson Welles's professional opportunities by the tone and matter of this book, let posterity be the judge.

CHARLES HIGHAM

Sydney-Los Angeles-Santa Cruz-
San Francisco-Los Angeles-Sydney-
Los Angeles: 1967-1971

CONTENTS

1. THE MAN, THE BEGINNINGS

How utterly American a phenomenon is Orson Welles! Able to work at his best only under ferocious pressures, with half a dozen projects in action at once, driven by a daemonic energy, excessively violent in his loves and hates, massively humanist yet capable of absorbing every ounce of his colleagues' personalities into his own consuming ego, undisciplined, extravagant, perennially adolescent, an artist possessed — he has swept through every aspect of the entertaining arts: he has been a magician, a circus clown, an impresario of music, an entrepreneur, producer, director, and editor of films and television shows, master of radio drama and documentary, and creator of the most staggering and disastrous stage productions in American theatrical history. His personality as an artist is on the scale of a Hugo, a Balzac: he is expansive, grand, capricious, sometimes gross in his style; maddeningly prone to dissipate his energies; baroque and Gothic by turns; romantic, journalistic, slapdash, and brilliant. *Citizen Kane* remains his masterpiece, as the world has said; but many who thought his a tragedy without a third act, a story of a genius burned out, have been proven wrong. In *Chimes at Midnight* — that tender elegy to the vanished past of England, echoing in its mood the lovely valedictory of *The Magnificent Ambersons* for the vanished past of America — and more recently in *The Immortal Story* — a reflection on the tragedy of old age — the most durable aspect of this prismatic artist was shown at its best: a contemplative aspect, a calm, autumnal quietness in contrast with the sounding brass of so much of *Kane, The Lady from Shanghai,* and *Touch of Evil.*

Welles's films often display a reckless sophomoric humor: the Disneyesque parody of nineteenth-century fashions in the first reel of *Ambersons,* the treatment of the stupid deposed newspaper editor Carter and the burlesque politics in *Kane,* the travesty of California law procedure in the courtroom scene in *The Lady From Shanghai,* the scenes between Susan Vargas and the elder Grandi in *Touch of Evil,* the dreadful facetious passages in *Mr. Arkadin.* Humor of a gently destructive, playful, sometimes shoddy kind has flashed through film after film, like the sound of Welles himself laughing in great arched caves.

An inflated display of visual and aural effects often works through the sheer accumulation of grotesque detail: in many of Welles's works we have the sensation of rushing in a ghost train through a plaster fun-fair labyrinth, surrounded by screaming and clutching bone figures. We are like Michael, the sailor in *Lady from Shanghai,* sent hurtling through the mouths of gross distorted papier-mâché figures to arrive at the shocked contemplation of our own face in multiple in a bizarre hall of mirrors.

Most of Welles's images and sounds reflect the destructive element of the grotesque. The smashing, rending, tearing sounds on his tracks, and the trick he has of closing in on a face to show its blotched, spotted, moral and physical decay, reflect an obsession with violence and barbarism. In his films the faces of the aged are observed with a horror at corruption: they have no beauty, none of that fine, pure line which time brings to some faces. In *Lady from Shanghai,* especially, the faces

1

have a nightmare brutality and ugliness: the first shot of the lawyer Arthur Bannister shows him with freckled, spotted hoods over eyes filled with despair, mouth as thin as a turtle's, skin splotched of a fungus; the body, twisted and shattered, crawls like a spider's. His partner, Grisby, forever sweats and leers, eyes peering murderously or furtively out of dewed and flabby flesh. Mrs. Bannister, as played by Rita Hayworth, has the silvery quality of decay, her skin and teeth glittering like ice, her eyes dead under the narrow furrowed brow. Even the minor characters — the old ladies who spy on the young lovers in the San Francisco Aquarium, the raw hillbilly sailors on the cruise — look stunted and distorted. Welles has a marvelous eye for the grotesque American face — and voice: the shrill "I just want to look at her!" of the old schoolteacher at the trial, the giggling and sniggering of Grisby.

Even in a film on which Welles was simply working in a supervisory capacity, his personality flashes through. I have it on the authority of Agnes Moorehead, who played Jane's aunt very much along the lines of her Aunt Fanny in *The Magnificent Ambersons,* that Welles's presiding genius was present throughout the shooting of Robert Stevenson's *Jane Eyre* (1943), in which he played Edward Rochester. By the lowering iron gates of Thornfield that introduce the work, we are reminded of *Kane;* by the lushly gloomy introduction of Aunt Reed and the fat boy gobbling sweets, we are reminded of *Ambersons.* Jane packed off to boarding school, the tramping of the children round the schoolyard in the rain, carrying the irons, Welles's first appearance as Rochester, riding with bat-winged cloak out of the fog on the lonely moor, the cry "Jane! Jane!" echoing through the house when the governess goes to revisit her dying aunt — these are unmistakably Wellesian in their sumptuous or delightfully austere physical detail. And so, above all, are the Gothic scenes involving the mad wife from Jamaica, the crazed maid appearing around corners with guttering candles; the claw hands of the incarcerated woman shadowed on the wall when Rochester flings open the door of the cell and shows the maniac to his kindred on his wedding day.

Yet through the humor and the mad imagery, through the stillness or the hurdy-gurdy din of the master's films, one unmistakable thread may be traced: his passionate, magnificent love of life and of human beings. There isn't a single vicious streak in his work: even Bannister, the spidery evil lawyer of *Lady from Shanghai,* is judged with strict fairness. Welles's warmth and radiant kindness, his sheer generosity, suffuse every frame of his films. His message is clear, and is greeted with enthusiasm by the young even today, in the age of Godard and Antonioni: the corrupt destroy themselves, and riches and power utterly corrupt.

Charles Foster Kane was wrecked by his inability to love, his belief that everything could be bought and absorbed into himself, even his wife. At the end, he is left remembering only Rosebud, the sled that represented the purity, the snow cleansed innocence of his childhood, before he knew wealth and fame. *Ambersons* shows us how the machine age wrecked a whole world's innocence, and once again the snow, lovely on the eaves of the Amberson house early in the film, becomes a symbol of lost purity. In *The Stranger* we are made aware that the innocent housewife, Mary Longstreet, in the last analysis has a greater strength than her husband, the former concentration camp commander Franz Kindler: here, the contrast between the haunted, "black" figure of Kindler and the pretty, quiet Connecticut town in which he has taken refuge could not be more meaningfully drawn. Power destroys Macbeth and Othello and the Bannisters of *Lady from Shanghai,* while Michael in the latter film is free at the end to rediscover the clean life of the sea. And in *Chimes at Midnight,* that lament, that marvelous echoing sigh, we see Henry IV weighed down and crushed by his crown, while in the nearby inn the good and simple led by Falstaff know a fleeting but real happiness.

Welles's drawing of character has the bold strokes of a caricaturist. His method with actors is reflected in their mannered, edgy playing; he drives them on and on, bullying, coaxing, wheedling as theatrically as any stage producer in a thirties Hollywood musical. His own performances — of Kane, of the sailor in *Lady from*

Shanghai, of Franz Kindler, of Hank Quinlan the gross sheriff of *Touch of Evil,* of Macbeth, Othello, Falstaff, and Mr. Clay in *The Immortal Story* — are vivid sketches of personalities ideally suited to the cinema. Welles's chief weakness as an actor is that he plays almost every part at the same volume — fortissimo — just as his chief weakness as an artist is that in his vision a single lamp blazes with the dramatic intensity of a Turner sunset.

Technically, Welles's films have a remarkable sophistication. In *Kane* his style was at its most dynamic: the boldness of the compositions and the daring use of light and shadow were designed to hypnotize the audience much as a magician might hypnotize a crowd with patter while producing fifty pink rabbits from a hat. Here, Gregg Toland's 24mm wide-angle lenses, stopped down to achieve deep focus, with every shot photographed on Super-XX film, gave the effect of moving three-dimensional pictures capturing seventy-eight years of America's past.

The Magnificent Ambersons, photographed by that supreme master of light Stanley Cortez, was more richly rewarding in style, based on Currier and Ives and other American sophisticated primitives. Welles was impatient with Cortez, preferring the quick, slashing approach of a Harry J. Wild or a Gregg Toland; yet the slow, careful artist we see in this film is in many ways the finest Welles has collaborated with. Cortez's images will stay with us forever: the network of shadow that shrouds Isabel Amberson's face as she waits for extinction on a white pillow, the close-up of Agnes Moorehead's anguished face as she weeps in pain at Isabel's death, at the loss of the beautiful past.

Alas, Welles was never to work with artists of quite this caliber again. But variable as it is, *The Lady from Shanghai* is splendidly done, Karl Struss ingeniously shot *Journey into Fear,* and in *The Stranger* and *Touch of Evil* Russell Metty, master of low key and high key, expert if unimaginative craftsman, gave much of what Welles needed.

Aurally, the American films are as exciting as they are visually captivating. The tracks leap and fizz like loose electric wires, full of screams, shouts, hisses, and explosions of music, designed by a man in love with sound. *Citizen Kane* begins beautifully with Bernard Herrmann's menacing chords and the voice of the dying man, whispering in an echo chamber; later, footsteps ring coldly on stone, a brass band blares in a party scene, and the voices of Kane's associates filter back through time at different levels as though heard down an infinite corridor.

In *Lady from Shanghai* Heinz Roemheld's arrangements of Latin American themes during the cruise counterpoint the endlessly bickering, squabbling passengers' voices. The introduction to the cruise is beautifully scored and mixed: a harsh series of chords, and the yapping of a pet dachshund, the newly arrived sailor and the wife of the yacht's owner softly breathing an exchange that hints at their developing attraction. For the beach picnic Roemheld uses a woodwind version of a pop song ("Baia") to introduce a party whose gay surface barely hides the misery of those taking part in it. The trial scene is brilliantly recorded: the sniffing, coughing, screaming, and shouting give one the impression of listening to a tape recording made in a cage full of predatory birds. But the film's finest use of sound — and I have not forgotten the splendid splintering of glass and rattle of shots in the final showdown in a hall of mirrors — comes in a sequence set in Acapulco. The wife races in terror down a long colonnade; her white dress flashes through black pillars in the darkness; a male chorus sings a frantic Latin American melody ("Ero"), and there is a rapidly accelerating rattle of drums, followed by two harsh and eerie chords from the brass section.

Touch of Evil offers an almost equal amount of aural pleasure. In the opening scene, Henry Mancini's drums tap-tap in an ironic musical echo of the time bomb almost nobody can hear ticking in the back of the doomed politician's roadster. Later, the characteristically feral squabbles echo and re-echo in the various stone rooms of the film; in the scenes when Susan Vargas is raped and pumped full of drugs in a motel, Welles once again uses a radio, this time blaring a savage example of early rock 'n' roll. And amid the brass notes and ticking, tapping emphases of Henry Mancini's score there is a splendid range of voices, from the shrill, edged charm of Janet Leigh and the low, sinister whispers through the motel walls of the predatory gang boy, to Marlene Dietrich's turtledove sigh and Welles's oceanic thunder.

Outside America Welles has not been able to control the aural aspects of his work. His habit of using his own voice to double for others' is a maddening one, learned in the cheeseparing days of radio. He cannot face dubbing and looping sessions, and even dodged much of the all-important post-recording that followed the disastrous completion of *Macbeth*. It is a wild impatience that has crippled him here; but he is also victim of a mystifying deafness to the way an audience *hears* a film. He evidently is indifferent to the way the sound track affects others when it is recorded. Perhaps the chief reason for his failure with the masses is that he has never quite calculated how an audience *sees* a picture — seeing it only, as it were, with his inner eye. Similarly, he evidently hears the sound track with his *inner* ear. It is a particular aspect of his genius that in such matters he is often closed off from the feelings of others.

Welles's genius fed on Hollywood's marvelous machinery; in Europe his dependence on American skill cruelly shows through. And he is an American artist in more than formal technique: all his American films show a profound understanding of the American character, of its ambition, its deceits, its absurdities, its humor and resilience. *Kane, Ambersons, The Lady from Shanghai,* and *Touch of Evil* explore facets of the native mind and emotions with great complexity. Welles's greatness has chiefly been thought to lie in his technical innovations or renovations, his experiments with lighting, cutting, and sound. But his true art was in breaking through the Hollywood conventions that shut out the truth about Americans or turned the authentic dramas of everyday life into comic strips of violence informed by cheap sociology. In breaking those barriers, he showed that the cinema could explore life as ruthlessly as the novel or the theater. If Welles's desire for truthfulness destroyed him, he will leave the truth as his monument.

And his films are not merely truthful — Rossellini's are truthful, too, yet time has dealt badly with them. Welles's are beautiful: the best of them are delectable artifacts. Their richness of visual texture remains unequaled in the cinema, even bearing in mind the films of Von Sternberg.

Welles is a bon viveur as well as a poet. In *Kane* when he shows us the vulgarity and emptiness of the lives of the American rich, he is unable to resist a gourmand's gobbling of detail. He laps up everything his art director, Perry Ferguson, gives him: echoing banks, offices dominated by faceless portraits and tables brought to a skating-rink polish, mirrors that face each other, their images reflective to infinity, the largest jigsaw puzzle in the world, cavernous fireplace and fake-baronial dining room, a bedroom like a parody of femininity, full of frills and mirrors and perfume bottles to be smashed by the tycoon in a storm of masculine rage.

In *The Magnificent Ambersons* Booth Tarkington's world is observed with piercing clarity below the surface; but the vulgar surface itself is loved. Welles broods with intense enjoyment over the Amberson house, its pretentious staircase leading nowhere, like American hopes; the plush, ferns, baroque ceilings; George's Fauntleroy velveteen suit, the cracking whips and muscled horses of a morning ride, the winter motor outing with its laughing crowd perched high, bells tinkling brightly, whirling snow, and hiss of parted ice.

Even *The Stranger* — a film rather better than Welles thinks it is — contains a refined poetry of surfaces, of the materialist beauties of small-town America. The Connecticut store, with its proprietor forever listening to the radio, the town square, dominated by a massive Strasbourg clock, the birch woods, with boys weaving through glades in a paper chase while a murder is carried out only a few yards away: a microcosm of American life is disclosed in the setting of a provincial town, violence and beauty juxtaposed, suburban pleasantries barely hiding a deadly cruelty.

The Lady from Shanghai displays a still more powerful imaginative force. For the first time, Welles moves from North America, taking in Acapulco, the coast of South America, the Caribbean. Of all his films, I find this one the most ravishing: a masterpiece of evocative imagery, conjuring up as no other film has done the feeling of the tropics, of the lazy movement of a yacht at sea, of the beauty of marshes and palms, and the misty calm of remote ports of call. For all its somber, characteristic sniping at the rich — at the symbolic little party of faded-liberal sailor, wicked lawyer, murderous wife, and *voyeur* partner sailing from the Caribbean to San Francisco — the film is essentially a romantic work. In the film's most beautiful sequence — when the wife lies on her back on deck, singing, and the two businessmen exchange brutal wisecracks about money ("That's good, Arthur!" "That's good, George!") — Welles's love of luxury, of ease and pleasure, seeps through the bitter social comment and shows him as a lover of the flesh.

And in *Touch of Evil* he stripped away the gilded surfaces to look into a foreign soul: Mexico's, as well as into the shallow turbulence of the southerner's. In a Mexican bordertown the local police chief, the American Narcotics Commission representative and his wife, the petty criminals, all are blighted in different ways by corruption. Here, the sweltering darkness, the jazzy electric signs, the sickly, dusty daylight of Los Robles are observed with a passionate interest in the physical manifestations of evil.

These films crystallize Welles's half-adoring, half-repelled observation of the American reality: outwardly lavish and well upholstered, inwardly rotted by sickness, an inescapable moral cancer. His deeply sophisticated humor, so seldom commented on, is even more penetrating than Von Sternberg's. At heart, he is a cynic slightly blunted by geniality; if people are brutal, he enjoys it. But not coldly, gloatingly, like Hitchcock or Wilder. He savors evil with the relish of a man in love with life, in love with all its manifestations.

A tension between a passion for luxury, for the sensual pleasures of life, and a fascination with corruption, destruction and decay gives Welles's films their dynamic and explosive force. In exploring below the American surface, seeing its viciousness and ugliness, he went too far, and America has ignored and rejected him. But he loves what he has derided, and it is a tragedy that America cannot find a place for him. It is his tragedy, too, that the marvelous Hollywood machinery he needs has for more than a decade been denied him. But he has nothing left to feed on elsewhere; it is his tragedy that the commercial world he so brilliantly exposes in his work cannot find room for an artist of his size.

• • •

George Orson Welles was born in Kenosha, Wisconsin, on May 6, 1915, the second son of the wealthy inventor Richard Head Welles and the pianist Beatrice Ives Welles. Both boys were remarkably precocious, and Agnes Moorehead told me how deeply impressed she was when she met Welles at the age of five, already an intellectual adult.

The Welles family warmly encouraged its astonishing prodigy as he consumed Shakespeare's plays, quoted Wilde, wrote poetry, and drew cartoons — all before the age of ten. From this childhood period came experiences he later used in his films: he gave the name of his mentor, Dr. Maurice Bernstein, to the manager of the Kane newspapers, and his grandmother lived in a bizarre wooden house, a miniature Xanadu. The conjuring sequence in the opening reel of *Journey into Fear* sprang from Welles's early mastery of magic, a skill learned in part from Harry Houdini himself, and *The Magnificent Ambersons* owed much to Welles's understanding of a provincial community in the Midwest of his childhood.

The boy (already known as a potential genius of theater, of magic, of art and literature) went to the famous Todd School at Woodstock, Illinois, where the equally famous headmaster, Roger Hill, became his guide and friend. Here Welles's knowledge of Shakespeare, born at the age of three when his mother gave him *A Midsummer Night's Dream,* developed and flourished, burgeoning in *Everybody's Shakespeare,* an edition of the plays with an introduction by Welles and Hill. Welles played on stage innumerable times at Todd; and it was during a holiday from school that he went to the Orient — to Shanghai, scene of the seamy origins of the Chifu-born Elsa Bannister in *Lady of Shanghai.* The operatic theme in *Kane* was presaged by an episode recounted by Peter Noble in *The Fabulous Orson Welles:*[1] at a musical party given by Welles's mother, a Chicago opera star descended on the company and sang. When she asked Orson what he thought of her singing (he was in his teens), he told her she had "a lot to learn." Earlier he had appeared as the son of Madame Butterfly in a Chicago Opera Company performance. It is not insignificant that it was at the Chicago Opera House that Susan Kane had her first and spectacular flop, and that both Welles and Joseph Cotten worked in their early days as newspaper drama critics, Welles reviewing operas.

At Todd, Welles dazzled everyone by playing parts in productions of the Nativity, in musical comedy, and in versions of Shakespeare, Marlowe, and Ben Jonson. It was here that he produced the genesis of his cinematic Shakespeare trilogy, and his doomed stage presentation, *Five Kings*. He returned years later to film scenes in a stage production of *Twelfth Night*. Yet another foreshadowing of the future occurred when Whitford Kane, Director of the Goodman Theatre, presented him with a drama prize, thereby unwittingly making his surname immortal through Charles Foster Kane.

In his teens Welles went to Scotland and Ireland. He crashed the Dublin Gate Theatre in 1931 by presenting the astonished director, Hilton Edwards, with a large sheet of paper on which was written: "Orson Welles, star of the New York Theatre Guild, would consider appearing in one of your productions and hopes you will see him for an appointment." Reading for the Duke in *Jew Süss,* he was bizarre, but Edwards and Micheál MacLiammoir, later to play Iago to his Othello, were sufficiently impressed by his personality to take him on. His first night in *Jew Süss* was marred by mishaps, but he won a standing ovation in a brilliantly erratic performance. He conquered Dublin; but he was unable to work in London because of labor restrictions, and he was snubbed by Broadway. Unable to get work, he went to Morocco, later to be the setting of much of his version of *Othello,* fought as a picador in Spain, thus gaining

experience valuable in preparing the unfinished *My Friend Bonito,* and returned to America to find the doors still closed.

But help was forthcoming: from Alexander Woollcott and Thornton Wilder, both of whom were impressed by Welles. Guthrie McClintic and his wife Katharine Cornell engaged him for a tour in the Cornell company, where he appeared successfully at the Woodstock Drama Festival, and in 1934 he made his New York theatrical debut, as Chorus and Tybalt in Katharine Cornell's production of *Romeo and Juliet*. Soon afterward he met John Houseman, who was to be his associate in the Mercury Theatre and script editor on *Citizen Kane*. Together they produced Archibald MacLeish's play *Panic,* about the Wall Street crash, for Houseman's newly formed Phoenix Theatre Group. Later, the two men presented an all-Negro *Macbeth* for the Federal Theatre — a notable success.

In 1937 Welles produced *Dr. Faustus* and a celebrated production, in defiance of an Equity ban, of Marc Blitzstein's famous opera *The Cradle Will Rock*. Plunging into radio performances and productions, Welles managed to raise enough money to realize a dream, the Mercury Theatre, in 1937.

The Mercury Theatre — a cliquey, passionately interlocking group — was intended to establish a solid and permanent repertoire of plays. At the old Comedy Theatre on 41st Street the company presented a *Julius Caesar* in modern dress against stark platforms and an almost bare stage modeled on recent news stories of European dictatorships. Joseph Cotten, Martin Gabel, and George Coulouris were in the cast. *Julius Caesar* was a success, and was later put on at the National Theatre. Later came *The Shoemaker's Holiday, Heartbreak House, Danton's Death,* a version of *Five Kings,* and the sensational *War of the Worlds,* which caused a panic when it was broadcast.

It was during this period that Welles made his first film, *Too Much Johnson*. William Gillette's comedy had first been presented in Brooklyn and then at the Standard Theatre, New York, in November 1894. Starring Gillette himself, and based on a French farce,

---

[1]London: Hutchinson, 1956.

it was the story of a rake, Augustus Billings, who has a brief fling with a passionate Frenchwoman. Forced to flee from the lady's irate husband, he sails off for Cuba by steamer, telling his own wife that he has bought a plantation there; on arrival, he fakes a land deed. Numerous complications follow until an unresolved duel with the Frenchman brings the amusing proceedings to a close. Despite critical disapproval, the play ran ten months on Broadway to cheerfully convulsed audiences.

Welles used a Keystone Kops-Mack Sennett approach, with white make-up and undercranked film. Among the players he cast was Marc Blitzstein, who appeared with incredible energy as a French barber in almost every scene. "We think," wrote *Stage* (September 1938) on the strength of his performance, "Mr. Blitzstein is not only an outstanding musician and composer, but an excellent comedian as well." Herbert Drake, drama reporter for the *New York Herald-Tribune,* later press agent for the Mercury Theatre, and finally its vice-president, played a Kop. Welles wanted to combine the film with a stage production — a plan later abandoned. Half an hour was to be projected before the curtain rose and about ten minutes shown later. The two portions together would make a fascinating cohesive picture, but it seems tragically to have disappeared, and was never shown to the public.[2]

The film was shot in and around New York in the summer of 1938 by a team that knew nothing about making films. Welles's own experience was restricted to his Todd School *Twelfth Night,* to reading Pudovkin, and to visiting Robert Flaherty during the filming of *Man of Aran* in 1932. Richard Wilson, Welles's production assistant, had according to his own report "not even read Pudovkin." The money was found by the film's producer, John Houseman, who successfully dunned friends and people interested in the theater.

The cast included Joseph Cotten as Johnson, a part played in the style of the *Comédie Française,* Ruth Ford, Arlene Francis, Mary Wickes, Edgar Barrier, and Virginia ("Anna Stafford"), Welles's first wife. The photographer was the late Paul Dunbar, a Pathé newsreel cameraman. Welles edited the film himself.

When horses were needed for some scenes, Wilson and others got them from livery stables at Haverstraw, New York. Gowns were conned out of New York costumiers. Rooftops were used for chases, in the style of the Keystone Kops with Joseph Cotten frequently risking his life as he hung from rooftops, Harold Lloyd style. A Bronx studio was used for the interiors.

The film went as follows.[3] Johnson, a notorious ladies' man, is walking down the street swinging his cane and tipping his stylish derby and looking to right and left. Finally he arrives at a New York apartment building and presses the bell. He is admitted to the house, which has potted palms in the hall (several "dramatic" cuts heavily re-emphasize the palms). Upstairs Arlene Francis is taking off her long, brocade dress and stripping down to black lace corsets. She looks over and there is an inset of a photograph of Johnson's head; she clutches it to her lovely and ample bosom, sighs deeply, and replaces the picture on a shelf. Cut to Johnson walking down the hallway and entering the apartment.

Now follows a scene of "flickering film and unflickering passion" (Wilson), then a quick cut to Edgar Barrier, the husband of Arlene Francis; the lovers hear the husband arriving, Cotten tries to get into his trousers, and he exits onto the fire escape. The wife greets Barrier and tries to distract him sexually to no avail, forgetting

---

[2] Welles is said to own the one remaining print.

[3] I am indebted to Richard Wilson for this description.

that Cotten's picture is on the bookcase. Barrier rushes and grabs the picture, and he and his wife tussle over it. There are about twenty set-ups as they struggle in a tug of war, and the picture tears across the eyes and the bridge of the nose; Francis thrusts her half into her cleavage. This scene is intercut with Cotten running down the fire escape and fleeing.

Holding his half of the picture, Barrier looks down, sees Cotten, and gives chase — across Central Park, over rooftops with Cotten jumping from building to building, through downstairs and upstairs, traversing chimneys, attics, and cellars. In one sequence Cotten is stuck in a line of people including suffragettes, and Barrier is caught up in the same parade. In another, Barrier is forced to stop by the passing of the American flag, which he has unavoidably to salute. Finally, Cotten runs up a gangway to a ship (the Statue of Liberty tour ferry as it happened, hired for the day to stand in for Gillette's ship to Cuba). At the last minute Barrier jumps and hangs onto the side of the ship as it draws away with Cotten aboard. The curtain was to rise as Barrier leaped from the screen onto the theater stage.

The second segment shows Barrier locating Cotten on board ship, and there is a long further chase on horseback in "Cuba," featuring Howard Smith as a "heavy." There are also scenes in which Guy Kingsley as an eager suitor chases Anna Stafford onto the same boat while her father, played by Eustace Wyatt (the archaeologist in *Journey into Fear*), fights to preserve her honor. Scenes were shot in "Cuba," using a rock quarry near Haverstraw decorated with rented palms. It was all hilariously funny, and too sad to recall.

2. CITIZEN KANE

By 1938 the Mercury Theatre group was thoroughly established: exhaustingly busy on stage and in radio, quirky, facetious, brilliant, with a pattern of funny, strictly intramural jokes that ranged from smoking room to barracks to green room in their caliber and references. The making of *Citizen Kane* came about because the Mercury Theatre group needed enough money to open its massive production of *Five Kings* on Broadway. It had failed on out-of-town tryouts, perhaps in part because it encompassed many of Shakespeare's historical plays (starting with *Richard II* and ending with *Henry VI, Part Two*) and took two successive days to perform — beginning at four in the afternoon and ending at eleven, with a dinner break and interludes read from *Holinshed's Chronicles.* (In the end, *Five Kings* was never again staged.) The huge *succès de scandale* of the notorious, panic-inducing *War of the Worlds* broadcast in 1938 resulted in a Hollywood contract: Welles, after refusing several prior offers, arrived in Hollywood on July 20, 1939, to make a film of Joseph Conrad's *Heart of Darkness* for RKO Radio Pictures. RKO, whose parent company, Radio-Keith-Orpheum, was under the enlightened presidency of George J. Schaefer, hired him.

His hiring was partly inspired by the studio's severe financial plight at the time. In 1939 it had been in receivership, saved at the last minute from total ruin by the financier Floyd Odlum. It was in fact the financially weakest studio on the Coast. It was hoped (ironically, as it turned out), that Welles would by virtue of his enormously famous name help to pull the company out of the red. Behind the move to engage Welles was the powerful Nelson Rockefeller, who, through his Rockefeller Center group, owned a sizable slab of RKO stock and had, in fact, pushed Schaefer into office (with the aid of shareholder David Sarnoff, head of RCA) and was sympathetic to the hiring of Welles.

Welles's contract ran to more than sixty pages and gave him unlimited powers short of actually issuing bodily harm to Nelson Rockefeller. He did not even have to invite RKO executives to the rushes. After *Citizen Kane* the contract was canceled and replaced by another that did not, apparently, give the right to approve the absolutely final cut, which the *Kane* contract gave (or Welles could have sued the studio over their cut version of *The Magnificent Ambersons*). A proviso that slightly compromised both contracts was that the studio must approve a project in finished script form before it began filming.

Heart of Darkness was to be told in the first person, with hand-held Eyemo cameras, and Welles was to play both Marlow, the seeker after truth in the African tropic jungle, and his quarry Kurtz, the mysterious recluse trader in ivory; others in the film were to be Everett Sloane, the Austrian actress Dita Parlo, Erskine Sanford, George Coulouris, Ray Collins, and Gus Schilling. Tests were done showing aspects of character — featuring Welles, Sloane, and Schilling — and trying out the first-person technique, with smoke coming from a pipe held in front of the lens and Welles as Marlow glimpsed in mirrors.[1]

[1]Interview with Richard Wilson, Santa Monica, 1969.

Already produced by the Mercury Theatre of the Air, *Heart of Darkness* was never made as a film: Dita Parlo was interned in France, and the studio decided the whole venture would cost too much (one million dollars) and present too many technical problems in the use of subjective filming. It was officially announced that improved hand-held camera techniques would have to be developed before the film could be made. Welles then wrote a script based on the novel *The Smiler with the Knife* by Nicholas Blake (pseudonym of C. Day Lewis), which in his version became a story about a society woman who discovers the truth about a fake nationalist organization; strong echoes of this, as well as of the style of *Kane,* were to be found in George Cukor's *Keeper of the Flame* three years later. The scheme was abandoned because Carole Lombard refused the role of the society woman, and Lucille Ball, whom Welles had chosen for it, was thought by the studio to be too "light." In the meantime, Welles narrated *The Swiss Family Robinson* for RKO and wrote the script for a film about Nazi influences in Mexico City, entitled *Mexican Melodrama,* which was based on Arthur Calder Marshall's novel *The Way to Santiago,* with first-person photographic narration to be done by Gregg Toland, who scouted locations in Mexico City. It was to deal with spies in Mexico to illustrate the menace of Nazi fifth columns there, and it was inspired by Nelson Rockefeller, who had deep interests in preventing Nazi incursions in that area. (Apart from business investments, he was spearheading a Rooseveltian move to consolidate North and South American relations and flush out Nazism south of the Panama Canal.) The scheme was shelved when the Mexican government refused to cooperate, and it was revived in 1942 only to be abandoned once more when a studio power reshuffle took place in May-June of that year.

It is now certain that it was not Welles but Herman J. Mankiewicz who first thought of *American,* the story which was later to become *John Citizen, U. S. A.* and, finally, *Citizen Kane.* Mankiewicz, brother of the director-producer Joseph L. Mankiewicz, had worked as a reporter, had been on the staffs of *The New York Times* and *The New Yorker,* and had become a well-known

A make-up test for HEART OF DARKNESS.

writer of Hollywood films. He also knew Hearst. As Pauline Kael has established in her contribution to *The Citizen Kane Book,* Welles met Mankiewicz socially and became excited by Mankiewicz's idea of a film based on the life of Hearst; he asked Mankiewicz for an outline. This Mankiewicz prepared, and Welles liked it. He asked Mankiewicz to develop it into a screenplay. Mankiewicz prepared the script with the aid of John Houseman. Certain of Welles's ideas given at the time of the outline were incorporated, including the idea of the *March of Time* framework. The script was somewhat changed around at Welles's suggestion in subsequent drafts and further changes were made during shooting and cutting. All the dialogue remained Mankiewicz's own and so did almost the whole of the structure. Later, Welles claimed sole credit for the script and in the original rough cut had a title which shocked Mankiewicz: "A Film by Orson Welles." Mankiewicz took the matter to the Screen Writers Guild, and enforced a shared credit, important particularly because they later shared an Oscar for the script.

A similar story had actually been told on screen before, in rather coarser terms: in the script (by Charles Kenyon and Sidney Sutherland) of Alfred E. Green's *I Loved a Woman* (1933). It is an account of the career of a meat baron obsessed with *objets d'art* who falls in love with a rather aloof, icy woman and marries her, but later he becomes infatuated with a struggling opera singer, whose career he sponsors when he becomes wealthy. When the *Maine* is sunk and the Spanish-American War breaks out, he declares that "the war is our oyster" and loots $50 million from the war by selling bad meat to the troops. Finally he is abandoned by everyone, and is left with only his collections of art treasures (seen in crates). The opera singer makes her debut sponsored by the meat baron in the *Chicago Opera House,* and the elections of McKinley and Roosevelt are shown in lantern-slide techniques foreshadowing the Wellesian montages in *Kane.* Other parallels could be found in William K. Howard's *The Power and the Glory* (1933) and Garson Kanin's *A Man to Remember* (1938).

The narrative was to deal with the career of a great tycoon and to form a fully documented attack on American acquisitiveness. Together with John Houseman, Mankiewicz developed a story sufficiently complex to form the basis of a masterpiece. Mankiewicz, with Houseman acting chiefly as editor and Welles going down on weekends, spent thirteen weeks with a broken leg in a motel in Victorville, California,[2] working on the screenplay, while Welles at RKO immersed himself in a study of film technique with the RKO technicians and of the works of Fritz Lang, René Clair, King Vidor, Frank Capra, and — especially — John Ford. Elements in the films of all these directors evidently affected him: the sense of the overpowering force of fate and the somber UFA-esque low-key style of Lang, the fantastic light comedy of Clair, the strong sense of the American milieu and the emotional profundity and honesty of Vidor, the brilliant energy and dashing style of Capra, the punch

of Ford, whose *The Informer* impressed and most deeply influenced him. UFA films also left their grim romantic mark. *Kane* has been called a revolutionary work, but it is in fact a creation in the mainstream of America's film art, a deeply traditionalist reflection of the native cinema's major virtues: energy and forcefulness, physical glamour, and strength of purpose.

Gregg Toland, who called Welles to ask for the job of shooting *Kane* and got it immediately, was born in Charleston, Illinois, on May 29, 1904. He began his career by leaving grade school and enrolling in technical school to study electrical engineering. At fifteen he again left school and went to Hollywood, where he worked as an office boy at Twentieth Century-Fox. Intrigued by cameras, he became an enthusiastic assistant to the celebrated photographer George Barnes. Eight months later he became an assistant cameraman and went to work for Goldwyn, who often loaned him to other producers: to Selznick for *Intermezzo,* which introduced Ingrid Bergman to the American screen, to Darryl F. Zanuck for *The Grapes of Wrath,* and to Walter Wanger for *The Long Voyage Home.* He won an Oscar for his photography in *Wuthering Heights.* Toland's earlier work foreshadowed *Kane*: in *Les Misérables* he used less light in the sewer scenes than any other cameraman had up to that time, and in *The Long Voyage Home* he introduced coated lenses to permit shooting into lights, Super-XX film stock, and low, partly or wholly ceilinged sets. This technique he developed fully in *Kane,* where some sets — not all, as Toland claimed — were built with unusually low, removable muslin ceilings, and camera angles were often from floor level. Some sets were built in parallels, so that sections could be removed. With the exception of some sets which had paper skylights or removable ceilings to allow the use of banks of small lights and junior spotlights from above (notably the *Inquirer* offices — see illustrations), all were built specifically to permit lighting from the floor.

At RKO, Welles, aided by Russell Metty, made a close study of lighting, while Toland learned from James Wong Howe's use of deep focus in William K. Howard's *Transatlantic* (1930), which included muslin set ceilings

---

[2]Which Welles may have recalled in the motel scene in *Touch of Evil.*

introduced by Griffith and Billy Bitzer to suggest the claustrophobic atmosphere of a ship.

From the beginning Toland and Welles wanted to achieve a flow of images so hypnotic that the audience would not be conscious of the mechanics of film making. Direct cuts were avoided wherever possible. Instead, the camera would pan or dolly from one angle to another. "In other scenes," Toland wrote in *The American Cinematographer* (February 1941), "we preplanned our angles and compositions so that action ordinarily shown in direct cuts would be shown in a single, longer scene — often one in which important action might take place simultaneously in widely separated points in extreme foreground and background." Some details were extraordinary: Toland showed the light changing on Joseph Cotten's face at three points of the sun to indicate the lapse of time in which he is recounting a story in flashback form.

To achieve great penetrating light power, twin-arc broadsides, normally used only in Technicolor, were used. These lamps were the backbone of the lighting, with various spotlights as accessories. To solve the problem of deep focus which could equal the depth of Flemish paintings, often with a man's head only sixteen inches from the camera while small objects were seen with equal sharpness two hundred feet away, Super-XX film was shot with 24mm wide-angle lenses, stopped down. The lenses — Waterhouse stop lenses, normally used for stills — were coated with a special substance and fitted with devices resembling irises. Time transitions were achieved by lap dissolves, in which people were lit through special dimmers. The fade-out began with background lights gradually dimmed, then the people themselves dimmed just as slowly. Fade-ins were achieved by raising the lighting on the set first, then the lighting on the players.

Toland made the following comments on deep focus in *The American Cinematographer* (February 1941).

One certainly learns surprising things about the behavior of lenses. For example, I discovered that a 24mm lens, stopped down to f:8 or less, becomes almost literally a universal focus objective at a certain point. If it is set to focus on a point 4 feet 6 inches in front of the camera, everything from 18 inches to infinity will be in acceptably sharp focus.

Lighting for a combination of ultra-fast film, coated lenses, and radically reduced apertures presented special problems, and a new system of lighting balance had to be developed. Fast film tended to flatten contrasts, but the stopped-down, coated lenses tended to increase them. Therefore, Toland explained, scenes had to be lit with "less contrast than would be the custom under more normal circumstances." He wrote:

The precise degree of change depends upon the stop used, but in general the shadows must be "opened up" with a more general use of filler light, the highlights must be watched, and when optical diffusion is used, diffusers such as the Scheibes, which tend to soften contrasts, are generally preferable. Obviously, too, when you are dealing with film of the extreme sensitivity of Super-XX, you will find that even at reduced apertures, extremely delicate gradations of lighting contrasts pick up, registering far more strongly than they do even to the trained eye. Yet, strangely enough, once a cinematographer has accustomed himself to this type of lighting, it becomes in many ways easier than more conventional lighting, for it is simpler, less artificial and employs fewer light sources.

Toland also wrote in *Theatre Arts* (September 1940), that he and Welles had to shoot Mrs. Kane's boardinghouse over a period of four days: "It was a complex mixture of art and mechanics. A table and chair on rollers were to behave with clock-like precision as a three-ton camera boom moved over them. In proper timing lay the difficulty. When the props behaved on schedule, a child actor Buddy Swann would blow up his lines. When those two items co-ordinated, the operation of the camera crane by nine men would be slightly out of synchronization. To bring all this action, dialogue, and mechanics into perfect time was the problem. But it was eventually solved."

Toland saw the film twenty-seven times in the projection room used in *Kane,* to check every aspect of the laboratory work. In one scene he resorted to an ingenious expedient not commonly used at the time: when after

fourteen takes a dramatic episode seemed not perfect, he suggested that Welles match the sound track of one take with the images of another to bring about a perfect result. Welles agreed.

Double exposure was used in the scene in which Kane finds that Susan has taken poison. The medicine glass was exposed, and the rest of the scene left dark. Then the film was rewound and the rest of the scene exposed. In a scene when a cockatoo screams on a Xanadu veranda, it was matted in against a set, with a processed beach behind the set.

The RKO art director Perry Ferguson was chosen by Welles as the architect of Xanadu, the El Rancho Night-

club in Atlantic City, the Thatcher Memorial Library, the newspaper offices and rally halls. His flawless taste allowed him to give a stylized but not overblown physical illustration of American materialism and vulgarity; many of his sets — for example, the long mirrored corridor where Kane walks, his image reflected to infinity — are masterpieces. Ferguson created an eerie and echoing shell for the scenes in Xanadu when Susan Alexander plays with her jigsaw puzzles, a sad, drab resting place in the hospital where Jedediah Leland ends his days, a twilit gloomy chamber for Bernstein's office as general manager of the Kane newspapers. Working closely with Ferguson, Darrell Silvera helped design the overall look of the film, its essentially Gothic splendor, the striking authenticity of its urban American ambience. There were 115 sets — some of them 200 feet long and using two adjacent stages. The fireplace at Xanadu was 10′x18′x 27′. In the final scene at Xanadu, 1,072 boxes and 263,450 feet of lumber were used and arranged to look like a broken jigsaw puzzle or a deserted skyscraper city when photographed from a crane. The make-up was entrusted to Maurice Seiderman, who gave Welles seventeen separate treatments (some of them too obvious). Welles told Seiderman that he was dissatisfied with the treatment of his eyes as an old man, and Welles bought contact lenses which gave his eyes a watery and blood-shot look.

With only a limited amount of money to spend in view of the studio's uniquely pinched conditions, Welles was economically forced into a position that made him create a remarkable eclectic artifact. Not merely did the plot owe its origin to a wide range of historical sources. The actual physical structure of the film drew from the materials of RKO's other films as well. And not only in the images and music of the newsreel. Xanadu in long shot was similar in "construction" and mountainous location to the castle in the RKO-released *Snow White and the Seven Dwarfs;* it was painted with the aid of former members of the Disney team. Its building was shown in clips from work on Notre Dame cathedral in *The Hunchback of Notre Dame.* The famous window that glitters in the darkness beyond Kane's bed as he dies was first seen in the introductory shots of John Knox in John Ford's *Mary of Scotland* (*un hommage,* if ever there was one), and the great fireplace at Xanadu was a conversion of Mary Stuart's at Holyrood House. The exterior of *The Inquirer* office was made over from a Holyrood gateway, and the door to the mirrored hall through which Kane walks after his wife leaves him came from *Gunga Din,* while the animated bats in the swamp at Kane's Everglades picnic are from *Son of Kong,* with the ape matted out and Kane's guests matted in. A surprising proportion of the film is constructed in this way—I have seized on references I have recognized, as these facts were not made public or even available from the participants—and the effect is not mere economy or ingenuity: it is to evoke in regular film-goers subliminal memories and echoes, as well as—the other side of Welles's talent—to give an intramural, half-joking plug to the RKO technicians as well as an extramural advertisement of RKO's historic and historical skills.

Bernard Herrmann wrote the score; he had begun composing for Welles in 1936, writing for the Mercury Playhouse Theatre on instructions from CBS, "music of definite form and in a rational idiom." His work was so successful that his assignment to *Kane* came as a foregone conclusion. The music was a triumph, from its first sinister notes that accompany Kane's death, through the ironically used Waldteufel-like waltz that mockingly underlines the breakdown of the Kane marriage, to the fortissimo strings that accompany the final destruction of the Rosebud sled, the end of Kane's life.

Herrman was given unusually free conditions for the composition: film music then being usually written in two or three weeks, the composer had little time to prepare his own orchestration; the sound levels and the dynamics of the score were not controlled by the composer in the finished film. We learn from a contemporary article by Herrmann in *The New York Times,* published shortly after the film's release, that he was allowed twelve weeks to write the music, which he orchestrated and conducted himself. "I worked reel by reel, as it was shot and cut. In this way I had a sense of the picture being built, and of my own music being part of that building. Most musical scores in Hollywood are written after the film is entirely finished, and the composer must adapt his music to the scenes on the screen." In *Kane,* he said, an entirely different method was used, and many sequences were tailored to match the music.

In the episode in the 1890's when *The Inquirer* starts to grow, Herrmann used a cancan scherzo, accelerating with the "montage" that illustrated a mounting circulation. The campaign against the traction trust is figured by a smart galop. When Kane and Leland arrive at the office there is the rhythm of early ragtime: the effect is of a ballet score in miniature.

Brass bands and hurdy-gurdy tunes were used. In the jigsaw-puzzle scenes the music simulates the ticking of a clock. Music cues occur in the film ahead of abrupt time transitions; often they are subtle and sometimes dissonant arrangements for bass flute solo, bass drum, or muted horns. There are two main leitmotifs: a simple four-note figure on the brass illustrating Kane's power, given out in the first two bars of the film; and the Rosebud motif, a solo on the vibraphone which appears first when Kane drops the glass ball and is heard whenever childhood images recur to evoke with pathos the sense of a lost and beautiful past. But the score's most thrilling musical moment has not been referred to by Herrmann in print: Thompson reads the pages of Walter Parks Thatcher's diary, and a sad melody changes to a brightly innocent flutter of woodwind and strings, indicating the pursuant images of Kane's childhood—whirling snow and an obstreperous encounter with a banker.

The music for the newsreel was compiled with the assistance of the RKO-Pathé Newsreel team using copyrighted materials in the RKO files. The title theme of *News on the March* was the British composer Anthony Collins's bold, brassy march for the Belgian war scenes in *Nurse Edith Cavell,* made by Herbert Wilcox in 1939. The voluptuous tropical theme behind the image of Xanadu fronted by waving palms as the first words of Coleridge's poem ("In Xanadu did Kublai Khan/A stately pleasure dome decree") unfolded on the screen was drawn from Alfred Newman's exotic *Gunga Din* score. Kane's death was accompanied by a variation on

Mendelssohn's "Funeral March" composed for *King Kong*. As Kane's newspaper empire grows, the ebullient rippling title theme from Roy Webb's score for *Reno* is heard. Three bars from Webb's sinister "head-hunters" music in John Farrow's *Five Came Back* appropriately precede shots of Walter Parks Thatcher's ordeal before a congressional investigation committee. As Kane faces political ruin over the Susan Alexander scandal, Webb's arrangement of *The Girl I Left Behind Me,* first used in *Abe Lincoln in Illinois* earlier in 1940, is employed ironically. Bars of the *Tannhauser* overture crash when Susan's opera career is referred to and we see the Chicago Opera House. Chopin's "Funeral March" accompanies the repeat of Kane's funeral, and the whole closes on Anthony Collins's *"Cavell"* march.

Herrmann used other composers' work in the body of his score. *In a Mizz,* a 1933 jazz composition, by Charles Barrett and Haven Johnson, is heard as a sad vibraphone accompaniment to Susan's first appearance in the El Rancho Nightclub, recurs faintly and sepulchrally as she attempts suicide, then emerges fully with lyrics ("There ain't no love/There ain't no true love") as a bitter commentary background to the scene in which Kane shouts at Susan in the Everglades picnic tent. Kane's campaign song was written by Herman Ruby to music (originally used for a song called *A Poco No*) by Pepé Guizer; it is at first a welcome song, and after its use as a campaign anthem it is heard mournfully as Kane sees the collapse of his political ambitions. It recurs over the final credits. Rossini's *Una Voca Poco Fa* is used for Susan's attempts to sing, and Herrmann used snatches of Handel's "Hail the Conquering Hero Comes" and George Root's "Battle Cry of Freedom" in the campaign scenes.

The fake opera *Salammbô* is a curious pastiche. Called *Thaïs* in the original script as a direct reference by Mankiewicz and Welles to the fact that *Thaïs* was composed for Hearst's first mistress, it was altered to *Salammbô* by Herrmann, who in fact in his own score contradicted the spelling of the title of Flaubert's novel by calling it *Salaambô*, possibly a facetious reference to its

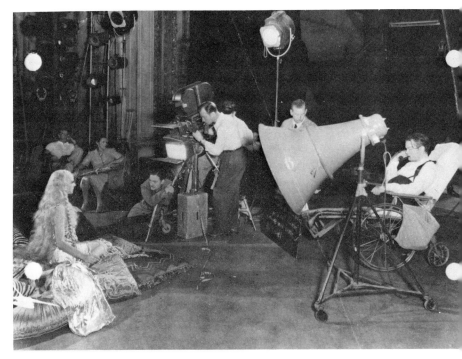

Welles broke his ankle during the shooting of KANE, *and had to direct some scenes from a wheelchair.*

pseudo-Oriental nature. It combines elements of a twenties production (and musical reorganization) of a Massenet-like French Oriental work of the 1890's and overtones of Richard Strauss's *Salomé* and Reyer's *Salammbô*, first heard in New York in 1900 (several other operas of this name were available to Herrmann). The libretto, drawn from Racine's *Phèdre* and sung by Jean Forward deliberately badly (she was a professional singer), makes a deliberate reference through being selected from a suicide speech to Susan's subsequent attempted act of *felo de se,* also by poison, and the professionally suicidal nature of her performance. It is typical of the Mercury team that they should have thought out this almost incredibly complicated musical and visual joke and have coupled it with a setting and array of costumes that would have horrified Flaubert. Of course it partly cheats: Susan could not have learned a complete libretto in French! The words of Phèdre's speech as presented in the libretto are as follows (somewhat cut):

Ah, cruel! tu m'as trop entendue!
Je t'en ai dit assez pour te tirer d'erreur.
Hé bien! Connais donc Phèdre et toute sa fureur:
J'aime! Ne pense pas qu'au moment que je t'aime,
Innocente à mes yeux, je m'approuve moi-même;
Ni que du fol amour qui trouble ma raison
Ma lâche complaisance ait nourri le poison;
Objet infortuné des vengeances célestes,
Je m'abhorre encor plus que tu ne me détestes.
Les dieux m'en sont témoins, ces dieux qui dans mon flanc
Ont allumé le feu fatal à tout mon sang;
Ces dieux qui se sont fait une gloire cruelle
De séduire le coeur d'une faible mortelle.
Toi-même en ton esprit rappelle le passé:
C'est peu de t'avoir fui, cruel, je t'ai chassé;
J'ai voulu te paroitre odieuse, inhumaine;
Pour mieux te resister, j'ai recherché ta haine.
De quoi m'ont profite mes inutile soins?
Tu me haïssais plus, je ne t'aimois pas moins;
Tes malheurs te prêtoient encor de nouveaux charmes.
J'ai langui, j'ai sêché dans les feux, dans les larmes:

Il suffit de tes yeux pour t'en persuader,
Si tes yeux un moment pouvoient me regarder . . .
Que dis-je? Cet aveu que je viens de faire,
Cet aveu si honteux, le crois-tu volontaire?
Tremblante pour un fils que je n'osois trahir,
Je te venois prier de ne le point haïr:
Faibles projets d'un coeur trop plein de ce qu'il aime!
Hélas! Je ne t'ai pu parler que de toi-même!
Venge-toi, punis-moi d'un odieux amour:
Digne fils du héros qui t'a donné le jour,
Delivre l'univers d'un monstre qui t'irrite.
La veuve de Thésée ose aimer Hippolyte!
Crois-moi, ce monstre affreux ne doit point t'echapper
Voilà mon coeur: c'est la que ta main doit frapper.
Impatient déjà d'expier son offense,
Au-devant de ton bras je le sens qui s'avance.
Frappe: Ou si tu le crois indigne de tes coups,
Si ta haine m'envie un supplice si doux,
Ou si d'un sang trop vil ta main seroit trempée,
Au défraut de ton bras prête-toi mon épée;
Donne.

without a break. In a film full of tiny skills, this example of sleight of hand is the most infinitely cunning of all. A typically inspired example of cutting shows the words of the butler trailing away, "His wife left him . . ." and a white cockatoo screeches. And the newsreel, matching scores of separate fragments, is an astonishing example of virtuoso parodistic cutting.

Wise and Robson, with the RKO-Pathé newsreel people, spent weeks on the newsreel alone. They treated the stock (not, it must be confessed, always consistently) according to the age it should look, often by winding it through sand-filled rags or duplicating the positive dozens of times to get a faded look. Toland aided them by shooting his matched-in footage without arcs or other artificial aids, and by simulating news-team methods, and employing Eyemos (as in the Kane wheelchair scene, shot with an imitation of concealed camera).

Wise, who had worked on a few films at RKO, was hired to replace an older studio editor on the picture because Welles, himself young, wanted a younger man. Welles was shooting "tests" for *Kane* at Pathé Studios in Culver City, which were in fact actual sequences. Wise talked to him while he was shooting the picnic scene in the tent with Dorothy Comingore and was a party from then on to Welles's making of *Kane* without the studio knowing it: the projection room scene, the Atlantic City nightclub scene, the newsreel itself, and three other sequences were all supposed to be merely tests for a projected motion picture.

Simultaneously, Welles did the "tests" for *Heart of Darkness.* Both sets of tests came in to Mark Robson and Wise; their work was aided by thorough preplanning, set-up by set-up, with Gregg Toland.

Changes in some lines of dialogue were made in New York when Wise took the print to George Schaefer at Radio-Keith-Orpheum. Paul Stewart and Ray Collins were in New York and re-recorded some words, and the newsreel had to be tampered with because it ran too close to reality. Wise called Robson long distance in Hollywood to make the necessary changes, and after six weeks a release print was ready.[3]

Robert Wise and the uncredited Mark Robson brilliantly edited the film. One wonderful example of their skill occurs in the scene introducing Susan Kane for the first time. Many critics have incorrectly described this sequence as being filmed in a single take: the camera climbing up to a neon sign, descending through a skylight without a break, and discovering Susan. Actually, the cutters with Welles play a brilliant psychological trick on the audience. The sound of thunder is very loud, conveying to our minds in a flash a feeling that rain is about, supported by Herrmann's chords (called "Rain" in his own penciled score). Rain breaks across our line of vision after an almost totally imperceptible fraction of a second, some frames blank. The instant the rain blurs on the skylight glass before us, there is a dissolve that is almost literally invisible because the rain blurring is just what we expect to see. The blurring is *on the dissolve.* Then the shot continues, apparently

[3]One small scene in the newspaper office was the only one cut.

Welles drew all save two of his cast (Ruth Warrick and Dorothy Comingore) from the distinguished Mercury Theatre Company, which had the double advantage of being new to films and of being fully unified to execute Welles's concept. Among them were Agnes Moorehead, (who played Kane's mother), Joseph Cotten (Jedediah Leland), Everett Sloane (Bernstein), George Coulouris (Walter Thatcher), and Erskine Sanford (Carter). Dorothy Comingore, altogether admirable as Susan Alexander Kane, had appeared in several films in the mid-thirties as an extra; discovered by Chaplin while playing at the Carmel (Calif.) Little Theatre, she was signed by United Artists under the screen name of Linda Winters; three months later she was summarily dismissed from that studio without a screen test. Later another studio tried her out, actually gave her a test, but used her only in crowd scenes and for stills; she was typecast as a beach beauty. She broke her contract, refusing to appear in films unless she could show her talents as an actress. It looked as though she was going to sink without a trace when Welles met her at a party, decided she would be ideal as the fluffy, vulgar, but sensitive would-be opera star, gave her a test, and signed her up.

William Alland, who played the shadowy reporter representing the audience in its search for Kane's true character and parodied *March of Time's* Westbrook Van Voorhis as the news commentator, had played the role of Marullus in Welles's production of *Julius Caesar:* he had secured that role after charging into Welles's dressing room, locking himself in, hiding the key, and rattling off some of Marullus's speeches with considerable *brio*. Paul Stewart, who played the cynical butler Raymond, had earlier actually discovered Welles for radio: he was a producer who had happened to hear Welles's voice at an audition. He drew Welles to the attention of a director at CBS, Homer Prickett, and later became Welles's production assistant on the Mercury Theatre of the Air before turning actor.

All these players were contracted by RKO; and the "official" post-"test" shooting began on July 30, 1940. Filming started in "absolute secrecy" — Welles's flair as a publicist had not deserted him. There was said to be

only one copy of the script (although this was patently absurd), and Welles was said to sleep with it hidden in his bed; only George Schaefer was supposed to have read it (apart, presumably, from the crew and players). Actors were said to have been given their own parts, and merely cues. Visitors to the set were barred, unless Welles himself gave special permission for them to see the shooting.

Work, carefully preplanned, went ahead smoothly for four months. More rumors about its subject matter leaked out as RKO's publicity department allowed public and press a series of furtive peeps into the mystery. It was said by some to be calculatedly based on the life of William Randolph Hearst, whose mistress, Marion Davies, had had a brief screen career; but the shrewd pointed out that Marion Davies had not been the failure that Susan Alexander Kane was said to be. Others claimed the story was based on the magnates Zaharoff, Kruger, or perhaps Jules Brulatour, head of Kodak — who had forced his wife, the fair-haired former movie star Hope Hampton, into a disastrous opera career. Some remembered Harold McCormick, whose wife, Ganna Walska, had achieved fame as an opera star, and Samuel Insull, who built the Chicago Opera House. The fact was that Mankiewicz, though he knew Hearst well, had produced a plot as eclectic as the film's style.[4]

By January 1941 Louella Parsons had decided that the film undoubtedly must portray her employer, William Randolph Hearst, and asked to see the film privately. Her request was refused, together with those of others in Hollywood, a community already filled with jealous enemies of Welles who envied his freedom — a freedom they themselves had never been able to attain. Finally, Louella Parsons did see *Kane* at a preview along with Douglas Churchill of *The New York Times,* and Jim Crow of *Look.* She stormed out after this showing, but later she repented and saw the film again, this time in the company of her chauffeur, and two Hearst law-

[4]Ferdinand Lundberg, author of *Imperial Hearst, A Social Biography* (New York: Random House, 1936) evidently disagreed: in 1948 he sued Welles and Mankiewicz for plagiarism of his work. The case was settled out of court.

yers, A. Lawrence Mitchell and Oscar Lawler. They viewed the picture in silence, and she left without a word.

Miss Parsons told Hearst that the picture blackened his name, even though Hearst himself had approved a script in September 1940,[5] and she attempted to force George J. Schaefer to withhold it. All mention of the film was forbidden in the Hearst newspapers. *The Hollywood Reporter* berated RKO for having made the film at all. Louis B. Mayer, characteristically, offered Schaefer $842,000 (the film's negative cost) if he would have the negative and all prints destroyed. (Hearst had been a major Metro stockholder until 1934.)[6] Schaefer refused. Hearst threatened to engage his entire newspaper chain in an onslaught on Hollywood morals, the employment of aliens in Hollywood, the alleged inclusion of sexually charged scenes and lines in defiance of the Hays office, and the nature of the private lives of screen moguls. The trial of Joseph M. Schenck of Twentieth Century-Fox in New York on income tax evasion charges would be run in full, and any similar stories he could get hold of. Welles was delighted with the flow of publicity: at a Los Angeles luncheon, he announced that he was planning a feature film on the life of the one and only William Randolph Hearst.

Hearst himself saw the film much later, with Marion Davies in San Francisco. When asked what he thought of it, he said it was a little too long: he told friends privately that he enjoyed seeing himself on the screen.

The Hays office announced that it would not get involved with the controversy over *Kane,* and Michael Sage in *The New Republic* (February 24, 1941) commented: "The neutral position of the Hays Office, which is supposed to defend the interests of RKO as well as those of other companies, is reminiscent of the sterling fortitude displayed by Neville Chamberlain when Hitler trampled Czechoslovakia."

[5]*Newsweek*. September 16, 1940.
[6]Henry Luce, however, offered to buy the film outright and bear the full responsibility of releasing it himself. His own *March of Time* was, of course, parodied in the newsreel, a fact that greatly amused him.

Schaefer's original attitude, as expressed to Louella Parsons when she first called him attacking the picture in New York, was that if anything was really offensive to Hearst the film would be "canned," while Welles was reported as saying that "rather than see George Schaefer in Dutch he would see *Kane* die unopened in the can." Finally, Schaefer and Welles issued a joint statement saying that the film was in no way connected with Hearst.

In January Hearst lifted the ban on mention of *Kane* in his newspapers (including the actual *New York Inquirer!*) and instead used space to attack it. Outvoted by his board, Schaefer was compelled to postpone the film's original opening date, scheduled for February, and a press preview set for March 12 was canceled. At an RKO sales meeting in Chicago in March, exhibitors were told that no decision had yet been made on *Kane's* release. Welles's statement was: "It is not based upon the life of Mr. Hearst or anyone else. On the other hand, had Mr. Hearst and similar financial barons not lived during the period we discuss, *Citizen Kane* could not have been made."

Later in March Welles called reporters to his suite at the Hotel Ambassador in New York (he was producing *Native Son* on Broadway) to announce that he would sue RKO if they did not release the film at once. He had, he revealed, a 25 percent interest in the profits and pointed out that this percentage was being jeopardized: "Under my contract I have the right to demand the picture be released and to bring legal action to force its release. RKO must release *Citizen Kane*. If it does not do so immediately I have instructed my attorney to commence legal proceedings."

Schaefer, after the furore that followed the conference, telephoned Welles to ask him to withhold legal action until they could meet in New York. At this stage there was an ironic footnote: the Hearst Press attacked the Free Company, an organization that had produced Welles's radio play *His Honor the Mayor,* as "communistic," in a style that recalled with precise accuracy the film's satire on political thought and particularly Walter Parks Thatcher's remarks about Kane himself.

Meanwhile, in what proved to be a last-ditch stand, Louella Parsons had telephoned the governor of New York and sought to prevent the showing of the film in New York City. Although Miss Parson's demand was naturally ignored, RKO — after Schaefer had told Welles he had no intention of canceling the film's release — had problems in finding a theater for the premiere run. Radio City Music Hall refused the film (for some reason Nelson Rockefeller, who owned it, yielded to pressure); there was trouble with the Warner circuits, and finally with the independents. At last the film was previewed for the press in April, and it opened on May 1 at the Palace heralded by the slogan: "Now you know . . . it's terrific," scarcely the most inspired of publicity blurbs for the most notorious of films. (The film opened a week later at the El Capitan Theatre in Hollywood.)

The reviews were warmly enthusiastic, although the Hearst papers not only failed to discuss the film critically but banned reviews of a current RKO soap opera, *Kitty Foyle,* as well. Charlie Chaplin said he would "back any picture which Mr. Welles may have in mind," and shortly thereafter bought Welles's treatment for *Monsieur Verdoux.* Hermine Rich Isaacs in *Theatre Arts* wrote: "An exciting work, vital and imaginative, full of the unbridled energy which Orson Welles brings to every new medium he invades." *Time* let fly with superlatives, apparently missing the hints of Henry Luce in the Kane character: "Lush with the leggy beauty of Publisher Kane's teeming love life, grotesque with his wholesale grabs of Europe's off-scourings." Bosley Crowther in *The New York Times* wrote: "Far and away the most surprising and cinematically exciting motion picture to be seen here in many a moon," while at the same time saying that the film failed to provide a picture of the character and motives behind the man "about whom the whole thing revolves." Kane, he added, is "cynical, ironic, sometimes oppressive and as realistic as a slap." Later, in the Sunday *Times* supplement, Crowther returned to the theme: no criticism was really made of Kane, he decided, and "there is no reason to assume from what is shown on the screen that he is anything but an honest publisher with a consistently conscientious attitude to society." In *The Commonweal* Philip T. Hartung went completely overboard: "He saw and he conquered. And *Citizen Kane* is proof." The only significant dissenting review was by Otis Ferguson in *The New Republic,* who found the film very much a mixed success (and later savagely attacked *The Magnificent Ambersons* in the columns of the same periodical). In England the response was enthusiastic: excited responses from the newspaper critics Dilys Powell and C. A. Lejeune, and William Whitebait of *The New Statesman* (then *New Statesman and Nation*) called *Kane* "A cross between a Pirandello play and *The Search* [sic] *for Corvo*," adding that the scene between the lawyer and the parents of Kane was "as vividly memorable as, say, a Camden Town Interior by Sickert" — a weird comparison if ever there was one — and that *Kane* was "Hard as nails in sentiment. . . . Makes a startling new use of violence, both on the eye and the ear." It received several Oscar nominations — all booed at the 1942 ceremonies — and one Oscar (for the screenplay).

The film flopped in the Midwest and the British provinces, but finally broke even; today, because of television, it can be said to have made a profit. If it is true that it synthesized rather than revolutionized Hollywood techniques, it is now an axiom that its influence struck deep into the American film of the period, helping to create a specific ambience in *films noirs:* dark, somber, heavily mannered, the flavor of American Gothic realized in settings looming and oppressive, in lighting low-key and *blafard.*[7]

One crucial question we must ask ourselves about *Kane* is: does the film accurately reflect William Randolph Hearst's life? Welles has in recent years continued to insist that Kane was not Hearst. He told the *New York Herald Tribune* (September 11, 1951):

He was a great figure. I didn't have a battle with him. He had one with me. *Citizen Kane* was *not* an exposé of Hearst as everyone believes. I didn't make a picture about him.

Hearst was raised by his mother. He had a very happy childhood. My man Kane was raised by a bank. That's the whole point of the picture. They were different types of men. For example, my man Kane would never have fought me the way Hearst did. Instead, he would probably have offered me a job.

Hearst and the people around him did me terrible harm after the picture appeared. Some day when I write my autobiography I'll tell of the damage that they did me, and the frame-ups they tried.

The big similarity between Hearst and Kane is that both of them had no responsibility to the people. But in spite of everything I hold no malice towards him. I don't see why anyone should hold any malice toward him.

We must admit, first, that the portrait is a caricature, and that the picture of Hearst's relationship with his mistress, Marion Davies, is not intended to be literal: her devotion to Hearst was absolute, and his death came to her as a bitter blow.[8] The real Hearst was capable of love, and life at San Simeon, his fabled ranch in California, sparkled in its heyday with a brightness and gaiety contradictory to the squalid luxury of Kane's ranch picnic and the echoing, tomb-like emptiness of Xanadu.

In other respects, the film follows Hearst's career with mixed fidelity. The plot adjustments are significant. Both Hearst and Kane were only children, born in 1863, and both were expelled from Harvard. Hearst's father and mother were not, like Kane's, poverty-stricken boardinghouse keepers. George Hearst was a well-to-do farmer's son, whose silver strike at the Comstock Lode made him a millionaire, and whose later interest in the Homestake Mine still further increased his massive fortune; he became a senator and earned a respected place in the American Dictionary of Biography. In the film these parents are left a deed to the Colorado Lode by a defaulting boarder, Fred Grange, and the Kane fortune is thus founded not by the acumen and push of a paternal figure but by blind chance.

---

[7]The influences of *Kane* struck into forties films, but disappeared with the onset of CinemaScope. They are not as extensive as some claim. Works like *Ivy, Caught, Keeper of the Flame,* and *The Devil and Miss Jones* are examples of the influences at work.

[8]Others have taken a grimmer view, hinting at homosexuality and other perversions and suggesting that Marion Davies was often kept a virtual prisoner at San Simeon. We will probably never know the truth, but I have preferred the more charitable view.

Hearst's love for his mother is echoed in Kane's love for his, and the Rosebud image — symbol of a lost childhood and the protection of a mother — is an apt reflection of the fact that Hearst was forever haunted by the memory of the charming, tender, and noble Phoebe Hearst.

The origin of the character of Susan Alexander Kane[9] has usually been attributed to Marion Davies alone, and the portrait is indeed visually based on her: the nervous doll's face, the aureole of blonde hair, the chirrupy voice. It is true, too, that through his Cosmopolitan Pictures outfit, first in New York and then in California, and by purchasing a major shareholding interest in MGM (and later Warner Brothers) Hearst secured for her a career in the cinema which she really didn't want, and was embarrassed to see applauded by every Hearst newspaper critic who valued his job. In fact, a stronger foundation of the character is in Sybil Sanderson, Hearst's first love, an opera singer whose initial American appearance at the Met was applauded in an exorbitantly large article in Hearst's *San Francisco Examiner* (prototype of Kane's *Inquirer*); for her the infatuated Massenet composed *Thaïs* and *Manon* — the mode of the former appropriately and perfectly parodied in Herrmann's *Salammbô* excerpts. Sybil Sanderson died ruined by drink and ill-health in her late thirties, her career dogged by scandals. Although Hearst's wife, Milicent Wilson, was a dancer and not, like Emily Monroe Norton, the niece of the president, much of her personality is echoed in the gentle, staid, and unexciting Emily.

Politically, the parallels with Hearst are often startlingly close, for instance in reference to *The Inquirer* having started the Spanish-American War.

Hearst bought the New York *Morning Journal* in 1895; it was originally an unsuccessful paper, and he changed it into a one-cent sheet of a popular type. He raided the New York *World* for members of Joseph Pulitzer's staff. The combination of sensationalism and jingoism elevated the circulation to 1,506,000 copies.

He attacked President McKinley (as Kane attacked President Monroe), and provoked war with Spain. Later came the Chicago *American,* paralleling the Chicago paper for which Leland worked. During the Depression, he sold or scrapped papers, like Kane.

The famous exchange of telegrams between Hearst and Frederic Remington, an artist whom he sent to sketch the Spanish butchery in 1896, is reproduced almost intact in the script. When Remington cabled the *Journal,* "Everything quiet. There is no trouble here. There will be no more. I wish to return." Hearst replied: "Please remain. You furnish the pictures; I'll furnish the war." Later, Hearst published a Remington drawing of a Cuban girl stripped for searching by Cuban soldiers; the rival newspaper, the *World,* managed to produce the girl herself, who confessed she had been searched under conditions of privacy by matrons, and that Remington could not have drawn her.

Once the film closely echoes an actual conversation: the remark Kane makes to Walter Parks Thatcher when the banker complains that the newspapers are losing a million dollars a year — "I'll have to close this place — in sixty years." This is directly drawn from Phoebe Hearst's comment upon learning that her son's *Examiner* and *Journal* were losing the same amount: "At that rate, he could last thirty years." Bernstein is based on two of Hearst's associates, Arthur Brisbane and S. S. Carvalho, and Jedediah Leland is based on John Francis Neylan, the Irish lawyer and political reporter who fought gallantly against graft and became Hearst's counsel and lawyer for the Hearst empire: a man of probity, he was often thought of as Hearst's conscience, and he is heartlessly parodied in the figure of the sophomoric, verbose, and often foolish figure presented on the screen.[10] There are parallels, too, in the character of Jim W. Gettys with Boss Charles F. Murphy, a political manipulator who opposed Hearst at the time Hearst ran for governor of New York; Thatcher is a caricature of J. P. Morgan. Kane's politics authentically

---

[9]Rita Alexander was the name of Welles's screenplay typist.

[10]Leland's dismissal for his unfavorable notice of Susan Kane's operatic debut echoes Hearst's sacking of many for similar "mistakes."

echo Hearst's: Hearst began as a Jeffersonian demo-crat, using *The San Francisco Examiner* as a radical organ to fight political corruption, big business, and monopolies, while at the same time deeply involved in business ventures of his own. Later, he became fascist, exploiting a fascist potentiality in the lower middle class, a class that had once been as Jeffer-sonian as he was.

As Raymond Gram Swing wrote in his *Forerunners of American Fascism*: "During the lifetime and power of this single man, the entire economic fabric was made anew. We see in him the beginning of the modern era, hear through him the social outcry against it, and find him today, no longer a rebel, but resigned to it and accepting its fascist implications."[11] Kane's speeches in the film echo Hearst's, and also Hearst's letters — like the famous one written in 1906 to Arthur Brisbane and quoted by W. A. Swanberg in his definitive *Citizen Hearst*:

We still maintain a republican form of government, but who has control of the primaries that nominate the candi-date? The corporations have. Who control the conventions? The corporations. Who own the bosses and the elected officials? Are they representatives of the people or the cor-porations? . . . If the corporations do all this — and they surely do — can we any longer maintain that this is govern-ment for the people?[12]

In his campaign for the governorship of New York, expertly condensed and parodied in the film, Hearst promised "government ownership" to restore to the people "everything the corporations have stolen from them." Later, when Hearst's Americanism — like Kane's — changed its meaning he began to admire Hitler and Mussolini. In the mid-thirties, after he had established his fascist stand and had visited Hitler, Hearst attacked the communist menace. So the changes were rung and the film mockingly rings them too.

And *Kane's* final conclusion is the same as Swanberg's, finishing his life of Hearst on a series of question marks.

Studying that life, Swanberg wrote, was for most of his contemporaries "as confusing as adding two and two and discovering for once that it did not make four." Swanberg concludes that Hearst would have been dan-gerous in high office and that his rejection by the voters was a fine proof of the democratic system.

He had integrity, on occasion. He had principles and beliefs which he firmly swore by at any given time but which could fluctuate as wildly as a compass near the pole. His crippling weakness was instability, vacillation, his inability to anchor his thinking to a few basic, rocklike truths that were immovable in his heart. . . . For all his potency of utterance, he seemed a creature of caprice, lacking real substance.

(In some ways an appropriate comment on the worst side of Welles himself.) Swanberg adds that Hearst was "unrivaled in the magnificence of his failure, the scope of his defeats, the size and scope of his disappointments." The film exactly captures this quality of magnificent catastrophe in a style not dissimilar to that which characterized Hearst's journalism — as Swanberg says, "Combining elements of the peep-show, the Grand Guignol and the foghorn." Welles's achievement was to blend those elements into art. As Swanberg says:

[11] Julian Messner, 1935.
[12] New York, Charles Scribner's Sons, 1961.

"Who but Citizen Hearst would have set himself up as a king, owned seven castles, fought for the common man, looted the world of art, squired a bevy of actresses through Europe?" The answer is no one. And who but Orson Welles, the explosive *Wunderkind* of American radio, theater, and film, could have brought his life to the screen? No one again. One is left only with the wish that Welles had drawn his own conclusions about this friend of the working man, the Jeffersonian, the fascist, the master of empires, instead of leaving us with an enigma as baffling as a great stone Easter Island face.

• • •

Threatening chords sound on the brass; a somber gateway bears the single, authoritative initial "K"; a hill is seen, cluttered with junk; and inside a tall sixteenth-century Scottish window glows with light. A man is dying, rubbery lips in close-up breathing "Rosebud"; a crystal paperweight bounces out of the man's hand, its snowflakes whirling; a nurse walking through the door

is seen refracted through a sliver of its glass. After this audacious Gothic opening, we are in a projection room — actually at Pathé — at a test screening of an episode of "News on the March."[13]

The commentator recalls the splendors of the Kane mansion, Xanadu, in Florida — a private mountain built from the desert flats of the Gulf country; 100,000 trees and 20,000 tons of marble used for the palace of the mogul, its contents "a collection of everything . . . the loot of the world," and, outside, the greatest private zoo since Noah. "Since the Pyramids, Xanadu is the costliest monument man has built for himself."

We are given the details of Kane's empire: thirty-seven newspapers two news syndicates, a radio network, grocery stores, paper mills, factories, ocean liners — a world built up from the fabulous seed of the Colorado Lode, the world's third richest gold mine, which a defaulting boarder left to Mary Kane, the tycoon's boardinghouse-keeper mother, in 1868 when Kane was five. At a filmed congressional investigation of Walter P. Thatcher, grand old man of Wall Street (based directly on the J. P. Morgan investigations) Thatcher recalls Mary Kane asking him to raise her son, and he savagely attacks Kane: "In every essence of his personal beliefs, and by the dangerous manner in which he persistently attacked the American traditions of private property, initiative, opportunity and advancement, Mr. Kane is nothing more nor less than a communist!" (A moment later we see a politician in New York's Union Square call Kane "a menace to the working man . . . a fascist," thus showing Welles's disregard of corrupted opinion.)

Particulars follow of the late despot's marriage to Emily Monroe Norton, niece of the president of the United States,[14] her death in a car accident in 1918 with their son, and his marriage two weeks later to Susan Alexander, then a singer at the Town Hall at Trenton, New Jersey, formerly a sheet-music salesgirl at Ziegel-

[13]Suggested, clearly, by Hearst's own Hearst-Metrotone newsreels, *News of the Day* as well as Henry Luce's *March of Time* distributed by RKO.

[14]A parallel, here, with the marriage of Hearst's Seattle publisher, John Boettiger, to a president's daughter.

Prelude "Citizen Kane" / Mill

From the projection room, slashed with the arc beam that flickers out with Kane's life, looming with the silhouette figures of the "News on the March" production team, Thompson, its leading reporter, sets out to look for "Rosebud." He tries without success to interview Susan Alexander in Atlantic City, where he finds her in a seedy cabaret, the El Rancho Nightclub; he enters the gray echoing tomb of the Thatcher Memorial Library, where a prim female custodian informs him that he must leave at 4:40 P.M. sharp, her voice distorted eerily by the marble halls.

Through pages 84-142 of Thatcher's memoirs, we are transported to the remote township of Little Salem, Colorado, and a lonely wooden boardinghouse on a wintry plain. Thatcher is telling Mary Kane how the fortune of the Colorado Lode left her by the defaulting Fred Grange is to be disbursed: $50,000 a year to her and Mr. Kane, the rest in trust to the boy, who is to come into control of it at the age of twenty-five. Outside, at that moment, Charles is playing with the Rosebud sled,[15] and as his mother introduces him to Thatcher,

man's. For Susan, Kane built Chicago's Municipal Opera House at a cost of three million dollars; for her, he suffered political ruin, when the scandal of their love affair destroyed his attempt to become independent governor of New York. The newsreel sketches in the Depression — eleven Kane papers merge, others are sold, or scrapped. Returning from Europe by ship, Kane is asked by the press on arrival in New York harbor: "How did you find business conditions in Europe, Mr. Kane?" "With great difficulty," is the fatuous reply. Disintegration sets in: Kane is shown in his old age, a shapeless mummy in a wheelchair, pushed through an orchard, observed by a concealed camera through the branches of a tree; then in the hollow pile of Xanadu. Lights out, and death.

[15]Sleds were at one time given trademarks or titles similar to "Rosebud." Welles himself had a bed shaped like a sleigh in his New York apartment, and in his Broadway production of *Native Son* in May 1941, he had a character drag on a sled with the name Rosebud on it.

the boy rams it vigorously into the horrified banker, thus symbolizing a contempt for authority, for power, that animates the character throughout the first half of the film, until he finally becomes a victim of power himself.

Charles rises to manhood in a series of Dickensian scenes (Welles next wanted to make *The Pickwick Papers*): his collisions with Thatcher, youth with its dash, energy, and irresponsibility contrasted with cau-

tious and respectable late middle age (an effect echoed in *The Magnificent Ambersons*). The Colorado Lode is elevated by Thatcher's wizardry into the world's sixth-largest private fortune, but Kane is interested only in one of Thatcher's innumerable acquisitions: *The Inquirer*, an impoverished, fuddy-duddy New York paper.

Thatcher explodes into rage at *The Inquirer's* new policy of concocting stories: "You know perfectly well there's no Armada off the Jersey coast," a reference to

Welles's own techniques in the Martian broadcast, as well as to several Hearst newspaper hoaxes. We see Kane informed by a correspondent in Cuba that he could write travel prose poems about the place, but that the war he was sent to cover does not exist. "You provide the prose poems," Kane says through an intermediary by way of reply, "I'll provide the war." At the same time Thatcher clashes violently with Kane over his expensive, idealistic front (Welles's playing here is miscalculated: it is too unambiguously sincere). In a direct reference to Franklin Delano Roosevelt's early career Kane says that if he does not look after the underprivileged, "somebody else will." Thatcher condemns *The Inquirer* as a philanthropic exercise, and Kane contemptuously announces that if it loses a million a year, as Thatcher predicts, it will have to close — in sixty years.

In the next scene Thompson visits Bernstein, Kane's favorite editor. Bernstein, in a sequence notable for its mood of elegiac stillness foreshadowing *The Magnificent Ambersons,* says that Rosebud may have been a girl; he brings up a reminiscence of crossing to New Jersey on the ferry in 1896 and seeing for a fleeting moment a girl in a white dress carrying a parasol; not a month has gone by since in which he hasn't thought of her. Thatcher, according to Bernstein, was "the biggest damn fool he ever met. . . . It's no trick to make a lot of money . . . if all you want is to make a lot of money." (Bernstein isn't over-bright.) Kane, Bernstein maintains, didn't want money; and he emphasizes the tycoon's early irresponsibility, his dismissal from Cornell, Yale, and Harvard for bad behavior.

A vivid, thoroughly Dickensian scene follows as Kane arrives at *The Inquirer* offices for the first time, and is greeted by the silly and fustian editor Mr. Carter with a pompous welcome message, the staff snapping sycophantically to attention. *The Inquirer,* on its last legs, is an old lady of a journal which keeps open only twelve hours a day. Kane seizes on an obscure story of the disappearance of a woman named Silverstone and turns it into front-page headlines as a murder case, with the husband named as the suspected killer, an echo of Hearst's activities in the Hall-Mills case. Carter is dismayed: "If we were interested in the gossip of housewives," he fumes, "we could fill the paper twice daily." Kane makes no secret of his tabloid ambitions: "Mr. Carter, that's just the kind of thing we *are* going to be interested in." Then he instructs Carter to send a crack reporter to the address of the missing woman, with instructions to tell the husband that unless he produces his wife *The Inquirer* will have him arrested: "If he gets indignant and asks to see his badge, the reporter will call Mr. Silverstone an anarchist, loudly, so the neighbors can hear!"

Shortly after this display of irresponsibility Kane suddenly announces that *The Inquirer* is to be a crusading paper that will be "as important to New York as the gas is in that light." He reads a "Declaration of Principles," extravagantly remaking the front page for the third time to give room for it:

I'll provide the people of this city with a daily newspaper that will tell all the news honestly. People are going to know who's responsible. They are going to get the truth, gaily and simply and entertainingly and no special interests are going to interfere with that truth. We are also going to provide them with a tireless and fearless champion of their rights, as citizens and human beings.

Jedediah Leland, Kane's close friend, saves this significant document.

Kane buys *The Chronicle's* staff. At a party to celebrate their switch to *The Inquirer,* a long table is crowded with staff members, chorus girls prance in, and the crowd breaks into a sycophantic song later adapted as Kane's campaign anthem. The leader, a comic in straw boater and striped blazer takes the solo role.

Solo:
There is a man — a certain man
And for the poor you may be sure that he'll do all he can!
Who is this one? — this fav'rite son?
Just by his action has the traction magnates on the run?
Who loves to smoke? — enjoys a joke?
Who wouldn't get a bit upset if he were really broke?
With wealth and fame — he's still the same —
I'll bet you five you're not alive if you don't know his
    name!

CHORUS

What is his name?

Crowd:

It's Mister Kane

Solo:

He doesn't like that Mister he likes good old Charlie Kane.

SECOND VERSE

Solo:

Now please tell me — who can it be

Who always has a pretty lady parked on either knee?

Who says a miss — was made to kiss

And when he meets one always tries to do exactly this?

Who buys the food — who buys the drinks?

Who thinks that dough was made to spend and acts the way he thinks?

Now is it Joe?

Crowd:

No, no, no, no!

Solo:

I'll bet you ten that you aren't men if you don't really know!

CHORUS

What is his name? Etc.

THIRD VERSE

Solo:

Let's have a toast — a good old toast

And let it be in honor of the man we all love most!

To shake his hand — is some event

Why if he cared to he could even be our president!

He'd rather be — one of the mob

He took the niece of the president but not his job!

Oh what a guy

Crowd:

Hi yi yi yi

Solo:

Come on and sing his praise as we all raise our glasses high!

Behind the words which knowingly portray an idealist-cum-common-man's man, Leland and Bernstein discuss the stark idea that Kane started the Spanish-American War with a news campaign (hinted at earlier in the reference to Cuba). Leland points to the fact that the

Chronicle men, now excited at working for Kane, once had an opposing policy. But Bernstein is cheerfully, heartlessly practical: "Sure. They're just like anybody else! They've got work to do, they do it! Only they happen to be the best men in the business! Mr. Kane, he'll have them changed to his kind of newspapermen in a week!" Leland has his doubts; he thinks *they* may change Kane.

On his first treasure-hunting trip to Europe Kane has collected "somebody who's collecting diamonds," the niece of the president, Emily Monroe Norton. Bernstein's reminiscence fades as the staff of the newly bought newspaper dash to the windows to see the pretty, genteel girl displayed for their benefit in a carriage.

Bernstein's concluding words are: "Mr. Kane was a man who lost almost everything he had. Old age is the only disease . . . that you don't look forward to being cured of."

In a drab hospital Thompson talks to Jedediah Leland, Kane's college friend, and later drama critic of the Kane newspaper in Chicago. Leland is frail and a little senile, opening with a gloomy observation: "That's one of the greatest curses of the human race, memory." Despite his age, he can recall every detail of his past in the Kane empire.

I was his closest friend, and so far as I was concerned, he behaved like a swine. Not that Charlie was brutal, he just did brutal things. I guess I was what you would nowadays call a stooge.

[Kane] had some private form of greatness, but he kept it to himself. He never gave himself away. He never gave anything away, he just 'left you a tip.' He had a generous *mind,* I don't suppose anybody ever had so many *opinions.* But he never believed in anything except Charlie Kane. He never had a conviction except Charlie Kane in his life. I suppose he died without one.

It must have been pretty unpleasant. Of course, a lot of us check out without any special convictions about death, but we do know what we're leaving, we do believe in *something.* Are you absolutely sure you haven't got a cigar?

Leland recalls Emily Kane: in dancing school she was a nice girl, perhaps the nicest of her group; and "It was a marriage, just like any other marriage," as we see the couple animatedly talking across a breakfast table, arguing ("Your only co-respondent is *The Inquirer*") and in successive time-lapse scenes subsiding at last into silence behind copies of *The Chronicle* (Emily) and *The Inquirer* (Kane). Kane's egotism is shown when Emily, complaining about *The Inquirer's* attack on her uncle, the president, says: "People will think . . ." and Kane furiously answers back, *"What I tell them to think!"*

Now Leland moves on to the subject of Kane's second marriage, to Susan Alexander: Charlie called her "a cross section of the American public . . . guess she must have had something for him . . . that first night [they met] all she had was a toothache . . . . " On his way to the Western Manhattan Warehouse to look at his mother's pitiful belongings ("I am in search of my youth"), Kane meets Susan. He has been splashed by a truck and has mud on his face, and she offers to clean him up; he makes her laugh by wiggling his ears: a trick taught him, he says, by the present president of Venezuela at the world's best boy's school. He imitates a rooster; affection draws them together. Kane exerts a simple charm ("I run a couple of newspapers. What do you do?") and a surprising sentimentality ("I guess we're both lonely people"). She discloses an ambition to be a singer, and Kane decides to make her an opera star; an accelerating allegro shows her singing for him in a parlor and trained by a distracted Italian teacher.

Now we are at 185 West 74th Street, Susan's new house, for the sequence that shows the beginning of Kane's subsequent political defeat in the confrontation with Emily Kane and Kane's rival for the governorship, Jim W. Gettys. Gettys threatens to expose Kane's relationship with Susan in every newspaper not owned by Kane in the state. He has already forced Susan to send a note to Kane also threatening exposure. Kane isn't fazed: "There's only one person in the world who decides what I'm going to do, and that's me." As Gettys and Emily leave, Kane calls down the apartment building staircase that he will put Gettys in Sing Sing; but he can't: Gettys exposes him.

The doomed campaign itself is conducted, Leland reminds us, on a workingman's ticket, on behalf of the "underpaid, the underprivileged, and the underfed." Leland warns him, correctly, that the workingman is apt to turn into organized labor, that the laborer is going to claim rights, not regard them as Kane's gift: "When your precious underprivileged really get together, oh boy! That's going to add up to something bigger than your privileges! Then I don't know *what* you'll do! Sail away to a desert island probably and lord it over the monkeys!" Kane's reply is soft: "I wouldn't worry too much, Jed. There'll probably be a few of them to let me know when I do something wrong." But Leland is tough: "You don't care about anything but

you. You just want to persuade people you love 'em so much they ought to love you back. You want love on your own terms. Something to be played *your* way, according to *your* rules." Leland asks to be sent to Chicago as drama critic, but Kane doesn't want him to leave New York: "You won't like it in Chicago . . . the wind comes howling off the lake and gosh only knows if they heard of Lobster Newburg." And he adds — determined as ever to get the last word in: "A toast, Jedediah, to love on my terms. Those are the only terms anybody ever knows."

Susan's Chicago debut is introduced with Matiste the singing teacher screaming "No! No! No! No!" As the opera begins, two men in the flies above the stage hold their noses (Welles is cheating here: Leland from his balcony seat could not have seen them). Leland, drunk, types his notice in the office: "Miss Alexander, a pretty but hopelessly incompetent amateur . . ." and Kane fires him. Leland contemptuously returns *The Inquirer's* manifesto of principles that no special interests are going to interfere with truth." Kane, with Susan's career in pieces, retires to Xanadu, and Leland makes a final observation: "He was disappointed in the world, so he built one of his own."

In the last section of the film Susan Alexander takes up the thread, emerging from a drunken stupor in Atlantic City, finally coaxed into talking by Thompson. She says she never wanted an operatic career (when in fact she did half-want one); we see the horror of her disastrous first night again from her point of view; she rages over the bad review by Leland (which Kane himself had completed). Kane, declaring that he has no intention of making himself ridiculous, orders her to continue with her singing. She does, the career fizzles out with the symbolic flickering of a bulb filament; the voice fades away on the sound track, and she attempts to commit suicide. She makes a last, desperate statement to her husband: "I couldn't go through with the singing again . . . you don't know what it means, to feel that a whole audience doesn't want you." He replies: "That's when you've got to fight them." But he relents; his essential humanity shows through: "All right, you won't have to fight them any more. It's *their* loss."

Now we are transported to Xanadu, where night is indistinguishable from day: "What time is it? 11:30 in the morning? Night?" The words are Susan's, and she is already trapped: "A person could go crazy in this dump!" Although Kane has evidently done his utmost to keep his wife happy — he tells her that if she looks in the west wing she will find a dozen of her friends still in residence — she is still miserable, longing for New York, for fun. She is working and working at a gigantic jigsaw puzzle ("Makes more sense than collecting statues"), and the monotony of their life is symbolized by Kane's brooding head in the foreground, her own work on the puzzle dominated by a vast imported Scottish Stuart fireplace.

In the garden Kane holds a picnic, a Negro symbolically moaning to a harsh jazz accompaniment, while in

their tent the Kanes quarrel with Susan taking up Jedediah Leland's point about Kane's inability to love: "You never really gave anybody anything in your whole life . . . you just tried to buy me into giving you something. You don't love me, you just want me to love you. . . ." As she talks about love, the screams of the guests outside indicate that at least somewhere in Xanadu there's a good deal of "loving" going on.

She packs, and Kane is finally threatened enough to scream at her not to go: "You can't do this to me!" Her reply is: "I see, it's *you* this is being done to!" But if she was pitiless then, in Atlantic City now she is full of pity: "Don't you think I'm sorry [for him]?"

The film's coda is formed by the narrative, brief and succinct, of Kane's valet, the sinister Raymond, who wants (but doesn't get) $1,000 for his pains. He remembers Kane smashing Susan's room to pieces, and picking up a snow crystal paperweight she left behind, with a cabin that might perhaps be Mrs. Kane's boardinghouse in the midst of whirling imitation snow. Kane has seen "Rosebud": the memory of the sled he loved, and the innocence and beauty it recalls bring tears to his eyes.

Disappointed, Thompson resigns himself to leaving Kane's secret untouched. The reporters pick cynically over the detritus of a lifetime and someone asks: "What did you find out about him?" Thompson replies: "Very little. I don't think anything can explain away a man's life." And that is all we are left with: the fire eats away

the paint from the Rosebud sled, the reporters walk off briskly to catch the next train back to New York, plaintive tones sound in the score; and the gate with its sign "No Trespassing" closes inexorably forever on a legend.

• • •

The opening sequence, even after innumerable viewings, still retains its power to haunt and disturb. A close-up of the "No Trespassing" sign dissolves to a slow exploration of the meshes of the iron fence secluding Xanadu from the world. This oppressive image changes to great flowers of iron; and then, in a very gradual, almost Sternbergian dissolve, to the massive single initial "K" framed in wrought iron, the crest of the gate. At the right, Xanadu towers distantly loom out of the mists in the faintly moonlit night.

Two spider monkeys sit watchfully in a cage to the left of the frame, a gate to the right balances the composition; gondolas gleam against the background of a pier, and the castle shimmers palely, reflected in the water of an imitation Venetian canal, precursor of a similar one in *Touch of Evil*. The figure of Bakst, an Egyptian cat god, stands before a bridge with a raised portcullis, and another gate is seen to the right. A golf marker (365 yards) for a mistily glimpsed course emerges. Almost subliminally we are made aware that a single window of the castle is lit up, casting a sliver of illumination in a bleak and towering tomb of stone.

The effect is brilliantly sinister, mysterious, and magical, pulling us forward in a series of hypnotic dissolves as though in a dream, each successive shot containing glimpses of the castle, a succession of gateways leading us on in our exploration of this secret and fabled world, Kane's strange legacy.[16] Now we get a closer shot of a crumbling gate, with palm trees around it, shabby and unmoving, a medium shot of the castle, and the lighted Scottish window. The light snaps off, and we cut to a

[16]There is an intriguing parallel in Hitchcock's *Rebecca,* made the same year and in the same studio, and originally adapted by Welles for his "First Person Singular" radio series. *Rebecca* was also a precursor of *Ambersons* in its use of narrative.

reverse angle shot of the interior of the window, with a figure lying stiffly on a bed like a medieval knight on a tomb: Kane. This image dissolves into a dazzling effect: the entire screen is filled with whirling snowflakes, blotting out everything. We draw back to see a little wooden house, and the camera retreats further to disclose that we are peering into the depths of a circular glass snowstorm paperweight; it is at that precise moment that the word "Rosebud" is spoken, and the lips, repeating the word, fill the screen. The globe bounces down steps, its tiny flakes whirling in water, a nurse comes in aslant the image; the little house lies sideways on the left of the frame and the screen is filled laterally by a piece of shattered globe, the nurse refracted through it. She folds the dead man's hands and pulls the sheet over his head, observed entirely in silhouette. Another dissolve leads to the lighted window and the figure, almost exactly paralleling the shot introducing the death chamber. Cut to a row of flags painted on a credit card: "News on the March."

This is apparently meant to be only a portion of a news magazine; the panel heading is "Obituary: Xanadu's Landlord." In rapid succession we see the words of Coleridge's poem; a series of shots of San Simeon, partly from the air, of people disporting themselves in the grounds; the construction of the building; a figure on a horse, vertical wipes removing a series of images of toil; four horses, two giraffes, birds, an octopus, an elephant, a huge aviary of glass, a cupid firing a bow and arrow. The funeral of Kane, his rise and downfall, and excerpts from his career, faultlessly blend deliberately scratched stock, artificially staged scenes shot by Gregg Toland, and newsreel photographs.

As the newsreel flickers off with a dying fall on the sound track, the figures in the screening room strike up matches in the dark. When Thompson receives his orders to track down the facts about Kane, his editor looms in the arc beam, the light streaming from his body in a series of fans, splitting the image into fragments. Thompson's first interview with Susan Kane is introduced with the camera probing through a violent electric storm to a huge illuminated sign announcing

her at the El Rancho Nightclub, then moving up "through" the rain-swept skylight, followed by a shot of Susan drunk at a table as indicated earlier.

At the Thatcher Memorial Library in Chicago — Thompson's diminutive entering figure is dwarfed by a huge gray echoing cathedral of stone pierced by dusty sunbeams; ahead of him a table stretches to infinity, like a gigantic coffin marking the resting place of the dead banker. A subjective camera representing Thompson explores the pages of the book, reflecting the audience's desire to peer into the secrets of the character. The tall, slanting, perfectly molded banker's handwriting is followed in a very gradual left to right pan, and we pick out the words slowly, as though groping in the dark: here is Bernard Herrmann's figure for woodwind, moving from faintly sepulchral bars into a gay childlike theme, innocent and tripping: "I first encountered Mr. Kane in 1871. . . . " The flutes and piccolos trip still more lightly, blending into a delicate passage for strings as the page fades away to a mass of snowflakes, as mind-filling as those which blotted out the image upon Kane's death: an eight-year-old boy is playing with a sled, coming down a hill; he throws a snowball at the sign on top of the crude wooden building to the right of frame: the snowball smashes against letters that read BOARDING HOUSE. Thus in a moment we have seen that Kane is obstreperous, rebellious; the setting of loneliness and shabby gentility has been permanently fixed in our minds.

The composition of the scene that follows, with Thatcher, the Kanes, and the boy, is very simple: while the sound track is complex with argument, the camera remains stationary at a table, Charles glimpsed through the window in a long-held take. A slow dolly shot introduces and closes the interior scene of the discussion, and at the end we are able to look lingeringly into the house: cheap vases, mats, pictures, an image of rural simplicity. Outside in the snow the grouping of the characters is again observed in a long take, with the camera absolutely fixed. Welles cuts to Mrs. Kane, the camera coming down to take in Charlie, followed by a dissolve to the sled, tossed away on a snowbank; then the sled more thickly covered in driving snow, a symbol of vanished innocence and purity, while a mournful train whistle beyond it brilliantly conveys Charlie's unhappy transference to Chicago.

The scene in Bernstein's office is played against windows streaming with rain, rain reflected in a desk which bears a magnifying glass — an indication of Bernstein's advancing years, his failing sight. A fire flickers in a grate, Kane's portrait dominates the scene, and Thompson is just in front of the camera, leaning forward as the audience's representative. Once more the camera remains still, except when it moves very slightly across the desk as Thompson leans forward: here is a scene of absolute firmness, economy, and sobriety — aspects of his talent for which Welles is all too seldom recognized. Bernstein's movements, too, are extremely economical: quietly lighting a cigarette, going to the ticker-tape machine near the window to look at the Wall Street results as he makes his point about Walter Parks Thatcher's financial career.

As Bernstein begins his story about life on *The Inquirer,* the camera glides down the side of *The Inquirer* building to a carriage, without a break; we dissolve to the interior of the carriage, disclosing Kane and Leland; the carriage moves out of frame as they enter the building — all observed in a single take. We catch a hint of Kane's continued involvement in the past, and a foreshadowing of the Rosebud image, as we see a simple iron bedstead and some chairs — possibly from the Kane boardinghouse — carried into *The Inquirer* editorial office by members of the staff, marked with auction tickets.

Anticipating the rather disappointing handling of all the *Inquirer* scenes, the opening one — in which the fussy editor rings a little bell and greets Kane's arrival with the whole staff standing — matches a certain facetiousness in the writing with a cluttered and dull physical handling: even the arrival of Bernstein, tumbling amid the newly arrived furniture, isn't handled with any notable wit. People interrupt each other pointlessly, and the showing off of the ceilinged set seems very much like "Look, no hands." During the conversation in which the editor refuses to indulge in a circulation-building stunt, the handling is so fussy and confused that the whole point is lost and understood only on a re-examination of the sound track: here Welles is indulging technique to such an extent that an important aspect of Kane's character — his brutal use of people for dramatic effect — is lost. In the next scene, as Kane leans against the office window to write his "Declaration of Principles," Kane, Leland, and Bernstein are arranged in posed triangular compositions that serve no useful purpose and once more distract the attention from the matter in hand: namely, Welles's statement to the audience that Kane is a fake idealist, or trying to be one.

As we see *The Inquirer's* circulation rise, the Declaration of Principles is printed on the front page in close-up, the camera withdraws, then there is a quick dissolve to Leland, Bernstein, and Kane behind a window showing the increased figures — a perfectly straightforward and acceptable narrative device. We move to a similar shot of *The Chronicle's* window as the three men discuss the possibility of Kane taking it over; and we see a photograph of *The Chronicle* editorial staff. As Kane says that he has bought the staff, like candy in a store, the photograph comes to life. We are at the party to celebrate the take-over: a new photograph is taken, the table crowded with champagne bottles and rioting staff members, with two carved-ice busts at the end representing Leland and Bernstein: they frame the screen for part of Kane's speech. As the band comes in wearing busbies, dressed in the costumes of Catherine the Great's Russia, and the girls rush in after them, the editing tempo appropriately increases, cutting from audience to girls and back again, taking in a chorus master with baton and striped coat in the style of W.C. Fields. In contrast with the excitement of the others as Kane dances with a girl in long-shot, Leland — in cut-in two-shots with Bernstein — looks thoroughly bored and unimpressed. The handling here is prosaic and straightforward, except for the shots of Kane and the girls reflected in the window bearing *The Chronicle's* name. Tragically, the main points of Bernstein's and Leland's conversation are utterly lost.

Welles returns to a more disciplined handling in the next scene, when Leland and Bernstein discuss Kane's visit to Europe: a long-held two-shot enables the points of the conversation to be fully grasped, and the welcome home is beautifully managed: a close-up of a cup as Carter reads the welcome message, the cup carried forward, a cut to the door with Kane framed in it, then

a reverse dolly shot of great length and ingenuity across the office, the camera staying stationary in a position below eye level, observing the group of editors from a distance. A cut to the window as we see the staff realize that Kane has brought home a bride; the carriage is shown in the window, which forms a frame within a frame; and, finally, we get a long shot of the whole staff waving a farewell to Kane through the windows of the office and the tall, gilt lettering of *The Inquirer* — one of the film's most hauntingly beautiful effects.

When we return to Bernstein's office at the end of his narrative, the light has changed: it is no longer twilight, but night, and it has stopped raining.

Now we are to meet Jedediah Leland, at the Huntington Memorial Hospital on 180th Street. We see Thompson below and looking up at a gigantically imposing bridge; dissolve to the hospital, two figures in a blown-up still in wheelchairs, silent, behind Leland, who looks thin and shriveled in his patterned dressing gown, hidden behind dark glasses, his head encased by an old tennis cap-cum-eyeshade. He has become tragically senile; his incarceration in the hospital, the feeling of paralysis that comes with old age, and the terrible isolation of the sick are all conveyed with great economy by the use of an apparently stationary, but in fact almost imperceptibly moving, camera, the dolly pushed forward inch by inch as we get infinitesimally closer to the old man's

face. (This effect is repeated in the sequence when Bannister and his wife talk outside the courtroom in *The Lady from Shanghai*.) The grey lighting echoes feebly the mood of the projection-room scene. The composition is divided into sections by diagonal beams of sunlight which move during the conversation, the background sad, drab, tomb-like: a wall to the left, windows at the back beyond the two huddled patients in their heavy rugged wheelchairs, and the figure of Leland nodding on like a scarcely animated mummy. The effect of using a still to freeze the background, instead of living people and a set, is to emphasize the approaching stillness of Leland's end. After this unusually prolonged and subtle take, we see Leland's face retained over the first shot as he describes Kane's marriage: the breakfast table dissolves in, and the old man's head nods, slowly disappearing.

The celebrated sequence of the Kanes' declining marriage is figured in rapid cuts from face to face, seen across a bowl of flowers, with "swish pans" giving a curious effect like a moving train at night or a succession of windows flashing between each successive scene as we see the room grow more elaborately furnished and filled with more lavish displays of tropical plants; finally, the couple is left reading the antagonistic newspapers; the camera draws away to show husband and wife posed at the table, utterly silent. As the sequence

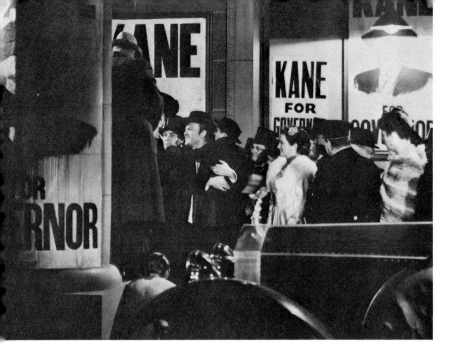

efforts gradually dissolves into the plaudits of a small crowd for Jedediah Leland's campaign speech — part of Kane's campaign for election as governor of New York — and then into Kane's own speech in a large hall, attacking his enemy, boss Jim W. Gettys.

The hall itself, populated by painted process figures, is an illustration of a tight budget, of Welles's necessary eschewing of extras: a far cry indeed from Capra's dazzling political rally in the rain in the not dissimilar *Meet John Doe,* made in the previous year. Welles's inexperience shows in the fact that he cannot conceal the obviousness of the process shot; he is not the equal of a Capra or a Curtiz in such effects, and for once the RKO special effects department served him poorly.

ends, we dissolve back to Leland in the hospital; he is observed with an entirely still camera as he begins to talk about Kane's first meeting with Susan Alexander. Now we are in a very "studio" New York street wet with rain, with Kane's shadow on the pavement and Susan giggling off-screen; reflections of the lights of a clothing shop glitter in the puddles. A long shot through the door of her rooming house frames the couple as they enter. Kane closes the door, and we are in Susan's cluttered room: she sits at a mirror, Kane wiggling his ears as she laughs in the reflection, and next to the dressing-table mirror and a portrait of Susan as a child the director has significantly placed the snowstorm glass paperweight that later turns up in Susan's room at Xanadu — it is not only a reminder of his youth, but of her innocence that he destroys.

Kane's fingers make rooster shadows on the wall; the camera slowly dollies towards the conversing pair, then remains stationary and holds them in two-shot. This is a very simple, beautiful scene in which we are made to feel the vibrancy of the young man and woman. This first meeting before a foredoomed marriage has a delicate poignancy, and the writing is unusually realistic and tender. As Susan begins her career as a singer, we see her struggling with a few bars while Kane sits, pipe-smoking and contented — and apparently tone-deaf — to the right of frame. His applauding of her

Kane's speech is rather conventionally handled, save for the total absence of close-ups — characteristic of the film as a whole, which up to now has featured only a handful of them — and a striking effect of puffs of smoke rising up from the old-fashioned camera flashes. At the end of the sequence, as Emily Kane announces that she is going to 185 West 74th Street (the house Kane has provided for Susan), there is a beautiful shot of Emily in her carriage, surrounded by an aureole of white fur.

At West 74th Street comes the confrontation scene between Kane, his wife, Gettys, and Susan Alexander: the compositions here are triangular, usually with three heads about midway in the frame, and one of the four protagonists kept out of view in each successive shot. Later in the scene the camera remains stationary for some time observing the four characters, a large picture of a sailing ship to the right. Dramatically, this is a tricky, ambivalent sequence: is Kane or Gettys the heavy?

At the end of the scene one of *Kane*'s most admirable

effects is achieved: surprisingly, it is one that has never been referred to in print. Following a shot of the door of Susan's house, as Gettys and Mrs. Kane disappear into opposite sides of the frame, the image almost imperceptibly freezes, the camera withdraws, and we are looking at the picture of the door in a newspaper photograph under the headline: THE HIGHLY MORAL MR. KANE AND HIS TAME SONGBIRD. Subheadings go: *Candidate Kane Caught in Love Nest With Singer, Entrapped by Wife as Love Pirate Kane Refuses to Quit Race.* This is a reverse of the earlier effect in which the still photograph of *The Chronicle*'s staff comes to life.

In *The Inquirer's* composing room, Bernstein reluctantly has to choose between two alternative front pages: KANE ELECTED and FRAUD AT POLLS: CHARLES FOSTER KANE DEFEATED. FRAUD AT POLLS is selected. A below-eye-level shot and the plaintive strains of the once jolly *A Poco No*, accompany Kane and his colleagues as they dejectedly quit the office. A shadow of venetian blinds across Kane's portrait suggests a canceling out of his career as a politician. The below-eye-level shot, beginning with some dramatic validity as a symbol of failure, becomes overindulged to

show us there is a ceiling. The subsequent conversation between Kane and Leland, in which Leland upbraids Kane for his using of the common people "as though you owned them," is handled without much effect, because the camera is at floor level; the main points are again lost in an effort to show Kane looming over his friend and colleague. Curious that, at the very point when the audience needs to be informed about Kane's fake idealism, the direction should muffle the point.

At the wedding of Kane and Susan, she is seen giggling helplessly, carrying a rather large and bedraggled bunch of roses caught in a bright new ribbon. KANE BUILDS NEW OPERA HOUSE, a front page headline shrieks as the singing teacher Matiste shouts "No, No, No, No!" A close-up of Susan has her made up — rather oddly — as Salammbô in a Brunhilde-ish hairstyle, with seventeenth-century Turkish turban. Clouds of incense float around her litter; we are on the stage of the Chicago Opera House. A cue light bobs up: the maid fixes the star's hair: Susan sprays her face with perfume. The camera seems to rise up past a curtain to a little house rather like the one in the paperweight, stored above the stage, then past a gondola, recalling the film's opening images, while Salammbô's voice echoes more and more distantly, until we see two men leaning over, high in the flies, one of them significantly holding his nose.

After the uninteresting scene in which Leland fails to write the review of Susan's performance and Kane completes it — the technique here, as in all the newspaper sequences, is much too labored — we return to the hospital. The transition is achieved with a very curious effect in which we see Kane typing to the right of the screen, illuminated with a kind of spotlight; a dissolve discloses Leland sitting in his wheelchair on the left of the frame, but for a moment the two images are retained together in a notably bizarre composition, followed by one equally strange as two nurses, their heads cut off by the top of the frame, come to wheel Leland away from the interview, back into the silence that precedes death. Here the still of the two patients behind Leland is replaced by a set from which the still was photographed, to admit his retreating form.

We return to the El Rancho Nightclub and move back through the sign to the broken skylight, cutting to a view of Susan at a table in a corner. A pianist is picking out the jazz notes of *In a Mizz* amid vaguely imitation-tropical decor with rather obviously painted holes in the plaster walls. Like the other narrators, Susan is examined in a very slow dolly shot that moves forward, with the audience and Thompson, exploring her ravaged face.

Now the condensed story of her failed opera career is retold. Her own face when younger dissolves in with Sternbergian slowness on the right, while her tragic one remains for a few moments at the left before dissolving away: we see Matiste's instructions, an argument between Kane and Matiste; and the shot of Susan's face as before on stage. A silver turban is fitted on her head, the camera rushes up to the cue light, figures race across the stage making last-minute changes. Shots of Susan are taken from behind her, looking out toward the cavernous darkness where the audience waits to destroy her career. The subjective point of view is also abandoned as we get a medium close-up of Kane's face in a box, Jedediah Leland tearing up the program into strips, and a below-eye-level view of her, legs moving in *lamé* past a glitter of footlights and the prompt-box. Bernstein nods off to sleep. Kane's view of Susan is contrasted with a rare close-up of Susan's face seeming to plead with him in an agony of despair, while he sits inexorably in the box. Finally she falls away to the cushions; she is exhausted, helpless. During the entire sequence we have not had a single shot of the audience from Susan's point of view: a major dramatic lapse, perhaps caused by economic considerations, even though physically the whole scene is brilliantly achieved: the vast shimmering mirage of the stage set, the dazzle of footlights, the group or single shots of the watchers all fusing into a beautifully accurate picture of a theatrical disaster. The sequence was shot against a battery of blazing bulbs, on an empty sound stage; the audience members were cut in later.

As Susan reads the notices in the hotel room, shrilly furious and vulgar, the direction is straightforwardly simple. A "montage" follows, illustrating her national tour too conventionally with express trains and successive headlines in Kane's newspapers, her voice struggling on behind the images, until on the headline NEW YORK SEEKS WAY TO CURB SPECTATORS her voice ironically fades, a filament goes out in a cue light, and her career is over. We dissolve to a bottle of poison looming on the left of the screen, a glass with spoon, while we hear the sound of Kane knocking on the door of her room. He finds her lying helpless; the arrival of the doctor is established by his bag in the foreground; each successive shot is taken just this side of the bed, and as Kane keeps a long vigil beside it, the handling is notably economical and emotionally touching. The conversation between Kane and Susan, in which she begs to be released from the burden of her career and he agrees, is exquisitely directed, achieving much of the warmth and accurate sentiment of his first scene with her.

Xanadu is introduced, all its lights aglow, with Herrmann's leitmotif figure on the brass. We dissolve to a gigantic jigsaw puzzle, representing what appears to be a huge, shapeless landscape. Two Egyptian figures are on our left, a baronial staircase on the right, Susan sitting by the fireplace (a continuity lapse here: in the introductory shot of Susan, the puzzle was three parts completed; in the new shot of her, it is scarcely begun). The shots are long, and we are given a series of dissolves over successive puzzles, illustrating lapses of time, an increase of boredom: a camel, a (significant) snowscape, a turreted house, a country scene, a river with boats and weeping willows, a ship at sea. Later, as the Kanes talk, a figure of a mounted medieval knight and a Gothic window tower over the conversation: in some shots Kane himself looks as stony and formal as any of his statues — an effect repeated in *Chimes at Midnight* in the scenes involving Henry IV.

The picnic scene is a masterpiece of cinematic strategy: Herrmann's Xanadu figure changes to a ragtime variant as Kane and Susan, dressed in costumes of the early thirties (he in striped blazer, she in white pleated skirt) are observed head-on in the back seat of a Düsenberg. From overhead we see a procession of cars making their way along a "Florida" beach, like a funeral cortège. There is a close-up of a sweating Negro singer, people dancing (from stock footage), and shots of the butler Raymond moving discreetly in the background. A pig turns on a spit as husband and wife quarrel (Kane, mysteriously, looks several years older here than in the preceding sequence of the car drive). As the quarrel reaches its peak, Kane looms enormously, threateningly over Susan, the band becomes more frantic, people slap their hands together in time to the tune, and to a background of flitting animated bats and jungle trees girls scream as they frolic with the male guests, their cries heard off-screen, symbolic of Susan's anguish as well as the sexual abandonment of the picnic.

As Susan packs to leave Xanadu, we are shown her bedroom, which is decorated like a child's nursery, with painted animals. (Now Kane looks far younger than in the picnic scene: can RKO have forbidden more retakes?) Back at the nightclub, chairs and tables are covered, and Susan's story is over. In half-darkness, against a stippled wall, she puffs despairingly at a cigarette lit for her by Thompson.

At Xanadu for the butler's version of Kane's life, the camera moves down the stairs in a very evenly managed long take as the butler pronounces the words: "I knew how to handle him; like the time his wife left him." A screaming cockatoo flaps off a balcony, indicating metaphorically the shock of Susan's departure and her virago-like character. As she moves off to the left of the frame, we see Kane in a long shot in a vaguely "Indian" corridor, framed in the door of Susan's bedroom, which he now almost ritualistically smashes to pieces, looming above our eye level. Phonograph, table, curtains, chests of drawers, chairs and bookshelves — one shelf concealing a bottle of alcohol — all are smashed. But as Kane lurches exhaustedly to the door he finds, next to a bottle of perfume, the snow scene paperweight Susan had owned when he first met her. He picks it up and looks at it in complete silence, the snowflakes whirling. Tears start in his eyes as he breathes the single word "Rosebud." The tears seem to be frozen on his cheeks. The butler comes up; a long dolly shot shows Kane walking past the guests and servants and along a mirrored corridor, his image reflected to infinity. The camera moves

forward to take in the multiple image; there is a dissolve back to the butler and Thompson.

As the reporters talk,[17] the camera moves back into a crane shot, taking in their figures moving through the statues and myriad crates, figures in the background in deep focus climbing up ladders, the camera tracking alongside a Donatello *Nativity,* a fourth-century Venus, across all the knicknacks, the cup ("value two dollars")

[17]Among them Alan Ladd and Richard Wilson.

given as a welcome present by the staff of *The Inquirer,* its message read out by a woman reporter. A long traveling shot follows the explorers of this monumental material; and as Thompson admits he has not solved the secret of "Rosebud," he puts down the box with a jigsaw puzzle — an obvious but legitimate symbol of Kane's unexplored reality. The whole of this scene takes place in a magnificent single take, the camera rising up again until all the boxes seem like the shattered ruins of a sky-scraper city, a vanished empire: a fantastic effect, and the film's greatest single stroke of genius. Finally, after its pitiless inventory of the worldly goods of Charles Foster Kane, the camera comes to the incinerator where trash is being burned.

Somber, eerie chords; a fluffy blonde doll lies sideways, like the broken life of Susan Kane; a violin case lies next to the Rosebud sled in the furnace; gradually the heat warps the paint, which looks almost as though ice and snow are melting on its surfaces. Finally the lettering and the ornamental rose above it are completely blistered away; the camera moves forward very slowly in to the sled; we dissolve to the chimney with its smoke writhing into the night sky; the smoke dissolves slowly over the wire fence, returning us to the "No Trespassing" sign. We have in fact trespassed, and we have been locked out, holding in our grasp only the last shot of the film: the huge initial "K" in its metal scrollwork, the castle, remote as a romantic legend, and the smoke wreathing out, carrying with it like a shadow, like Kane's spirit, everything that he sacrificed for, everything that he struggled to gain.

• • •

From this close analysis of *Citizen Kane,* we can draw certain conclusions. In this great but unequal work, sometimes immature, raw and rash, at others confident, mature, and spacious, the contrasts are extreme. The lapses are not the least extraordinary things about the film: for example the artistic cheats whereby witnesses to Kane's career describe visually things they cannot possibly have seen. Even if we allow that Kane's descriptions of things that happened could have been echoed by Leland, we cannot accept that Leland would have been able to describe in detail the confrontation between Kane, Mrs. Kane, Susan, and Gettys at which he was not an interloper; nor can we swallow the device whereby Susan is able to describe what Jedediah Leland did with his program in his seat in the stalls, or that Bernstein went to sleep in the balcony.

In his handling of the narrative parts of the film — most notably, the opening and closing passages — Welles's command of visual effect is altogether striking. In his poetic images, such as the recurrent allusions to the snow scene, and the wonderful use of dissolves throughout, he is the complete master. He is weakest when he handles the important dialogue scenes involving Leland and Kane either in a mode of heavy comedy or in showy cadenzas with the camera seemingly lying on the floor. Too often he lets his technique draw attention to itself, permitting us to look at a muslin ceiling (not always convincing anyway) when we would be better engaged in looking into the characters' faces as they emphasize points in a phrase. It is, no doubt, a mark against his technique that one often notes things while listening to the sound track that were altogether lost while watching the film unfold.

How much do we really know about Kane after Thatcher, Bernstein, Leland, Susan, and Raymond have filled in their own sections of the puzzle? First, through the newsreel, we are made aware of Kane's greed, his passion for possessions, and for making the grandiose gesture, symbolized through his construction of Xanadu: the stentorian commentary is in itself a satirical commentary on his ambitions and achievements, and a symbolic representation of Kane's pride.

We learn that, politically, he is a cynic, taking up many political ideas in turn and wringing each dry. This cynicism and opportunism, attractive when seen in opposition to the stiffly correct Thatcher, later look vacuous and futile; *The Inquirer* is simply a tabloid rag posing as a crusading organ, trumpeting its ideals as a prankish circulation stunt. Kane's growing egotism is pointed up by Leland, who also does not miss the tender side of Kane, shown in his feelings for Susan in the early stages. Susan shows us Kane's loneliness and lovelessness, and indeed she sees precisely eye to eye with Leland (who never had much time for her) in noticing that Kane needs love but cannot give it to others.

Kane is a selfish opportunist with delusions of grandeur; yet somehow, and partly through Welles's performance, he emerges as almost altogether likable, even lovable. He has energy, dash, humor, charm; and he shares with the director himself a youthful contempt for the fuddy-duddy, the respectable, the dull. We are made to feel that although *The Inquirer* is worthless as a political organ, it is probably a lively and a first-class newspaper. Kane's furthering of Susan's career can be seen as an act of kindness, as well as of defiance; and his belief in her talents is not in doubt. He is not intrinsically evil; his riches finish the work begun by his bank schooling.

The portrait is a generous one; but it is not altogether in the round: it is a brilliant sketch with the defects and virtues mapped by dashing strokes, yet the essence of the man is not quite there. We know, despite all the commentaries, too little about Kane: and here we see the limitations of the film. Kane's conversation almost throughout is staccato, a series of shouts across echoing rooms, mere illustrative noises in a void. We see only a dazzlingly illuminated cartoon figure, as two-dimensional as Colonel Blimp. The other characters are even more caricatured, made to live by performance rather than by the writing. Kane's parents are just a taut, nervous woman and an irascible old man in the script; Kane's mother, though, is brought to life by Agnes Moorehead as vividly as any crofter in *Man of Aran,* so that we see a lifetime of drudgery reflected in the shiny cheekbones, the tight mouth of the hoarder of cash. Thatcher, the great New York banker, is made to seem in George Coulouris's clever but hammy performance a stuffed shirt, an overbearing, crude, foolish figure of fun — even, oddly, in his own eyes when he is narrator through the pages of his diary.

Bernstein, the editor, is a faithful lapdog, sycophantic, silly, and finally a tired old man talking nostalgically about a girl he saw on a ferry. Leland is at best a genial stuffed shirt, at worst a pompous fool who declines into pathetic senility, trying to sneak cigars past the nurses in a hospital. Susan — beautifully played by Dorothy Comingore — is, like Kane's dull and genteel first wife, a disagreeable character, who fails to enlist our sympathy: at first a mindless girl, then later a loud-mouthed and vulgar middle-aged woman whose screeching is parodied in the image of a white cockatoo, flapping and crying as she walks out of Xanadu for the last time.

Dickens in his humorous mood sets the tone of all these characterizations, as well as that of much of the pace of the first half of the film, with its boisterous allegro clip, its procession of grotesques wonderfully observed in graphically compact images of greed, lust, and humor, marred only by the occasional ponderous writing.

The second half is taken at an altogether slower pace, a long *andante* in keeping with Kane's declining years and the somber setting of Xanadu. The film goes beautifully in these quieter passages: the last scenes with Thatcher, the still, poised sequence shot against rain-swept windows in Bernstein's editorial office.

But despite such simple moments when the film seems to go deeper, into a more poetic and evocative mood, it is for the most part a display of epic journalism, its flair expressed in vivid evocations of successive periods from the stuffy nineteenth-century interiors of Kane's pre-Xanadu house to the tawdry worthlessness of Susan's nightclub.

Kane is a work of confidence and excess, as bold as a fresco, and it reminds one again that the cinema has continued a nineteenth-century fiction tradition of size and grandeur when the novel (in English at least) has largely shrunk to the trivial. It is the story of a man haunted for a lifetime by the memory of the purity of a childhood of poverty, frustrated at being raised by a bank, stripped of a normal boyhood and given only the severe tutelage of the commercial East. Yet it is a film obsessed by the material splendor it attempts to deride, as are almost all Welles's films. The uses of the image of the sled and the snow symbols of "innocence" indicate Welles's profoundly American nostalgic romanticism; he cannot shake off the myth of the beauty of youth, or of an America that no longer exists, that perhaps never existed except in the imagination: the snow scenes when Charles is separated from his parents have all the concentrated frosty nostalgia of a *New Yorker* poem or winter short story.[18]

---

[18]The Australian magazine *People* reported in its issue for January 30, 1952: "Residents in Stockholm were shocked in January of 1950 to see Welles rolling in the snow that blanketed one of their most fashionable streets. He was snorting and laughing happily. He got up, shook his snow encrusted body and said in his famous voice: 'I've wanted to do this since I was a little boy.'"

Yet if much of the film reflects a sentimental romanticism, its structure is cynical. This cynicism lies in the technique of having people comment on Kane who are themselves comically overdrawn witnesses to a serious career. If we cannot take them seriously, we cannot take their views seriously; and if Kane emerges from their accounts making any sense at all, it is in spite of them.

The film displays a split personality: on the one hand attracted to splendor, on the other attracted to deprivation. Kane says that if he had had no money, he would have been great; Welles is saying that Kane's fabulous acquisitions mean nothing, that all they symbolize in the end is the broken jigsaw puzzle of emotional ruin that dissolves into the smoke rising sluggishly from the chimney of Xanadu. Yet if this is a film that seems to criticize the heartless acquisition of riches, it reflects its creator's almost lascivious dwelling on the appurtenances of riches as well.

If *Citizen Kane's* basic mood is anti-American, or at least anti-Middle West, it is also a wholly American work in its energy, opulence, ambition, and drive. It takes in a range of types, which, though Dickensian, are also of the America of cinema, comic strips, and radio: from the crumbling Bernstein to the hysterical caricature of the singing teacher Matiste. It moves across an American scene from the timeless, antique-laden world of the Florida castle to the El Rancho nightclub, from the drab offices of *The Inquirer* where Jedediah Leland makes his career to the silent hospital where he ends his days. Welles takes in vivid fragments of a society, if not the whole of a man — and all in a series of searchlight glimpses, reminding us as well of mortality, looking hard at the face of old age, of dissolution. Xanadu becomes a tomb as much as the El Rancho: a tomb for lost American ambitions, for a childhood dream of hope at the turn of the century, buried somewhere deep in the material splendor of 1940.

3. THE MAGNIFICENT AMBERSONS

Like *Citizen Kane, The Magnificent Ambersons* is a valedictory to the American past, filled with regret for the coming of the industrial age. Welles had always had a passion for Booth Tarkington's novel: he had brilliantly presented it in an hour-long version on the Mercury Theatre of the Air, on October 29, 1939, and there is in existence a silent film version he may well have seen as a child of ten — which was entitled *Pampered Youth,* directed by David Smith at Vitaphone in 1925. The earlier film, with its perfect evocation of Tarkington's midland town and Amberson house and addition, its titles drawn from the text, and its finely observed playing by Alice Calhoun, Emmett King, and Ben Alexander among others, in many ways foreshadows Welles's work (see Appendix I).

The subject also attracted Welles because it echoed his own earliest childhood in a town that had moved reluctantly from sleighs to Sears Roebuck motor buggies. He decided to incorporate into it his radio method of narrating the story, although on radio the tale was told, not by an impersonal disembodied presence — a more lyrical version of the "News on the March" commentator — but by Welles as George himself. He recorded the whole of the script on discs, and the actors were able to study it minutely for tiny vocal flaws; he intended to have them mouth, as in a musical, to the played-back words, a technique later used in *Macbeth.* The scheme was abandoned after tests on the first morning. But the whole recording was played to an RKO executive, to prove that the film could be done (some say Joseph I. Breen, vice president in charge of production on the West Coast, others George Schaefer, the president in New York).

Stanley Cortez, the film's superb cameraman, had had little chance to show his skill up to that time, although early in the thirties he made a beautiful abstract film about water, *Scherzo.* In 1941 he was at RKO doing photographic tests of various players who were later to be part of Selznick's "stable," and he dropped in to see Welles rehearsing the actors on all five of the *Amberson* house sets. Cortez knew Jack Moss, Welles's manager, and heard from him that the intention was to use an RKO camera staff on the picture. Meanwhile, it turned out that Welles had seen several of Cortez's films, *Danger on the Air* and *The Black Cat* among them. While preparing *Kane* Welles suddenly asked Cortez to shoot *Ambersons,* after accidentally seeing some Cortez tests before Selznick scrapped them; but Cortez was in New York, preparing to work with Selznick on a new project. Cortez had to locate Selznick in New York on a Saturday night to tell him about the Welles offer, finally tracking him down at Henry Luce's house; Selznick grumblingly agreed to let him go, and Cortez got in touch with Welles to accept the offer.

Cortez arrived in Hollywood on a Monday night and met Welles for the first time on the set the next day, when he started shooting the photographically beautiful dinner party scene with considerable distress. Cortez, a slow, literal-minded, careful symphonist of light, had never felt so rushed. When Welles saw the first shots, though, he flung his arms round Cortez in gratitude, and there was an immediate rapport — slightly dented later when Cortez's methods seemed to Welles a trifle slow.

The sleigh-ride scene was staged in a Los Angeles ice plant, so that the breaths of the people could be shown steaming the air. It took twelve days to shoot the scene, which presented enormous lighting problems: the bulbs even broke in the cold, and the 4,000-watt lights melted the snow. To simulate sunlight, a shimmering effect had to be achieved, and this was done by having arc lights glancing onto the snow at angles like sunbeam glare.

Cortez aimed at a "Currier and Ives" look which triumphantly came off. Normally, snow scenes were done on sound stages, with snowflakes made of uncooked cornflakes and powdered gypsum mixed in hoppers and blown around in wind machines. The RKO workers gutted the interior of the plant, surrounding the central set with a painted cyclorama of snowy Indiana countryside, and fed 5,000-pound cakes of ice into a cruncher, which spewed snow over everything like a firehose. Welles said *(Modern Screen,* April 1941): "Phony snow

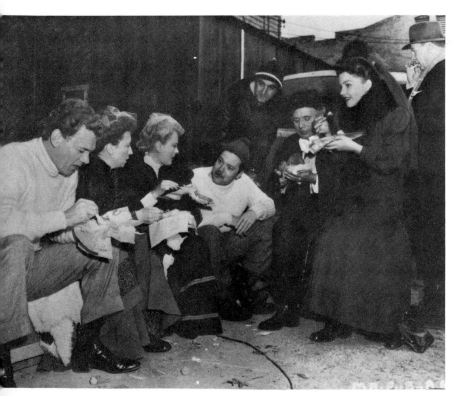

Lunch break during shooting at the ice-house.

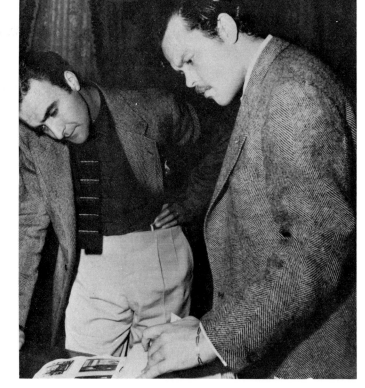

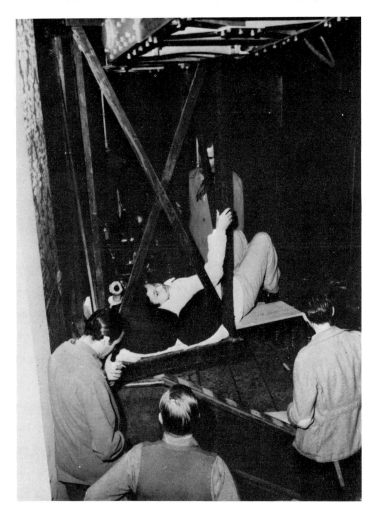

*Welles trying out the complex camera platform
used to achieve camera movement
in the mansion.*

just won't do. I want the real thing, so that we can make snowballs and people can get smeared with it and have it drip."

One of the most magnificent of Cortez's effects was cut from the picture. In a spectacular moving shot a hand-held camera wanders around the deserted Amberson mansion, past the bare reception hall, up the stairs to the second-floor hall without a break, going to the door of Isabel's room. The door swings open, and nothing is there. A 65-pound Mitchell camera with a periscope finder was strapped to the operator's chest, and he walked with it shoeless, while assistants moved mirrors, doors, and furniture out of his way. The shot ran 400 feet, or four and one half minutes. Nothing of it is left. (See Appendix II for details of the material dropped from *Ambersons*.)

In another shot, little of which is left, the camera went through eight successive rooms in one shot. It was Cortez's idea, and he told Welles it would be a gamble. Each time the camera was in a room, the camera saw four

walls and a ceiling. This presented enormous problems of shifting walls and even floors to accommodate the changing lights. As each wall moved, a light would be pushed in by Cortez's assistants on a predetermined mark. "It was," Cortez said, "a symphony of movement, noise notwithstanding." It presented a problem for the actors: they had to emote in the midst of this enormously complex set shifting and light arrangement. Mirrors had to be reversible on hinges, so that they would not show the cameras. They had to be twisted back, then returned to their original position, with split-second timing. Each room had to have an entirely different kind of lighting, to convey the fact that the Ambersons, following a contemporary custom, liked to have each of their rooms in a different style.

About halfway through shooting Pearl Harbor was bombed by the Japanese, and the United States entered the war. Just after that Welles received an invitation to make a Pan-American film (detailed in Chapter 5 on *It's All True*). He had to rush *Ambersons* to its conclusion, and he had to finish a third picture, *Journey Into Fear* (Chapter 4), at night in a three-picture deal with the studio. He also had to record his *Lady Esther Radio Program,* begun, crazily, just before shooting *Ambersons,* and broadcast each Monday evening. So he began using second units on other sound stages; Robert Wise, Welles's manager Jack Moss, and Joseph Cotten prepared some scenes in committee, and Harry J. Wild and Russell Metty were called in as auxiliary cameramen.

What happened to *Ambersons* is now a black legend, climaxed by the humiliation of its final release on the lower half of a double bill with a Lupe Velez comedy, *Mexican Spitfire Sees a Ghost*. The studio, involved in a power battle ending in the dismissal of George Schaefer, was unhappy with Welles's Rio carnival footage and with his reportedly wild behavior in Brazil (the most extravagant rumor had him urinating on a crowd from his hotel balcony). Exasperated by audiences' bored reactions to *Ambersons* in out-of-town previews (often in hick towns on the second half of lengthy double bills), the studio refused to let Robert Wise fly to Rio and work

with Welles on bringing the film down from its 148 minutes to a double-bill length of some 88 minutes. He got as far as Miami, then had to come back. Welles did his best to edit the film by telephone and telegram from Rio, running off his own rough cut in synchronization with Wise's copy, but, as Wise says, "it was hopeless. I simply couldn't follow his instructions, they made no sense. One telegram he sent me was 67 pages long. I couldn't follow it at all."[1]

In June Charles Koerner, head of production in Hollywood, told Jack Moss, Welles's manager, to supervise massive cuts. First, all the important documentary sequences of the growth of the midland city were eliminated, thus accounting for about two reels. Then the final long sequence in which Joseph Cotton visits Agnes Moorehead in the boardinghouse that was once the Amberson mansion was cut out. In this scene Eugene speaks to Fanny about the past, and as he does so, a record plays in the background. This record is a vaudeville duet, played in weirdly distorted voices by Cotton and by Norman Foster — who wrote it together. It is a new version of the vaudeville sketch, once made popular by the Two Black Crows, in which a master returns after a journey, and is met by his servant. He asks if there is any news (the title is "No News, or, What Killed the Dog?"). He is told that the dog has died. But when he hears the cause of death he learns by degrees that a whole city has been destroyed; the theme is based on the "for want of a nail" premise. The duologue comically underscores the tragedy of the Ambersons and the loss of the old city. At the end, as the record scratchily concludes and Fanny sadly says good-bye, Eugene goes out and the last shot shows him looking up at the skyline of a great industrial town beyond the old house's eaves.

Another scene, of Eugene O'Neill-like length and tone, was removed. This had the family sitting on the veranda in darkness, talking about their crumbling fortunes. Nothing whatever could be seen, only their voices heard plaintively under the trees. Worst of all was the

[1] Interview with Robert Wise, Sydney, Australia, 1968.

excision of the great silent sequence when the camera, strapped to the operator's chest, explores the stairs and the empty sheeted rooms in a repeat of the great take with which it earlier explored the same setting filled with dancing and carousing figures.

In the matter of the scenes in *Ambersons* over which doubt has hovered, let us try to dispel the mysteries. No one in the Mercury group recalls exactly who directed what in the picture, so that one must draw one's own conclusions from the evidence offered by all concerned. And my conclusions are as follows: Robert Wise directed the scene of the death of Major Amberson (under Welles's guidance), and, without Welles, the conversation between Eugene and Lucy in the garden, and the final scene in the hospital corridor, which was photographed by Russell Metty. A committee headed by Moss and including Cotten, Wise, and others, "directed" one or two small linking scenes including Tim Holt's prayer by the bed. Wise with Cortez to Welles's recorded instructions directed Isabel's reading of the letter to Eugene. Jack Moss bore the brunt of recutting most of the picture, with Wise's and Robson's aid, and supervised much of the Wise footage previously mentioned. Harry Wild and Russell Metty shot the additional scenes in consort, and Harry Wild lit the railway station scene (sometimes attributed to Foster, but probably directed by Wise) in a style similar to that of Stanley Cortez.

What we see today is a fragment only, but a dazzling one. If *Kane* is a vigorous journalistic work, then *Ambersons* is a poetic one, carried forward in a slow, somber movement in contrast with the razzle-dazzle energy and pace of its predecessor. Like the figures in the Waldteufel-like waltz with which Bernard Herrmann embellished the ballroom scene, it is a doomed, beautiful thing. Its darkness, its nostalgia, fill one still, like the knowledge of its partial destruction, with an unbearable sadness.

Booth Tarkington's novel, published in 1918, was part of a trilogy *(Growth)* which delt with life in a midland town, an anonymous version of Tarkington's native and beloved Indianapolis. The novel won the Pulitzer Prize and remains, together with Tarkington's beautiful story of small-town boyhood, *Penrod* (1914), as a touching and sadly underrated record of a vanished world. One of the central themes was that of the obstreperous youth who, through making a fool of himself, learns humility; George Minafer, the spoiled young villain who dominates the record of the Ambersons, had a literary precursor in Tarkington's Hoosier boy in *His Own People,* who was given his come-uppance and purification by the realities of Europe.

Tarkington's deep love of Indiana and of its youth and beauty endeared him strongly to the American public, if not always to more sophisticated critics. He had the commercial knack of ending his chronicles on a note of strong American optimism, despite all his nostalgia for a vanished carriage age, his hints of doom in his description of the approach of the machines. Even the whippersnapper heir George Minafer, drawn without a trace of

pity, ends up discovering the power to ask the forgiveness of his arch-rival and representative of the machine age, Eugene Morgan.

The Magnificent Ambersons is a film that shows the radical changing of an order, and the conflict of materialism with the romanticism of those still enmeshed in the past. It represents, too, a central conflict in Welles himself: between nostalgia and thrusting ambition, between mild inertia and a desire for action, between a love of the past and a hunger for the excitements of the future. On the one hand he is drawn to the youth and beauty and vigor of the young people in the story, yet on the other he is attracted to the fading older figures pushed aside by the thrust of commerce. Yet the conflict is not dialectically iron-cast; the situation contains an irony. The Amberson house is not really beautiful despite Welles's affectionate treatment of it. The tragedy of the Ambersons was not merely that they were blind to "progress," but that what they clung to was in itself the product of an earlier materialism, as insubstantial as a dream.

What prevents the film from working quite satisfactorily as a work of social comment is Welles's ambiguous response to the material. Tarkington suggested the irony of the Ambersons' predicament more firmly; the local people's regard for the magnificence of the Amberson household was meant to be a trifle absurd, since its grandeur was an expression of vulgarity. Welles, by falling in love with the house, makes the story more tragic, but he removes an important element from it. He mirrors the novel's surface, though, with extraordinary fidelity, capturing to perfection its elegiac tone, mirroring its sober North American poetry in a style less baroque than *Kane's.* The camerawork of Stanley Cortez shimmers with a beautiful nostalgic glow, moving as effortlessly as a waltzing figure through the tall and genteel Amberson house, catching the shine of lace, the gleam of stained-glass windows, the polish of expensive wooden balustrades.

The technical execution of the images is simple and functional, for all its sumptuous richness of texture. Even a virtuoso effect, when the camera (running on streetcar tracks) leisurely traces a journey by George and his inamorata by carriage in one take, has its meaning; it shows us the ugly telephone poles that are beginning to sprout in the growing city — ironical black figures of doom beyond the old-fashioned ride itself. Elaborate compositions are few, and the more effective for that: George looking into the mirror when his Uncle Jack takes a bath, with George to the left and Jack to the right, framed between bathroom knickknacks; George watching Jack leave the house after George's mother's death, a repetition of the same shot in reverse, with George's face and the reflected figure below as it gets into the carriage beautifully counterpointed. The staircase conversations are all elaborately composed; for the most part, though, this is a film of deliberately subdued, plain photographic character based on the methods of the photographers of 1905.

The groupings throughout are symmetrical, with a preponderance of three-shots, often with a man framed between two women. The heads form very frequently the points of an equilateral triangle, another gesture towards period formalism. In the ballroom scene the figures form into twos, threes, and fours; the scene itself is carefully choreographed. A conversation between gossips at a dressmaker's shows one woman framed in a sewing machine. In a discussion on the first floor corridor of the Amberson house, and in the farewell to the guests after the ball, deep focus effectively shows us two knots of people at different levels, each of equal interest to each other, in perfect counterpoint. Here, ceilinged sets serve a more valid and functional purpose than in *Kane* (and the ceilings look more genuinely solid) because they convey the oppressive nature of the house.

The camera's movements are more fluent and graceful than Toland's in *Kane*. The marvelous dolly shot that accompanies George and his aunt Fanny as they move out of a boiler room into the shrouded living room of the Amberson mansion shows Cortez's virtuosity at its height, since Fanny's hysteria is followed in an unbroken progression through four rooms. Editing here would have destroyed the emotional balance of the scene. The visual narration is frequently taken wholesale from the text, as in the farewell of George's Uncle Jack at a railroad

station. The sleigh-ride scene mirrors Tarkington's prose to a fault: "The sleighbells tinkled but intermittently. Gleaming wanly through the whitish vapor that kept rising from the trotter's body and flanks, they were like tiny fog-bells, and made the only sounds in a great winter silence." Though we may perhaps regret that the fashion in Hollywood at the time was not to use locations, the realism of the recreated ride is masterfully achieved.

The film carefully renders an American past, creating with affection a world as formally nostalgic as a cameo brooch. A tram stalled by a house, its horses champing; snow on eaves and heavy on winter's bare trees; the shine of a window where a woman stands listening tenderly to the tripping melody of a serenade; a hat fixed in a cheval glass; faces shining with the glow of cold, and voices raised high as a horseless carriage jigs away on its first journey under a shaking tasseled canopy, while a sleigh forms more delicate swooping parabolas in the snowbanks nearby; the early part of the film has an autumnal lyricism, the mood of a Frost poem. But the second half is even richer, in its deep shadows, its wintry colors, as the swarming darkness of the Amberson mansion presages death for Isabel Amberson Minafer, for her husband, for the General who is the house's most formidable living ghost. As each door closes, whether it bears a glistening black wreath or not, it seems to close forever on all possibility of escape from fate. As each white face fades away in the night, it is like watching the interment of corpses, and we are listening to their last requiem.

The film is composed in scenes which are given theatrically visible exits, but these are not "merely" theatrical. They serve a purpose: they show that the figures in the film's formal dance are forever retreating into shadows, into death. It is a film of vanishings; as when the figures at the end of the Amberson ball, two knots of people, one in the foreground, the other "rhubarbing" in the background, move out into the windy night, leaving the polished hall silhouetted behind as the musicians pack up their instruments. The Morgan Motor, too, vanishes over a hill past a giant wintry tree, and an iris out blots its image forever, to be followed by a black wreath, fixed to the door of the Amberson house.

All through the film people are leaving, drifting away like leaves before the wind. In the ballroom scene, the dancing figures seem to recede into infinity, an effect partly achieved by the judicious use of mirrors. Upright struts and pillars constantly create frames within the frame, so that the people seem to be fixed like moths on plates, fluttering and trapped. A variant on this method occurs in Isabel's deathbed scene, when the shadows of the bedstead and the lace curtain trap her in a spider's web of doom, and a sudden, shocking change of light into near darkness as someone draws the curtains, more firmly involves her in death.

The sound track, too, has the effect of isolating the people in the film, of withdrawing them from us. Voices are constantly heard "off" — not quite an innovation, since Wyler had used the method in *These Three* — but here more extensively employed than ever before. Just as we constantly see people not only framed in uprights but half glimpsed through doorways, reflected in mirrors or windows, so we hear their voices almost muffled through doorways or in the far distance of rooms, floating down a remote stairway or mingled with the measures of a dance, the hiss and clang of a factory. It is part of the film's evocation of a deathly atmosphere that, apart from Aunt Fanny's whine, everyone should speak in subdued, sad, falling tones, words with a dying fall in this film of dying falls, of an endless dying.

There are curious lapses in this lovely elegiac work: in the early passages illustrating in montage the passing of the years before George Minafer's birth, we see George himself fully grown, in a boat with his mother, who looks no younger than she does in the main body of the film. Agnes Moorehead is seen among the Greek chorus townspeople, commenting on the Minafers' behavior — an astonishingly slipshod touch (similarly, in the projection room scene in *Kane*, Welles showed Joseph Cotten and other members of the cast among the reporters in the near-darkness). These lapses illustrate the essentially private nature of Welles's art, and his (reciprocated) contempt for the audience, which, he feels sure, will not even notice these peculiarities.

Moreover, the film is full of unexplained introductions

of characters, so that the audience is never informed about the precise relationship between the Minafers and the Ambersons, whether Jack is Fanny's brother, and how Major Amberson is related to them. Welles's obliviousness to the audience's needs has never been more clearly evidenced than by this film, his most withdrawn hermetic work; and the recutting of the last part was not merely due to the need for a shorter film but to the studio's desire for clarification.

It is, too, a fragmentary work, and the fragmentary nature of it does not entirely stem from its re-editing. Welles himself lays claim to the first three reels as they stand, and these, too, have a fragmentary character. The reason for this lies in the very heart of Welles's nature as an artist. His secrecy, his recessiveness behind the braggadocio, and his emotional detachment, his inability to move into an audience's mind and hold it, are here clearly shown. Audiences failed to respond to the film because it has no clear emotional binding thread, the thread that made so ersatz a work as *Gone With the Wind* a huge success. There is no single character to identify with; the development of the characters we have instead is shown in hectic glimpses; we cannot love what we cannot fully understand; and as the audience sees these creatures fade and die and face their ruin, it is intrigued but not moved. For those who understand Welles's nature, for intellectuals not dominated by a need to identify at a cinema performance, the film works beautifully; for the common run of people, it works far less well.

The performances in *Ambersons* have a complexity and power rare in the cinema: and of them the most famous is Agnes Moorehead's definitive portrait of Aunt Fanny. Although she is not quite the Fanny described in the book, "who, rouged a little, was like fruit which in some climates dries with the bloom on. Her features had remained prettily childlike. . . ." And although the screenplay does not allow her Fanny's violent changes of mood, or her ability to look twenty at one minute and sixty the next, Agnes Moorehead moves deeply inside the frustration and misery of the character, convey-

ing in high-pitched whines, in querulous outbursts of rage, and in her whole taut, cramped, tightly corseted body and pinched hawk-like face, in every movement of her hands, in every fit of hysterical tears, a life wrecked on the rocks of repression.

George Minafer is stiffly but accurately played by Tim Holt: the black, curled hair, the spoiled pretty face, the suggestion of plumpness and impending fatness, the ramrod back, head held haughtily high in defiance of progress. Here is an aggressive masculinity barely concealing a vulnerable feminine streak, the cruelty and vanity conveyed in the strutting gestures. It is a portrait that precisely embodies the Booth Tarkington character, despite Holt's lack of experience (he had previously been seen mainly in Westerns).

Dolores Costello as Isabel, wan, with the vestiges of a great beauty, is a trifle too old for the part (in the novel, she is in her late thirties at first), but she conveys the correct degree of delicacy, the frailty and the melting sadness, her face at all times lit with exquisite softness by Stanley Cortez.[2] Ray Collins is brilliantly apt as Uncle Jack, the epitome of Midwestern behavior: fat, tough, but sentimental, with a shrewd, exact calculation of how much and how little George Minafer is worth. His harsh voice and gross physique — unpleasantly discovered in a bath at one stage — are unfalteringly conveyed.

Joseph Cotten, not as indulged as usual, is perfect as Eugene Morgan, a representation of the ideal husband imagined by Fanny, rejected but still loved by Isabel; but, genial and gentlemanly, he seems to belong more to the old generation than to the one that produced the horseless carriage. As a manufacturer of robust tastes and simple toughness, we cannot wholeheartedly accept him.

For the most part, the cast plays with an impeccable period sense, guided by a director at the height of his powers. The art direction of the late Mark-Lee Kirk is beautifully apt: the great Amberson ball, with its "flowers and plants and roped vines brought from afar" is perfectly conveyed, admirably restored; and the house

---

[2] And, of course, Russell Metty and Harry J. Wild.

is achieved without a flaw: "a house of arches and turrets and girdling stone porches," boasting "the first porte-cochère" (in Indianapolis). It is on the black walnut stairway, against the stained-glass windows and heavy drapes, that the main action of the film often takes place; a doomed, opulent setting for a drama of threatened splendor.

Welles's narration begins with an expert adaptation and condensation of the long nostalgic passage that opens Tarkington's novel:

In those days, all the women who wore silk or velvet knew all the other women who wore silk or velvet. And everybody knew everybody else's family horse and carriage. The only public conveyance was the streetcar. A lady could whistle to it from an upstairs window, and the car would halt at once, and wait for her, as she shut the window, put on her hat and coat, went downstairs, found an umbrella, told the girl what to have for dinner, and came forth from the house. Too slow for us nowadays, because the faster we're carried, the less time we have to spare.

During the earlier years of this period, while bangs and bustles were having their way with women, there were seen men of all ages to whom a hat meant only that rigid, tall silk thing known to impudence as a stovepipe. But the long contagion of the derby had arrived; one season the crown of this hat would be a bucket, next it would be a spoon. Every house still kept its bootjack. But hightop boots gave way to shoes and congress gaiters, and these were shaped through fashions that shaped them now with toes like box ends and now with toes like the prows of racing shells.

Trousers with a crease were considered plebian; the crease proved that the garment had lain upon a shelf, and hence was ready-made . . . with evening dress a gentleman wore a tan overcoat, so short that his black coat tails hung visible five inches below the overcoat; but after a season or two, he lengthened his overcoat till it touched his heels, and he passed out of his tight trousers into trousers like great bags.

In those days, they had time for everything. Time for sleigh rides, and balls, and assemblies, and cotillions, and open house on New Years, and all-day picnics in the woods. And even that prettiest of all banished customs, the serenade.

On a summer night, young men would bring an orchestra under a pretty girl's window, and flute, harp, cello, cornet and bass viol would presently release their melodies to the dulcet stars. Against so homespun a background, the magnificence of the Ambersons was as conspicuous as a brass band at a funeral.

Over this tenderly and nostalgically read passage, a period, a way of life are beautifully evoked. The opening shot shows the Amberson's house, miraculously correct, a streetcar traverses the frame from left to right, stops, and the passengers gather with leisurely movement around it as it waits for Mrs. Amberson to descend the stairs, give instructions to her daughter, and take her place in a seat. The camera remains at a precisely calculated distance, as though framing a mezzotint: the whole scene — like every subsequent one — edged in soft focus, in a haze of memory.

We see hatted men in a saloon drink heartily as the narration turns to hats, the saloon door swinging to and fro; a young man in a stovepipe hat sits in a boat with a girl twirling a parasol; Eugene Morgan stands in a mirror trying on hats, using a bootjack. The mood becomes increasingly comic, almost Disneyesque, as, like Goofy in an RKO cartoon comedy, Eugene struggles into successively more absurd trousers and overcoats at the mirror.

Then the mood becomes more tender and elegiac, the music more slow and stately. As Welles speaks the words, "In those days they had time for everything," we see the Amberson house covered in snow, richest of Welles's symbols of vanished purity, and as the serenade is mentioned, the house on a summer night, strung with pretty lanterns, a moon hanging behind the eaves. Then the image darkens, the moon is gone, and only a lamp glows on the left of the frame, big as a harvest moon.

As the serenade is played, Eugene Morgan runs forward with the men carrying the instruments to play in honor of Isabel Amberson, trips, and falls over. Isabel, through the lace curtains, is at once amused and withdrawn, cut off in the splendid darkness of the house from the comic little scene outside.

As the narrative ends the mood progresses to an *allegro vivace,* various townsfolk describing the splendors of the mansion: "Hot and cold running water, stationary washstands in every last bedroom of the place." A Negro butler opens the front door to Eugene, announcing that Isabel Amberson is not at home to him; his next call is equally fruitless. Outside the house another group of people — including Fanny Minafer — is talking about

Eugene's awkward courtship. ("Stepped clean through the bass fiddle.") Finally, we see Eugene luring Isabel at last out of the house: he in driving gear, she in big floppy hat, ringlets, and rings. But, ironically, even as this happens, the bystanders, acting like a Greek chorus, disclose that Isabel is not going to marry Eugene, the up-and-coming young horseless-carriage manufacturer, but Wilbur Minafer, a solid young businessman.

A woman neighbor describes to a group, as in a chorus, the splendors of the Amberson-Minafer nuptials: "Raw oysters floating in scooped out blocks of ice . . . and she'll be a good wife to him . . . but they'll have the worst-spoiled lot of children this town will ever see."

As she utters these words, a living illustration of her prophecy — George Minafer, in velveteen and ringlets — is seen making a thorough nuisance of himself. In his tiny carriage, he upsets a gardener with hoe, the horse trotting vigorously along, all observed in a brilliant succession of stylized, heavily angled shots which emphasize the nervous obstreperousness of Georgie's career, while the commentary indicates that everyone in town lived in expectation of the boy's ultimate "comeuppance."

A boy Tom Sawyerishly hoots at George a derisive reference to his curly locks, and the pair grapple, rolling

over and over on the lawn while a lawyer parent (Erskine Sanford) is seen in his typically Wellesian pose of infuriated gentility and exasperation, at first rapping peremptorily on the window, then descending to the lawn to drag the two boys apart. George punches him in the stomach, just as Charlie Kane rammed Walter Parks Thatcher.

A postmortem on the fight takes place in the garden of the Amberson mansion in a long-held shot as posed and formal as a Landseer: George in kilt and tam-o'-shanter, Isabel in white by a tree, Major Amberson crusty and wound tightly in a cocoon of age. George promises not to use bad language again (the phrase "Unless I get mad at somebody" immediately cancels out the validity of the promise), and a tripping woodwind passage in Bernard Herrmann's score indicates that George has no intention of improving at all.

The transition to George's adulthood is handled with a magical long dolly shot through the front door of the Amberson house, the wind sweeping with us as we move forward into a world of lost elegance and beauty, a wind that moves the chandeliers in a swaying sad dance, that ruffles and tinkles the Christmas tree's bells and baubles with a sweet, sad melody. Here everything is solid, rich, cluttered with the collections of generations, yet shining with an effulgence that already gives a hint of decay.

In the body of the hall the vines are festooned, the couples moving to and fro. "It was the last of the great, long-remembered dances that everybody talked about." George looks ideal, "white-gloved, with a carnation in his buttonhole," his young unlined face with "nothing to offer except . . . condescension."

Hearty greetings and robust exchanges accompany a subtle series of group shots often formed into triangles, while all the time we are aware of the couples moving, moving, in graceful procession, an endless parade through the house, accompanied by a minuet playing softly in the background.

A fine, long, gliding movement accompanies the Morgans — Eugene and his daughter — and the Minafers and Ambersons; the camera retreats before them, taking in richly flowered wallpapers, chandeliers, the shimmer of brasswork. We move up the stairs, past the orchestra playing the minuet, past stained-glass windows to an upper landing, in an awestruck exploration of American materialism, "of solid black walnut, every inch of it, balustrades and all. Sixty thousand dollars' worth o' carved woodwork in the house!" (Tarkington)

And the ascent continues, in a long dreamlike take, "among the gleaming young heads, white shoulders, jewels, and chiffon," Eugene dancing with Aunt Fanny, George expressing his contempt of automobiles to Eugene's daughter, Lucy, while unconscious of her identity.

Lucy and her father, George and his mother: they form into intricate patterns, a formal dance of long gliding takes and a shot of a punch bowl, the figures grouped symmetrically around it, and a discussion of relationships, of leisured days and ways. And in the mirror, as Eugene moves into a dance with Isabel, we see reflected the passing of time, as we recall the way they must have danced when he was courting her, long ago. And by contrast, as the sequence ends in a flurry of two- and four-shots, the obstreperousness of George Minafer, who condemns the uselessness of the rich businessmen surrounding him; asked by Lucy what he wants to become, he says, fatuously, "A yachtsman!" as he dances with her into the throng of figures on the dance floor, already blended with them, bringing the sequence of the Amberson ball to a brilliant close.

Now it is night, and the ball is over, the orchestra playing a plaintive air, and Eugene and Isabel still gliding in the shimmering light of the last lamps and the glow of the moon through the stained-glass window. The sequence ends upon an evocation of frost and snow, a window thickly rimmed with white faces in shadowy profile against it, presaging the beautiful journey through the snow that follows in a later scene.

An argument follows between George and Fanny on the various landings of the house's great central stair-case: George is suggesting that Eugene Morgan is using the Ambersons to obtain financing for the horseless carriage that George hates; Fanny, who has always been infatuated with Eugene, tells George peremptorily that Eugene is perfectly capable of looking after his own affairs. In the deep shadows the figures wrangle. George whines plaintively: "What makes you and everybody so excited over this man Morgan?" and in the playing and direction what could have been merely an empty grumble about a family rivalry becomes symbolic of a way of thinking that clings to a motorless past. And an opportunity, too, for Aunt Fanny's hysterical attachment to Eugene to be expressed in parrotlike screeches of rage, expostulations of shrill disapproval at George's failure of appreciation: "You're trying to insinuate that I get your mother to invite Eugene Morgan here on my behalf!" Here is a woman whose whole life has been wrapped up in the noble image of one man, and who is doomed to know only loneliness, never to be sexually fulfilled by him.

By contrast with this tense dark scene — staged in the swarming shadows of the house, the arguing figures perched above each other on balconies as though on clifftops — the next has a wonderful sense of release, of

dazzling frost, sunlight, and dashing movement; reflected in a frozen pool, with giggling on the sound track and the pretty tinkling of Herrmann's instruments a sleigh whirls round a bend in a road. The festively beautiful, poetic, motorless movement is set in exquisite contrast with the foundering of the horseless carriage — a vintage 1905 motor buggy hopelessly bogged down as Eugene, Fanny, and Isabel struggle to set it free. At last Eugene gets the Morgan Motor going, but George calls out from the sleigh he is riding in with Lucy, "Get a horse! Get a horse!" — a play on the old cliché, and also a perfect summary of an attitude to life. But the sleigh tilts over, and the couple roll down a mound of snow.

The camera delicately moves through the branches of

winter trees as George and Lucy are taken by Eugene to the horseless carriage to continue their journey, George's first sampling of travel in the New Age. The rattling monster stops again, quivering under its tasseled canopy, but progress cannot be stilled, and soon it is bearing its laughing cargo through the wind on an odyssey at eight miles an hour. They sing — even Fanny sings — "The Man Who Broke the Bank at Monte Carlo." And the screen, as at the ball, is continually broken up into patterns of heads, each face beautifully contrasted and compared, the sequence closed on an exquisite iris-out as the car vanishes over the horizon, and an era is over.

After the spontaneous excitement and gaiety of this scene comes the shock of reality: a black wreath on the door of the Amberson house indicates that Wilbur Minafer, the colorless man we have glimpsed only briefly, and whom Isabel threw over Eugene to marry, is prematurely dead. Sinister chords; as the Negro butler who once refused entrance to him opens the door to Eugene, we see as from Wilbur Minafer's coffin, the family looming above us, paying its last somber respects, a particularly striking close-up of Aunt Fanny's face reminding us of Welles's debt to Eisenstein; it is a shot that could have come straight from *Strike* or *Potemkin,* of a newsreel vividness and immediacy.

Rain sweeps across the building, thunder rattles, and George and Fanny sit at the table in the huge Amberson kitchen, observed by an almost motionless camera; according to Welles the actors improvised the dialogue of the entire scene, but in fact much of it is drawn from Tarkington. Fanny begins by bringing strawberry shortcake, "first of the season," and she warns George that he will become fat; she complains about his eating fast. There is a desultory discussion of family affairs, and the question of Eugene and Aunt Fanny comes up. When Uncle Jack comes into the room, he takes up the theme, and the two men tease Fanny unmercifully in a way that they have probably been teasing her for years, pretending that Eugene has been touching up his haberdashery for her benefit. She is deeply distressed, cries, and slams the door as she goes out. And a moment later Jack regrets his cruelty: "Really don't know of anything much Fanny has got, except her feeling about Eugene."

Following this reference to Eugene, there is a startling transitional cut from the two men talking to a sparkle of fire, a clanging of an anvil: we are in the Morgan Motor workshops. The Ambersons excitedly explore the cars, Fanny in particular enchanted by the horseless carriage. We are made to realize the passage of time in the film by the introduction of the first Morgan auto, in museum style, with its canopied hood ("How quaint!" one of the women says). Eugene is deeply pleased by the delightfulness of his guests, even thinking of reviving his flair for poetry. Standing between Isabel and Fanny, but looking only at Isabel, he thanks them for turning a factory visit into such a "kind celebration."

In their carriage George proposes to Lucy, be he is rejected, and not for the first time; this is observed in a long tracking shot down the main street of the town. George is boastful about his intentions: he will not enter a business or profession, but will "lead an honorable life." He will "take part in movements . . . whatever appeals to me." In the fatuity of this, and in the precise

tone of his voice, George presages the character of the left-wing intellectual in *Journey into Fear,* rambling along about his amateur's idealism.

A dinner party: Eugene is the guest of the Ambersons, and there is talk of someone else opening another horseless-carriage shop: the revolution has begun. Eugene predicts that soon automobiles will make this a very big town. "Automobiles will carry our streets clear out to the county line." Jack fears that if this happens people will move to the new part of town, and real estate values in the older section will be stretched too thin. George is rudely critical, deliberately offending Eugene who, he believes, disapproves of his marrying Lucy: "Automobiles are a useless nuisance." Jack reprimands George, but Eugene says:

I'm not so sure George is wrong about automobiles. With all their speed forward, they may be a step backward in civilization. It may be that they won't add to the beauty of the world or the life of men's souls. I'm not sure. But automobiles have come. And almost all outward things are going to be different because of what they bring. They're going to alter war and they're going to alter peace. And I think men's minds are going to be changed in subtle ways because of automobiles. It may be that George is right. It may be that in ten or twenty years from now, if we can see the inward change in men by that time, I shouldn't be able to defend the gasoline engine but would have to agree with George: that automobiles had no business to be invented.

It is a beautiful speech, beautifully delivered by Joseph Cotten, and it is followed by an understandable silence before Eugene excuses himself from the table, as each of those present weighs the significance of his words. When Eugene goes, Isabel mildly reprimands George, who is adamant. "What makes you think he was hurt?" George asks her, winning the deeply felt reply, her eyes brimming with reminiscence: "I know him."

Following the party George and Fanny clash over

George's criticism of Eugene. Fanny complains bitterly about her fate, wallowing in self-pity as she describes her loneliness since her brother died. (This confession elicits little more from George than "Omigosh!") Then she moves on to another tack: "People are talking about your mother. . . . Of course, I understood what you were doing when you started being rude to Eugene . . . I'm sorry for her, George." And George, fiercely resenting the insinuation that his mother is again setting her cap for Eugene, and that people are saying that his mother loved Eugene even when her husband was alive, says that the only gossip has been about Fanny herself, and her own pursuit of Morgan. And she cries, as she climbs the stairs, the pair of them again poised one above the other on the successive landings, "Yes, it's always Fanny, ridiculous old Fanny, always, always Fanny! . . . He always danced with me as much as he did with her . . . It's just that I didn't count, that's all. . . . Everyone in this town knows that Isabel never really cared for any other man in her life." George is shocked, and Fanny is astounded that he did not know. He becomes hysterical, and slams out as Fanny leans down from the balustrade, screaming the words, "What are you going to do?"

Storming across the street, George invades the parlor of Mrs. Johnson and charges her with spreading malicious gossip about his mother. The camera probes into a cluttered living room as Mrs. Johnson, at first a welcoming if haughty, straitlaced presence, gradually becomes more and more defensive and then furious. ("This isn't a courtroom, and I'm not a defendant in a libel suit!") She throws him out.

Now — in a scene introduced with a pouring tap and a puff of steam from a bath — George invades Uncle Jack's bathroom. Jack, seen in a mirror in an involved and beautifully managed composition, a hulk of flabby flesh arguing with George, receives the tirade calmly, pointing out that there can be nothing harmful in a marriage of Eugene and Isabel anyway. When Eugene arrives to call on Isabel, we see George's pugnacious face at the window, and a moment later at the door George tells Eugene he is unwelcome at the Ambersons. He slams the door in Eugene's face.

A dissolve takes us from a doorknob, symbolizing Eugene's failure to gain admittance, to Isabel withdrawing nervously behind thick black lace curtains, while the camera in a magnificent crane shot takes in Fanny and George on the stairs. Fanny condemns George for stirring up trouble and weeps uncontrollably. "Leave her alone!" He moves into the corner of the frame leaving her lonely, distraught.

At a table (a model of a car lies on the right, dogs to the left) Eugene is writing a letter to Isabel, "the dearest woman in the world," saying, voice over, in a technique that presages *Journey into Fear's*: "Now we are faced, not with slander, not with our own fear of it . . . but someone else's fear of it, your son's."

A slow dissolve introduces — in one of Welles's most beautiful transitions — Isabel in a room full of ferns, reading the letter, Cotten's voice continuing from one scene to the next, her eyes brimming with tears. As the words of reassurance against gossip and cruel tongues continue, she moves forward, her sad face shadowed, the whole mood autumnal, calm.

George enters after having read the letter. He taunts his mother, "You don't care what people say!" Thus he breaks the whole mood of the preceding scene with an air of contemptible arrogance and self-righteousness, though his mother remains oblivious to his faults. She responds to his viciousness with a tenderness and forgiveness that are wholly undeserved, and she agrees to go away with him; we thus see that the influence of her son upon her is subtly incestuous and as powerful as her true lover's.

As George and Lucy promenade along the main street of the town, past a movie house where Jack Holt is starring in *The Revenge*, George tells her about his impending departure for a trip around the world; he is shocked that she doesn't seem in the least concerned about his leaving. She smiles as he theatrically says, trying to wring some tears from her, "I think it's good-bye for good, Lucy," and all she can do is smile and say, "I hope you have the most splendid trip." Furious, he stalks off to the left of frame. But as we see her face revealed in close-up, we note that it is desperately sad.

She goes into the chemist's shop for some spirits of ammonia, and while it is being fetched, she faints dead away.

At Eugene's house, several months later, Jack Amberson reveals that Isabel, whom he has seen abroad, is not well; but we learn that George, "in his grand, gloomy and peculiar way," is enjoying life in Europe. But, with the camera stationary as we observe Eugene, Lucy, and Jack in a long, long three-shot take, Jack explains that George virtually has his mother prisoner now; "They say he won't let her come home. Don't think he uses force . . . he's very gentle with her."

At a railway station for Isabel's return, as Isabel leaves the train we see she is now seriously ill. The carriage moves off with its clopping horses. As sunlight

flashes across the carriage, making diagonal shadows, her face pale and withdrawn under its tulle hat, Isabel says: "It's changed. It's so changed." Jack says: "You miss the town? This town will turn into a happier place, old dear, now that you're back." But by his expression, and hers, we know that she is already doomed.

In the following scene Fanny is in tears in the gloom of the stairs, and there is a superb shot of George's face in a window, with Eugene, reflected far below, climbing into a horseless carriage. The music echoes that for Kane's death as a nurse hovers in a background of plush and high pillars and George enters his mother's death chamber.

Isabel is tenderly solicitous, even when half delirious at the end: she asks George, "Darling, did you get something to eat? Are you sure you didn't catch cold, coming home?" As the curtains are drawn, the light changes in complex patterns of shadow, the metal bedstead's shade like a spider's web of darkness catches her in an echo of the shot which showed Susan Kane ill from poison: Stanley Cortez's fantastic virtuoso skill has never been more spectacularly displayed than here. Not far away, Major Amberson sits in a stupor, near death himself: the elegance and order of the past are nearing extinction.

As Isabel dies, Fanny in anguish hugs George and says, "She loved you!" It is a moment of sharpest pain.

Once again, we see Major Amberson, the flickering light of a dying fire illuminating his wizened face, a face that still has remnants of an old military force and fire. The dark commentary is from Tarkington: "Major Amberson was engaged in the profoundest thinking of his life. He realized that everything that had worried him or delighted him during his lifetime, all his buying and building and trading and banking, that it was all trifling and waste, beside what concerned him now." He was preparing to enter "a country where he was not even sure of being recognized as an Amberson," the country of death.[3]

And immediately after we have seen Isabel die and

[3]This one-shot sequence was directed by Robert Wise.

the Major prepare for the end, as our minds have been filled with images of romantic dissolution, Welles shocks us by bringing Jack onto the scene to discuss with the Major, immediately after Isabel has gone, the complexities of the probate problems involved, and whether Isabel has the deed to the house.

But the Major is too far gone into senility to care: in a speech drawn directly from Tarkington he rambles on disjointedly, "the earth came out of the sun . . . the wheat came out of the earth. . . ." The screen goes completely black; the Major's life is over, like wheat shriveled in the summer sun.

A farewell at the railroad station: Jack leaves George on a journey to seek a new job (Tarkington has it placed in Washington). Like Bernstein, Jack Amberson remembers a girl he once knew in Tarkington's exact words:

Once I stood where we're standing now to say goodbye to a pretty girl. Only it was in the old station before this was built: We called it the depot. We knew we wouldn't see each other again for almost a year. I thought I couldn't live through it. She stood there crying — don't even know where she lives now. Or if she is living. If she ever thinks of me she probably imagines I'm dancing in the ballroom of the Amberson mansion. She probably thinks of the mansion as still beautiful. Still the finest house in town. Ah, life and money both behave like loose quicksilver in a nest of cracks. When they're gone you can't tell where, or what the devil you did with them.

After expressing an ambivalent attitude to George, half of praise, half of blame, Jack moves away into the steam under the great dome of the station.

In a garden Lucy and her father walk toward the camera through showers of weeping willows. She describes a parallel with George, the story of a bad Indian chief who "wore iron shoes and walked over people's faces"; they banish him, but can find no replacement. We learn that Lucy has resigned herself though, not to a life with George, but to a life in her garden; as Eugene says, "like a pensive garden lady in a Victorian engraving." She has had, she says, too much excitement in her life, she doesn't want any more. "I don't want

anything but you." And Eugene says finally he hopes she can forget even the name of the chief — or George — she talked about.

A tense discussion takes place between Fanny and George in the shuttered and sheeted Amberson house: he is only going to earn $8 a week in a law office, and she reveals that she has lost her money: she has $28, because she invested every cent in the Headlight Company, and it went broke. She cries desperately: "I know what you're going to do! You're going to leave me in the lurch!" She slumps into an attitude of defeat against the boiler, complaining: "I knew your mother wanted me to watch over you, and try to make something like a home for you, and I tried. I tried to make things as nice for you as I could. I walked my heels down looking for a place for us to live. I walked and walked over this town. I didn't ride one block on a streetcar."

As George tells her to leave the boiler, Fanny breaks into hysterics: "It's not hot, it's cold. But I wouldn't mind if it was burning!" He pulls her up, she laughs frantically, and there is the brilliantly achieved shot as

the camera rushes ahead of them through a door as they continue to argue over Fanny's opening up a boardinghouse. Settling on this, George invades his law firm to tell the boss, played by Erskine Sanford, bumbling like all Wellesian officials ("The law's a stern mistress . . ." is one phrase in lines bristling with pompous clichés), to tell him that he cannot take up law, he must do "something that pays from the start, . . . in a dangerous trade, dealing with chemicals, high explosives. . . ." He reveals that he wants to do this to help Fanny start her boardinghouse, with "games of bridge, the kind of harmless gossip that goes on in such places." The lawyer promises to help: "You certainly are the most practical young man that I ever met."

As George walks home, now by his very choice of occupation committing himself to the machine age he had despised so long, we see images of the growing city, and the commentary emphasizes the grim strangeness of the new landscape. Machinery is seen leaping up with the steel fury of a new kind of animal. Telegraph poles deface a once gracious road. Dissolves throw metal struts against a bleak gray sky as the commentary speaks a valedictory, predicting that by tomorrow an era of serenades will be over forever. The screen goes completely dark, and gradually we see George kneeling beside the bed where his mother once died, saying a last prayer, a last farewell: he has got his come-uppance at last. ("He got it three times filled, and running over.")

The next we hear of George he has been run over by an automobile, crushed finally by the New Age. In the newspaper *The Indianapolis Inquirer* a headline announces: "Auto Casualties Mount." (Here is an "in" joke: the paper is a Kane paper, and on the left of the front page is a theatrical column written by Jedediah Leland.) On the right we read: "Serious accident, Geo. Minafer, Akers' Chemical Co., both legs broken." In the final hospital scene Eugene talks to Fanny outside George's room, and Eugene says that George has asked for forgiveness. Eugene says "I never noticed before how much like Isabel Georgie looks." Tears sparkle on Fanny's cheeks, and, in a sentimental glow, she moves out of frame as Eugene talks about being finally "true at last to my true love."

This scene, directed by Robert Wise, has been much maligned, but it echoes, to the tune of a sad, final Herrmann waltz, the precise words of the ending of Tarkington's book: "For Eugene another radiance filled the [hospital] room. He knew that he had been true at last to his true love, and that through him she had brought her boy under shelter again. Her eyes would look wistful no more."

4. JOURNEY INTO FEAR

When war broke out in December 1941, Welles's position at RKO was uncertain. *Citizen Kane* had opened to a rather shaky public reception, and it had closed quickly in many theaters. *The Magnificent Ambersons* was nearing completion. To finish his three-picture contract and get on to *It's All True* in Rio (see Chapter 5) he had to fit in yet another production in a hurry. Somewhere in his mountainous reading amid half-a-dozen projects he found Eric Ambler's *Journey into Fear* and decided that he could make this quickly. But obviously, with *Ambersons* to finish and cut, he had no time to direct it himself. So he took the drastic step of recalling Norman Foster from *My Friend Bonito* (see chapter 5) to direct the film and hired Joseph Cotten to help him write the adaptation. Dolores del Rio, then involved in a stormy affair with Welles, was to star.

The sets, supervised by Welles himself, were partly made over from those prepared for *Heart of Darkness,* partly from other RKO films. The cameraman was the veteran Karl Struss, who had helped photograph *Sunrise*. Mark Robson was selected as editor (by that time, Robert Wise was fully engaged on *Ambersons*). Welles shot scenes, did retakes and inserts and cut *Ambersons* in the daytime; then, sometimes after lunch, sometimes as night fell, he turned up on the *Journey into Fear* set to oversee Foster and appear in the part of Colonel Haki. No special incidents marked the shooting (which was entirely within the studio), except for one brief moment of near-tragedy when the stand-in for Jack Moss, who

played the villain Peter Banat, fell and broke both legs during the shooting of the balcony fight in the rain.

The film had one curious feature: its casting. Jack Moss, who was Welles's manager, had never played a screen part before and agreed to play the villain only on the understanding that he would not utter a word (and he did not). Welles's secretary, Shifra Haran, played Mrs. Haller, wife of the "archaeologist" in the film, and Robert Meltzer, a close associate and friend who was killed on D-Day, was a steward. Others in the cast included Welles's chauffeur (as a driver!), cook, writing assistants, and his publicity men, Herbert Drake (who had been in *Too Much Johnson*) and Bill Roberts as stewards.

Karl Struss confirms that Welles was initially as deeply involved in the direction as Norman Foster. The two men discussed every scene in detail together, and although Foster did the actual direction, Welles undoubtedly controlled every one of his effects until he left for Rio. Struss was maddened by the constant retakes dictated by Welles in the scenes in which Welles appeared. At midnight on one occasion, they were shooting the forty-ninth take of the sequence in which Colonel Haki, played by Welles, is standing at the foot of the gangway of the Greek ship. A midnight call came for supper, and Welles still insisted on doing a number of further takes.

The lighting of the ship's interiors presented enormous hurdles for Struss. He had a further test: the scenes took

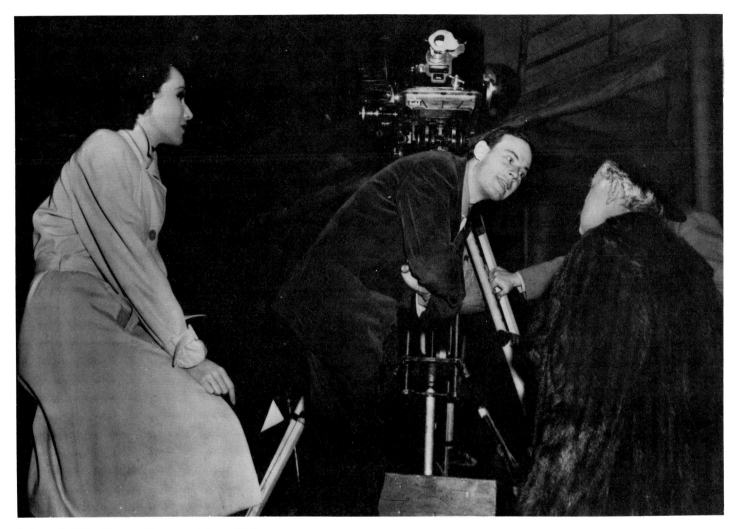

Dolores Del Rio, Norman Foster, and Orson Welles.

place on a ship at sea during wartime, which meant that wartime lighting arrangements, almost to blackout level, must be followed for authenticity. The only advantage in this extreme low-key lighting for Struss was that "normally you had the problem in ship scenes of showing the tank and matte processes used to represent ocean, or the lights hanging over the funnel from the studio roof. This time the problems were removed."[1]

In tracking out of narrow corridors into light during

the few day scenes at port, Struss was faced with getting cables out of the way and loaded onto a truck just out of frame level, because there was nowhere to shift them to on the set itself. There was one scene in a cramped cabin in which Foster and Welles specified there must be no light at all, but "the figures must be made out." A conversation was taking place off-screen, and there must be a feeling of danger in the air. Struss suggested that tiny lights be used that would filter under the door, causing the faintest of glows to cast the cabin's occupants into vague silhouette. Welles and Foster agreed.

[1]Interview with Karl Struss, Hollywood, 1969.

In an interesting innovatory technique, Struss achieved fades by bringing a black object up to full screen and replacing it by a similar object which then receded to show a new scene.

Karl Struss's problems, though, were as nothing compared to those of Foster himself. He started shooting the day after he arrived in Hollywood from Mexico, and hated the day-to-day script pages given him, which he found — despite his friendship with their authors — "silly and wordy." He was upset, also, at being withdrawn from his beloved Mexican project. Moreover, he had to shoot all Welles's scenes first so that Welles could leave for Brazil.

Welles said to me before we started, "Don't read the book." I said to him, "This is ridiculous." And he said, "We've changed it." And I often didn't know what the hell it was all about. . . . I remember for instance that nobody could remember how to pronounce "Kopeikin," the name of one of the characters. Usually it came out as "Kopenkin" — to rhyme with the battleship, you know.[2]

In New York when Welles returned from Brazil, he was shocked to find that *Journey into Fear* had been previewed without a proper concluding scene. Luckily, RKO relented sufficiently to allow Welles to recut the last scene but one of *Journey into Fear* (the hotel balcony) and to reshoot the final sequence with himself and Joseph Cotten in their final encounter in the hotel. The letter-reading framework was also added by Welles. All release prints, involving an investment of $25,000, had to be withdrawn to permit the changes. Some critics even reviewed the film twice, with five months' interval in between. It came out in its second version in March 1943.

Eric Ambler's *Journey into Fear* was published in 1940 and was admired by critics. "Only a bomb," wrote Maurice Richardson in the London *Observer*, "will be able to tear you away from *Journey into Fear*." The novel was a powerfully tense thriller, set in the Black Sea, Istanbul, and Batum. Howard Graham is an engineer enjoying a seedy sojourn in Istanbul. Easygoing, a bit naive, traveling alone, he is ill at ease in the Middle East. In Istanbul, he visits — with Kopeikin, a local representative of Graham's firm — a cabaret, Le Jockey, where he meets José and Josette, an adagio dance team; returning to his hotel, he narrowly dodges an attempt to shoot him. From Colonel Haki, the local police chief, he learns that he has become a target — because of his special knowledge of armaments — in the newly developing war. Welles's chief departure was to introduce the character of Graham's wife, who in the book was in England.

On board a steamer bound across the Black Sea, Graham undergoes an unsettling succession of experiences,

[2]Interview with Norman Foster, Beverly Hills, 1969.

superbly described by Ambler. He again meets the dancing partners as well as a tobacco salesman named Kuvetli, Mr. and Mrs. Haller (an apparent archaeologist, and his faded wife), and Mathis, a railwayman married to a shrewish Frenchwoman.

At Athens the paid assassin who attempted to kill him earlier comes aboard in disguise, and the tension develops considerably, as Graham, unused to violence and never previously asked to use a revolver, unable to convince the crew and officers that he is being pursued, dodges the killer, Peter Banat, all over the crowded ship. These details were freely adapted by Welles, with the Greek scenes altered.

To much authentic dialogue closely modeled on the novel, Welles (with Joseph Cotten's aid) added a number of striking inventions: the killer's pebble glasses, his habit of preserving complete silence, and his obsessively played, cracked phonograph record; the magician's act in Le Jockey — based on Welles's own interest in magic — the weird complexities in the character of the left-wing "intellectual" discovered on board the seedy ship; and the superbly unsettling climactic gunfight on the slippery, rain-swept balconies of a Batum hotel.

Physically, the film equals Ambler's brilliant descriptions of the cramped and claustrophobic life at sea, the muffled purgatory in which the passengers live surrounded by paper-thin bulkheads and throbbing hot pipes.

The playing convinces: Joseph Cotten's simple, honest hero; Dolores del Rio's mysterious, tragic dancing partner heading for some destination she only half-believes in, accompanied by her cut-rate-Valentino partner; Edgar Barrier's nervous, bespectacled, and sparrow-brained intellectual; Agnes Moorehead's cleverly observed Frenchwoman, all shapeless but stiff bourgeois pride. Karl Struss's camerawork, prowling about the ship unnervingly, is certainly beyond praise, while the sound track is a masterpiece, with its muffled voices, vibration, pounding engines, and ever-recurrent French music-hall song carrying with it a hint of death and destruction.

In the precredits opening the camera moves up slowly to the Hotel Istanbul, remaining fixed at a window: Peter Banat like a leprous slug in sinister glasses, a hat squeezed low onto his forehead, is listening to a scratched phonograph record of a male singer struggling through *"Chagrin d'amour"* at the wrong tempo. He puts a gun in his pocket as the needle jumps from groove to groove, repeating certain phrases nerve-scrapingly over and over again. He turns the light off as he goes out, and to the closing of the door, the credit titles come up, accompanied by Roy Webb's crudely enthusiastic score. Baskets move away from the camera, disclosing an Istanbul street scene; Banat also moves away, as Howard Graham reads the contents of a letter to his wife on the sound track over the image of the Adler Palace Hotel doorway: "If this letter ever reaches you, I want you to believe every word of it, and try to understand. It all began that night we arrived in Istanbul. . . ." The rest of the film is told in flashbacks, framed within the letter, a device which was added to give the film more structure after it was previewed to the trade and press.

The flashback begins with Graham and his wife meeting in Istanbul Kopeikin (Everett Sloane), a business associate representing an armaments firm. Using

the excuse of not wanting "to bother Mrs. Graham with business matters," he lures Graham out to Le Jockey, which is introduced with a startling shot of Dolores del Rio in a leopardskin costume, a Kurt Weill-like theme of Webb's on the sound track. A woman sings "Three Little Words" in Turkish, while Graham, disliking the place, keeps insisting uncomfortably that he must get back to the hotel and to his wife.

Graham's boredom only disappears when Josette Martel, the club's dancer, is introduced to him and joins the two men at their table. As she announces that she is about to leave Istanbul, there is a puff of smoke from the stage, and a magician materializes to an exotic musical background, managed with expert seediness by the composer. A loud bang on a Chinese gong announces the arrival of a Chinese midget carrying a coffin, while first in French, and then in German the magician announces: "Ladies and gentlemen, I will present to you an unbelievable miracle, that I heard in the mountain passes of India," and he pulls Graham from the audience for an unwilling participation in the act.

Helpless and afraid, but mysteriously compliant, Graham is tied to two pieces of wood which have been carved into the shape of a St. Andrew's cross. Peter Banat comes down the staircase silently as the Magician climbs into a trick coffin. As the lights go up we see that a transference has been achieved: Graham is now in the coffin, and the magician is straddled on the St. Andrew's cross. Just as we grasp this fact, we hear a scream and a shot half-muffled by the hubbub of the crowd. Graham climbs out of the coffin alive. But the magician is slumped on the cross in the attitude of death, his shirtfront splashed with blood: the assassin has killed him from the stairs, aiming at, but because of the transference failing to kill, Graham.

In the wake of his miraculous escape, Graham fatuously protests about not having a topcoat or being able to telephone his wife (like so many of the characters played by Cotten in Welles's films, he appears to be almost a simpleton). Cutting across our line of vision, the Turkish police chief Colonel Haki enters the club, a passively dominating figure in fur hat and coat as played by Welles, and Kopeikin comments: "He's the head of the secret police. He was a deputy in the provisional government in 1919." Someone else says: "There is a legend: he can drink two bottles of whiskey without getting drunk." And Kopeikin adds: "There is also a legend that he kills prisoners by tying them together in pairs and throwing them in the river with some food and ammunition." All this follows Ambler's text very closely.

Haki summons Graham to his office, Graham's entrance interrupted by the thin pipi-pipi of a Morse signal. At this stage Welles indulges a typical dramatic gimmick: Haki shouts across a room so loudly that only the stone deaf would not hear, and then Graham asks for the words to be repeated: they are at twice the volume. This method is presumably used to give added tension to a poorly written scene, but it merely results in the spectator's distress.

Graham discloses that he is an engineer, with naval ordinance his subject: he is engaged as a munitions expert in an armaments company and has just received orders to return to the United States. Haki tells him that his special training makes him a military objective:

Mr. Howard Graham, you are a careful driver. And an imaginative pedestrian. You never ride horses nor climb mountains. You do not hunt big game. You never felt the slightest inclination to leap before an approaching express. I'm sure you never think of death, or if so, only on those occasions when you take out an insurance policy. Has your excellent brain grasped what I'm trying to say to you? It's perfectly simple. Someone is trying to kill you. . . .

Exhausted, Haki sits slumped at his desk, overcome with the headache induced by a heavy load of work. Haki discloses that Graham's would-be killer at the nightclub was a Nazi thug normally operating with an Axis organization in Sofia: Banat, a professional assassin, whose price for killing a man is 5,000 francs. Haki is concerned that Graham should get safely back to the United States, but Graham contemptuously rejects his offer of safeguard: "I'll get safely back to America, don't you worry." Haki nevertheless arranges for Graham to be placed on a small, twelve-passenger cargo boat to Batum, warning of its awfulness, however: "It's little better than a floating swamp." He points out that if Graham goes by train, he will arrive dead. The alternative to complying with Haki's instructions is arrest, and an unceremonious bundling aboard the ship under guard.

When Graham arrives at the ship, Haki is standing at the foot of the gangway, making sure that Graham gets aboard. ("You have a big advantage over a soldier, Mr. Graham," he consoles him. "You can run away without being a coward.") The set of the quay, the atmosphere of departure in muggy clinging heat, are very well managed.

The gangway is removed, and we enter a labyrinth of corridors aboard the cargo boat, presaging the maze of Dunsinane in *Macbeth* several years later; Karl Struss's photography is here at its most complex and ingenious, moving fluently through Mark-Lee Kirk's inspired ship set. Only the failure to suggest the ship's movement in a swell (which would be particularly pronounced on a low-tonnage freighter of this kind) detracts from the sense of realism.

Graham lies down on the lower bunk of his cabin and lights a cigarette, while the camera observes him from the back of the bunk. It is seemingly fastened to the bulkhead and barely moves, repeating the same unblinking Wellesian stare with which it confronted Peter Banat in the film's precredits scene. A *Heart of Darkness*-like reflection in a smoky mirror shows us Graham's face; this again parallels the opening scene. Whether consciously intended or not, the effect here is to remind us subtly that Banat himself is in the offing, and as Graham loads his revolver the parallel is altogether too close to be missed, opening the second act, as it were, of the film, with Welles's familiar theme of the hunter and the hunted.

In the ship's corridor Graham meets the dancer Josette, now even more striking in a camel's hair coat, sweater, and tight beret; she is on her way to some unknown destination ("India, perhaps"). Like all the screen's mysterious and dangerous women, she seems driven by a fate she cannot comprehend.

The ship's dining saloon is beautifully observed, with bored passengers picking away at third-rate food: a peculiar collection of flotsam. The German "archaeologist," Dr. Haller (Eustace Wyatt) tells Graham, "I am a

good German, of the former Germany. This steward is an imbecile." A Frenchwoman, Mrs. Mathis (Agnes Moorehead, dressed and coiffed to perfection for the role, with black hair piled in ringlets, shawl hugged tight, and face scrubbed clean of make-up) and her husband are at the next table, cynically commented on by the German. The husband is a left-wing "intellectual" railwayman ("War is the last refuge of the capitalists"). Mrs. Matthis says: "He talks like a fool but you should take no notice, monsieur. He was a brave soldier. He won this silver war badge." To which Matthis's jaundiced riposte is: "It's the women who should fight these wars . . . they're more ferocious than the men." Josette's dancing partner, Gobo, (Jack Durant, José in Ambler's book) is an aging lecher ("he always has great success with pretty little girls and old women") who always wins at cards. The overpowering impression is one of seediness, with each character brilliantly drawn but somehow out of focus; a succession of clever sketches, acted to perfection, but never quite fleshed out.

During a conversation with Haller on the ship's deck

— shot in a similar manner to the hospital interview with Jedediah Leland in Kane — the sound of Peter Banat's scratched phonograph record echoes from a cabin. In the new sequence the passengers are packed tight at a circular table in the saloon, while Banat's bespectacled shape slithers down a companionway toward them. As Graham sees Banat enter the saloon, he spills the salt but throws it over his shoulder for luck, and Banat revoltingly crumbles a huge biscuit, scattering the smashed pieces into his soup from the palm of his hand, shoveling masses of spaghetti through his blubbery lips.

Disgusted and afraid, Graham goes out of the saloon and to the crew's quarters. He asks to be put ashore at once, bringing intoxicated laughter from the captain (who is in bed). The purser tells him: "This is a ship, monsieur, not a taxi. We carry a cargo around on a schedule." Helpless laughter also is the only response from the purser and the Captain as Graham explains that a paid assassin is aboard. As the purser asks Graham to go, the Captain says: "Boom! Boom!" and laughs drunkenly.

After this rebuff, tense and badly upset, Graham has to put up with the shrill virago cries of Mrs. Mathis down the ship's corridor, and her husband's maddening insistence on airing his dreary personal problems. The tension, achieved partly by the tight, packed, claustrophobic compositions in the ship's corridors and the oppressively long takes, is added to by Mathis's whining, hectoring, inescapable voice. Mathis's speech to Graham here is at once pathetic and funny, and beautifully delivered by Edgar Barrier:

Has your wife got a bad temper, Mr. Graham? For years I lived in misery. Then one day I made a great discovery. There was a socialist meeting and I went to it. I wasn't a socialist, you understand. I went to this meeting because I was curious . . . . I repeated what I had heard. My wife laughed in a very peculiar way . . . I discovered that my wife was a snob and even more stupid than I dreamed. . . . Mr. Graham, I bought books and pamphlets to make my arguments more damaging . . . I, a capitalist by instinct, became a socialist by conviction.

She was, it turns out, afraid he would reveal his socialism to her *bourgeois* friends.

As this absurd harangue-in-a-dressing-gown continues, we remain painfully conscious of the presence of Banat along the corridor only a few feet away. Finally Graham manages to pry himself loose and goes into his cabin. He feels under the bunk, and realizes the pistol is missing. He leaves, pushing past Banat in the dark shadows of the passageway, and sees the flapping of a tarpaulin protecting the passengers from a squall.

In the saloon, the passengers are restless, nervous and grumbling, Mrs. Mathis whining about the poor ventilation, saying: "I've had nausea and a headache since I got on this ship. We should complain."

Josette senses Graham's fear, expressing her feelings superbly: "People who are afraid . . . look different . . . their faces are very small and grey around the mouth." As they walk around the decks, the camera follows them in an enormous and extraordinary traveling movement, a take that superbly seems to go on forever, while Graham describes the cause of his terror, the threating presence of Peter Banat on board. Josette offers to help

him in whatever way she can, and we sense the beginning of a close friendship between them. She will see that Gobo engages Banat at cards to allow Graham to search his cabin for the revolver.

A moment later Graham runs into Haller — who has eavesdropped on his conversation with Josette — on deck. Haller talks like the true Welles creation he is, of dissolution, of the threat of death: "To see a ship from the land, or to see the land from a ship: I used to like both. Now I dislike both. When a man reaches my age, he grows to resent subconsciously the movement of everything but the respiratory muscles, which keep him alive. Movement means change, and to an old man, change means death. I think I will say good-night, Mr. Graham."

Graham begins his search of Banat's cabin, and a figure passes the door. It is Haller, who waits for Graham in the cabin, and confronts him with the revolver, which he himself has purloined; he admits that his name is not Haller but Müller, and that he not an archaeologist and a "good German" at all, but a Nazi agent.

Müller tells Graham that on arrival at Batum he will be taken to a small private hospital, ostensibly to hide him from Banat, but "suspected of typhus"; the purpose is clearly to torture him and wring the secrets of new armaments from him. Graham goes out on deck and sees farm animals huddled in pens. There he meets the salesman, Kuvetli, hired as an agent by Colonel Haki, who advises him to avoid being murdered at Batum by hiding in a spare cabin until the ship docks and then slipping ashore. In the meantime, to keep Müller quiet, Graham is to tell him that he will accept his offer of hiding in the hospital. A few moments later Kuvetli is found dead, with Banat's scratchy recording marking his sudden murder. Against the thudding of the ship's motors, as insistent as a heartbeat, Graham searches the dead man's belongings, and the awful record starts again, with its whining tenor, its thin screeching strings. A close-up shows the spinning disc with the needle grinding into it from the metal arm, while Banat narcissistically and obsessively combs and recombs his hair, as in the opening shot. In desperation Graham asks Mathis to take a message to the Turkish consul in Batum, which will indicate to Colonel Haki in Istanbul that he is in trouble. "In the event of my death, ask him to notify the American consul."

Batum is introduced expertly by a shot of Graham looking through the porthole of the cabin he is hiding in. But here the plot suffers from one of its inexplicable lapses: instead of lying low, Graham absurdly goes all over the ship asking various passengers — including Josette's dancing partner, Gobo — to lend him a revolver. More sensibly, Gobo suggests that Graham should leave the ship with him and with Josette, to have adequate cover. There follows a moment of incongruous and inexplicable comedy, as Matthis calls Graham into his cabin. He apologizes again for not being able to offer him a gun, "But I do have a knife," offering him a tiny, useless penknife and an umbrella. This almost fatally snaps the mood of the film.

At the dock Banat is waiting for his prey, and there is an extraordinary shot from the gangway upwards to Graham, his figure diagonally dividing the frame, looming above us. An extremely well-directed sequence follows, as Graham — who has been captured off-screen — escapes from the car in which Banat, Müller, and another are driving him to the torture hospital. Dogs and goats scatter in the Batum streets. We have a shot across a horse as the car dashes through the market, horn honking loudly, scattering people to every side. A Stalin poster looms on the wall behind. As the car has a flat tire, there is general hubbub; Graham finally finds his penknife useful and thrusts it into the car horn. A struggle takes place in the back with Banat. Horses rear and buck, their bodies strikingly shot from below eye-level. Then Graham manages to drive the car right through a shop window: the car seems almost to strike the camera, hurling over a cash register as it plunges almost on top of us. The whole sequence can be compared to the barroom fight in *Touch of Evil* and Elsa Bannister's flight through the Acapulco streets in *Lady from Shanghai* as a dashing scene of action and violence.

Graham runs into the kitchen of an adjoining house, where a cat is licking itself lazily in the foreground, and

a startled cook stands in the background. Lightning flashes; rain teems down; umbrella-carrying figures sweep past doorways. In a hotel lobby Graham asks for his wife. When they meet again, she prattles on ceaselessly in the doorway until Banat and Müller, wet from the rain, put in an appearance in the suite. Müller says: "I hate to take your husband away from you, Mrs. Graham." She agreeably discloses that Colonel Haki has arrived at the hotel, and Müller brazenly asks her to go down to the lobby and engage Haki in conversation while he concludes some "private business" with Graham in the suite.

Maids go into the suite, carrying fresh towels, and Graham uses the opportunity to slip out onto the balcony in the rain. There follows a masterly sequence as Banat and Graham and finally Colonel Haki all meet for the death struggle on the slippery ledges under the dripping awnings of the hotel. They edge round pillars; awnings flap; the watching crowd is seen directly from overhead, rain seemingly pouring out of the camera;

Banat wounds Haki, who crashes back through a window; Banat's spectacles are misted with rain, he can't see properly, he wipes them desperately; Banat's last bullet has gone, and he flings his revolver at Graham. The earlier vertiginous shot of the crowd below is repeated; and a moment later, in trying to push Graham to his death, Banat slips and falls five floors to a silent death in the street.

The final scene — added by Welles after his return from Rio — shows Graham concluding the letter to his wife (although she is resident in the same hotel). Colonel Haki comes in with his arm in a sling, and Graham writes the last words, saying, "I wonder why you always finish the letters you're going to tear up?" Haki says he turned out to be a dangerous man. Graham says: "I got mad. I spent too much time running away." The doors to the hotel lounge flap and close, and the film is — rather unsatisfactorily — over.

• • •

Journey into Fear is a film of a peculiar cramped tightness, so crammed with action and conversation that no one viewing can permit a full journey through its labyrinth. We find here the characteristic comedy which often seems to be carried into Welles's films by the presence of Joseph Cotten (with his bumbling requests for a topcoat and a chance to contact his wife when his life is falling to pieces), and we also find a sharp vividness of visual observation. There may be discrepancies of continuity and character, odd shifts of tone that don't work. But the success of the film, though flawed, is real: it may be crude and unsure, but it creates a world of its own.

The opening — Banat listening to the cracked 78 rpm record (owned by Norman Foster) with its scrambling of the words of *"Chagrin d'amour"* observed with an almost motionless camera as though seen from a facing window across a court — is masterly in its evocation of seediness, a cockroach life lived in shadows; and the visit to the nightclub has all the queasy, unbalanced feeling of real nightmare, with Hans Conreid a brilliantly mannered and sinister magician.

It was an inspired touch to have — as the sound track jangles with an unsettling rearrangement of the score — a version sung in Turkish of "Three Little Words," and the murder of the magician again comes off with tremendous flair. The feeling of being trapped in hell is a powerful one, and the nightclub itself, with its horrible transference act from cross to coffin, is a creation not inferior to Welles's hall of mirrors in *Lady from Shanghai,* his bead-curtained *boîte* in *Touch of Evil.*

The ship is marvelous: throbbing and pulsating, stiflingly claustrophobic, with its low ceilings and cramped cabins, its shabby saloon and irritable passengers squabbling in dressing gowns, its impression of bad and interminable meals eaten against portholes looking out onto the Black Sea, and, its cabin holding the murderous Peter Banat, beetle eyes black and empty, playing his record over and over again. These sequences aboard ship concentrate emotion to an almost unbearable degree, especially when the socialist bore, so brilliantly played by Edgar Barrier, corners Graham in the corridor.

But the film's most impressive, as well as its most famous, sequence is the ending on the balcony of the hotel at Batum. As the rain streams blindingly down the killer's glasses, as the figures edge past flapping awnings, as the crowd below is seen emphasized by the rain at an astonishing vertical angle, the film's virtuosity is at its most extraordinary. We have been released from the sweltering labyrinth of the ship to air and rain and light-slashed darkness, but we are still trapped in a nightmare, the murderous intensity of an evil dream.

5. IT'S ALL TRUE

No more disturbing episode, not even the recutting of *The Magnificent Ambersons*, exists in the Welles saga than that of his doomed Latin American project, *It's All True*. From the beginning of the RKO period Welles and his team, immersed as they were in *Kane, Ambersons*, and the abortive *Heart of Darkness*, were constantly casting around for new subjects. Some time in 1941 the idea came up for a multipart film stemming from a then-current enthusiasm for Julien Duvivier's *Carnet de Bal* and his omnibus Hollywood film, then in preparation by Sam Spiegel, *Tales of Manhattan*.

The title of Welles's new project — entirely North American in ambience — was to be *It's All True*, and the studio agreed in theory to a multistory Welles film. Two subjects came from Robert Flaherty works. *The Captain's Chair* was a novel, strung loosely together from Flaherty's travels in the frozen North. Welles had bought it in 1938 and adapted it as the story of a Hudson Bay trader captain who is given the command of a new vessel and clashes with a Hudson Bay official on board; when the official takes his chair at the table, he threatens to sink the ship. George Coulouris was to play the captain. This story was never filmed.[1] *My Friend Bonito* had its origins in Flaherty's excursion to Mexico with Leon Shamroy in the late twenties, to make a now vanished — and unfinished — film about the Acoma Indians, *Acoma, The Sky City* (Fox, 1928), co-shot by Floyd Crosby.

Flaherty was casting about for a boy to play the lead, and heard about a famous episode in which a youngster's pet bull was spared by the mercy of the crowd at a corrida. He turned it into an anecdote called *Bonito, the Bull*, and planned to film it with Korda, many years later. Korda, however, thought it better to make the story that of an elephant, doomed to be destroyed by a maharajah, which is spared by the intercession of the maharajah's servants; and from this it was only a step to deciding instead to make Kipling's *Toomai of the Elephants* as *Elephant Boy*, with Flaherty directing. The Flaherty story reverted to the author, and in 1941 he sold it to Welles for $12,000 (Welles had taken an option on it in 1936, but this apparently had lapsed).

A third episode was to be entitled *Love Story*, based by John Fante on an episode in his parents' lives. It dealt with a bricklayer who pretends to be wealthy to impress his young bride, spends the wedding night with her in a borrowed house, then tells her the truth. The three stories dealt with man's pride and dignity in relation to his work. The fourth story was to be the history of jazz, based on Louis Armstrong's ghosted memoirs and inspired by Welles's love of Negro life. The script was written by Elliot Paul and David Stuart, and color scenes were sketched and tests shot.

The only one of these episodes to start shooting — in the fall of 1941, as it happened — was *My Friend Bonito*, directed by Norman Foster from a script by Foster and John Fante. Foster flew into Mexico without papers. Al Gilks, later to co-photograph *An American in Paris*,

[1] It was adapted for BBC television by Denis Johnston in 1938, with Flaherty himself narrating.

went down to Mexico with the unit as chief cameraman, but when war broke out he was called for active duty and was replaced by Floyd Crosby, who had worked with Flaherty on *Tabu,* which won him an Oscar. Shooting took place in many of the great bull ranches of Mexico, including the celebrated La Punta. Welles flew down to supervise shooting on the earliest Gilks sequences, then flew home to start *The Magnificent Ambersons;* thereafter he only flew down on occasional weekends. The child star's name was Jesus Vasquez, but Welles renamed him "Hamlet." His friend, an old man who also had a passion for bulls, was played by the distinguished Mexican actor, the late Domingo Soler.

Foster was a little-known director of Charlie Chan and Mr. Moto B-pictures, who had a strong sense of exotic atmosphere that Welles had recognized in looking through his work during the period of day-and-night movie viewing that preceded *Kane.* Floyd Crosby, of course, had the unimpeachable qualification of having worked on two previous Flaherty subjects. The Mexican cutter, the late Joe Noriega, was a superb technician, and the Mexican cameraman Alex Phillips, who did additional shots, had a large local reputation.

Shooting proceeded smoothly through November and December, first with Gilks, then with Crosby. But in December, following Pearl Harbor, Nelson Rockefeller had an inspiration that unfortunately developed into a catastrophe. Rockefeller, who had been behind the hiring of Welles by RKO in 1939 and was still a major stockholder, was now Co-ordinator of Inter-American Affairs, spearheading a Rooseveltian propaganda drive in Latin America to improve cultural relations with his own nation. Nazi fifth-column activity was rife south of Panama, and a German invasion was feared. Latin American countries had banned Chaplin's *The Great Dictator* because of its parody of Hitler, and countries that had shown it had suffered from pro-Nazi riots. Moreover, several Hollywood musicals "portraying" Latin American life (e.g., *That Night In Rio, Down Argentine Way*), which were made with Rockefeller's encouragement by Darryl F. Zanuck, had been booed or laughed off the screen all over the continent for their

MY FRIEND BONITO: *Jesús Vasquez at La Punta.*

absurdity. Rockefeller had even been forced to hand Zanuck $40,000 dollars of CIAA money to reshoot portions of *Down Argentine Way* offensive to Argentinians and had supervised some Disney projects.

Nelson Rockefeller decided that Welles could act both as a cultural ambassador and as an artist by making a documentary film that would demonstrate North American interest in South America and illustrate South American customs to the people of his own country. On January 2 he and John Hay Whitney, head of the motion picture division, officially approached Welles, who was fortunate in having already embarked on *My Friend Bonito.* Welles decided to scrap the North American episodes of *It's All True* and to keep only *My Friend Bonito.* Rockefeller suggested that the film should start with a documentary of the Rio Carnival and should include a cartoon by Miguel Covarrubias; a Simon Bolivar episode was mooted.

Unfortunately, Welles allowed himself to be pressured into agreeing to get to Rio for the Carnival, which started on February 13. And he made a very serious mistake. Instead of pointing out to the RKO chiefs that he would

Welles arriving at the Rio airport.

Welles and Richard Wilson in Rio.

have to have his contract extended to permit him to make the third film due under it by June 1942 after *It's All True,* he went ahead and rushed his third film through. He recalled Norman Foster from Mexico in mid-shooting to make *Journey into Fear,* as we have seen, thereby ruining *My Friend Bonito.* Welles planned to continue *My Friend Bonito* later, but even this idea was abandoned, only to be taken up again when he returned to North America in August and talked about "three weeks Mexican shooting still to be done." Years later Foster tried to complete the film, with the same actors, but it was, of course, impossible; the Mercury had schooled Jesús in Los Angeles, and he had gone into the army and disappeared.

And Welles himself left for Rio — via Washington, Miami, and Recife — on February 5, with the editing of *Ambersons* uncompleted. *Journey into Fear,* with the

Colonel Haki scenes finished except for long shots using a stand-in, was, of course, still shooting. One would have thought that before leaving Welles would have made firm arrangements for Norman Foster to return immediately to Mexico to finish *Bonito* after he had completed *Journey into Fear,* but incredibly Welles announced instead that Foster would direct Dolores del Rio in the previously abandoned *Mexican Melodrama* in April.

Welles said before leaving Hollywood: "We have pretty well in mind what we are going to do in Brazil.[2] And we also know that we are going on from there to other Latin American countries. My definite plan is to attempt a movie for all the people of all the Americas. It will be a polyglot movie, by which I mean we are

[2]Only "pretty well." There had been no time to prepare a script or even a story or treatment, a fact that resulted in the fatally haphazard nature of the material when it was actually shot.

designing it to be completely understandable, no matter what the language of the audience. Some of it will be silent, part will be in color, but we intend to make it so that it can play in its original state in all of the Americas." A press release issued by Mercury Productions halfway through shooting (May 5, 1942) added: "[The film] will be comprehensible to the eye and not necessarily the ear of the audience. It will not be necessary to be able to read to understand. This means a venture into the revival of silent-film techniques. The film will be full length, released as a normal feature by RKO and will appear in its original form in every country where it gets exhibited." A full score, using Latin American themes, was commissioned from Paul Misraki, but never used.

Welles's hastily assembled team for the Brazilian project included Richard Wilson, his faithful assistant for many years, the cameramen Eddie Pyle, Harry Wellman, W. Howard Greene (the Technicolor man called for by Herbert and Natalie Kalmus, who had the Technicolor patent and supervised all of its uses), and, as director of photography, Harry J. Wild. On January 20 the first group, headed by Wilson, flew down in two chartered airliners, taking with them four Technicolor cameras, while another twelve planes left with other equipment. A ship arrived much later with more material, including, absurdly, the all-important arc lamps, which arrived after the carnival; meanwhile Welles had been forced to use local military searchlights for night dancing scenes, using every carbon electrode needed for possible antiaircraft defense.

From the moment he arrived, Welles made an immediate sensation in Rio. His personality inflamed enormous local enthusiasm, and he embarked on a round of nightclubs, performing his magic act, and appearing with famous Rio beauties, as well as plunging with enthusiasm into the days and nights of Carnival and dispatching second units all over to shoot the people arriving to take part in it.

He used the light Eyemo hand-held cameras, and Eclairs, light French cameras not then commonly used in America, fitting in his footage to all that Richard Wilson had shot, just before his arrival, of the first devotees on their way from inland. This episode, first called simply *Carnival,* was changed to *The Samba Story* or *The Story of the Samba,* when Welles decided to introduce something of the origins of the dance form which was sweeping North and South America and tie an account of it in with the Carnival. Second units went into villages and jungle areas, capturing the frenzied excitement of a nation afire with violent erotic rhythms, voluptuous and pulsating. Welles's teams showed crowds sambaing through dirt roads, swamps, and great rain forests. And when Welles, with his passion for elaboration, found it necessary to flesh out even this incomparably exotic material, he reconstructed the Carnival in a local theater and in the largest studio in Rio on a still more staggering scale than the real one.

Improvising the story with bold dramatic strokes as he went on, his genius at full stretch, Welles created the story of the samba schools, the samba's appearance at clubs and at public dances. To bind the whole story together he engaged the chunky, ebullient Negro enter-

tainer Grande Otelo (Sebastiâo Prata), whom he photographed leading the crowd like the Pied Piper of Hamelin, together with a little boy not unlike Jesús Vasquez. These scenes, gone forever, evidently had a legendary quality, formalized and poetic.

One sequence relieved the flowing rhythms of the rest. As Otelo and the boy reach the Plaza No. 11, a notorious haunt of prostitutes and thieves, and a place of marvelous color and vibrancy, Otelo sings a lament, the "Plaza No. 11 Farewell," a hymn to the destined vanishing of the square to make way for a new highway. Finally, Otelo and the boy are seen exhausted, the crowd drifts away down the streets like the ebbing bubbles of a dried-up river, and the boy leans against a lamp-post, sits down on the pavement, and, his hat tilting over his brow, snoozes happily away. Carnival is over.

This part of *It's All True* was to take thirty or forty minutes to unfold. Casting about for a story to accompany it and *My Friend Bonito,* Welles either now in Rio or (some say) earlier in Hollywood found the ideal subject in the December 8 issue of *Time.* This was a true account of four fishermen known as *jangadeiros* who had sailed their primitive, sailed seining *paiva* tree trunk raft, the *Sâo Pedro,* 1,650 miles without a compass from Fortaleza, a primitive port on the hump of Brazil, to Rio. They had been inspired by God to bring word of their wretched working conditions and lack of pension funds to President Getulio Vargas, dictator of Brazil. As their journey continued, oppressed Brazil went wild. The *jangadeiros* became national heroes when they at last sailed into Rio harbor, were greeted by every vessel in the bay, and were paraded, after receiving improved conditions from Vargas, in triumph through the city streets.

The leader of the *jangadeiros,* a small, rugged man named José Olimpio Meira (or, more familiarly, Jacaré, the Alligator), and his tough little fishermen companions Tata, Mané, and Jeronymo, fascinated Welles. He flew with Robert Meltzer to Fortaleza in March and signed them up. He decided to update their story from October 1941 to February 1942 to link them, albeit artificially, with the Carnival.

The structure was then as follows. *My Friend Bonito* was to be followed by Covarrubias's animated cartoon (on the conquest of Mexico), which would lead in to Welles booming in a "travelogue" voice like those in the James A. FitzPatrick shorts. When the audience was on the point of exasperation, the voice would fade and the image it accompanies — "Rio's scenic beauties" — would change to a group of attractive girls on Copacabana Beach. They are looking out to sea. Following their gaze, we note a tiny speck, far out in the ocean. Now the whole beach crowd looks, boats put out, and we see the *jangada* raft, which is greeted by a great fleet and followed by the cameras as it docks. The raft is hoisted by crane from the water, and the *jangadeiros* are greeted by the populace.

Jacaré then takes up the story, squatting in front of the camera as he describes to us the origins of the *jangadeiros,* and their brave battle in the past against the slave trade. He excuses himself, gets up, and announces that he is going to Carnival. This links him with the Carnival itself, which forms the next portion of the film.

During the shooting in March Welles saw a superb sight: as he crossed Rio Harbor from Niteroi across the Bay, he saw the moon glowing behind the great Christus statue on Corcovado Peak. He sent a cameraman onto a ferry the next night to cruise up and down until he obtained some perfect shots. They are magnificent; and they still survive.

Often, at night, Welles talked to the *jangadeiros* about their lives in Fortaleza and their lack of compasses. Jacaré told Welles that he thought a compass was a thing of pity. He added that a *jangadeiro* did not even need a chart. He had the sun, the stars, and the wind.

Shooting of the *jangadeiros* episode proceeded smoothly — then an extraordinary disaster took place. On May 19 a second unit was filming Jacaré and his companions off the coast when an octopus and a shark suddenly burst out of the water, locked in a death struggle. The crew eagerly shot this astonishing sight, and the *jangadeiros* stood up to look, thereby tilting over the raft.

They fell into the sea. Tata, Mané, and Jeronymo were powerful swimmers. They reached safety, hauled aboard a film crew boat. But Jacaré was a poor swimmer. As the great creatures sank in a bloody foam, reports ran, he was sucked into the vortex and vanished. Six days later, the shark was caught. Inside it, half digested, were portions of octopus and the head and arms of Jacaré.

Welles was stunned when he heard the news. He immediately scrawled across the script of *It's All True* the words: "Dedicated to the memory of Jacaré, an American hero." But many people unfairly blamed him for the tragedy.

Even before the shock caused in Washington and Hollywood by this incident, storm clouds had been gathering at home. The trouble began in February, just after Welles's departure for Rio, when Joseph I. Breen, the former motion picture censor who had assumed office as RKO vice president in charge of production in Hollywood, went on vacation to Mexico. In Breen's absence, Charles Koerner, a hard-driving New York executive of Radio-Keith-Orpheum, the parent theater company that controlled RKO Radio Pictures, came to Hollywood to take temporary charge.

Koerner, general manager of the theater circuit under George Schaefer, president of Radio-Keith-Orpheum,

was brashly opposed to Welles's policy of directing "big" two-hour films. Completely steeped in the idea of double bookings — a drama doubled with a comedy, say, to be on the safe side — Koerner saw this method of selling films in harness as an answer to the grievous problems of his company, still the shakiest in Hollywood. He hoped, too, that double bookings would provide a solution to the agonizing problem caused by a recent government consent decree which forbade block bookings of films in large numbers over chains of theaters — a decree that foreshadowed the severance of the theater chains from their studio owners or subsidiaries a decade later. Hence, he had *Ambersons* cut to fit in a double bill.

After Breen's return to Hollywood, Koerner stayed on to clash with Breen, who wanted a policy of high-quality pictures, carefully sold on particularized publicity campaigns one by one, and was against the cutting of *Ambersons*. Breen brought in two "quality" producers, Jed Harris and Reeves Espy; and he hired, in April, much against Koerner's wishes, Pare Lorentz, the brilliant documentary filmmaker *(The River, The Plow That Broke the Plains)* to direct a film entitled *Name, Age and Occupation,* based on an unfinished novel and an unfinished government documentary of Lorentz's own, about a farm boy who becomes a sergeant in World War I and later returns to the land, as much a symbolic representation of the simple American rural people as *Citizen Kane* was a representation of the ambitious American. Robert Ryan was brought from the stage to play Lorentz's leading character, and Floyd Crosby engaged to do the photography.

For months Breen and Koerner and the other members of the board of directors on both coasts were locked in a death struggle over studio policy. Stories about Welles's profligacy in Rio, followed by news of the death of Jacaré, gave strength to Koerner's arm. In May, realizing the situation was hopeless, Breen resigned and returned to his post of censor. The Lorentz project was canceled, after weeks of location shooting in and around Detroit, and the unfortunate Floyd Crosby again found himself with an uncompleted feature on his hands.

In New York the company was controlled by three

immensely powerful men: Floyd Odlum, president of the hundred-million dollar Atlas Corporation, who had saved the studio from bankruptcy in 1939; Nelson Rockefeller through his Rockefeller Center group; and David Sarnoff, the dynamic head of the Radio Corporation of America. Odlum, we may safely assume, was out to bat for Koerner, while Rockefeller and Sarnoff — particularly the former — were in favor of that policy of "quality pictures" which Breen had been happy to execute. Through his Atlas Corporation's incredible resources, Odlum assumed more and more control, and by June he had a 47 percent holding in the company. The pressure was too great; Rockefeller resigned, and with him Sarnoff and Breen. This left almost no one on the board with the slightest sympathy for Welles's venture, and in June an executive flew to Rio to recall the unit, while Koerner took the reins in Hollywood.

Widely reported, the death of Jacaré caused a sudden upsurge of Brazilian public feeling against the Hollywood film company in its midst. According to more than one member of the production team, they were unable for days to risk coming out of their Rio hotel. Nor were relations with RKO improved by Welles's notoriously eccentric behavior, which included throwing his furniture out of a hotel window in protest at a bill, with the aid of the Mexican ambassador, and nightclubbing on a prodigious scale. Worse still, the footage that came back to Hollywood was an inchoate jumble, with the stories of the *jangadeiros* and Grande Otelo so carelessly woven into the fabric of *The Samba Story* that only a masterpiece of editorial juggling could have knitted the threads together.

The studio emissary packed up the unit, seized the color cameras, and flew everyone home with the exception of Welles himself, his assistant Richard Wilson, Wilson's wife (the writer Elizabeth Wilson), and Welles's secretary. This little group traveled to Fortaleza and, on studio instructions, did their best to shoot — with the aid of a young Hungarian cameraman, George Fanto — the opening scenes of the picture, which showed the fishermen preparing for their journey south. Incredibly, they were not lynched, but liked; they used a stand-in for

the dead Jacaré and shot from 4:30 in the morning until midnight.

Welles and his small team, with the aid of local researchers, set out to create nothing less than the traditional life of an entire community. He showed hundreds of *jangadeiros* leaving Fortaleza each morning at the first glimmer of light, looking for their daily food. Storms came, destroying their hope of provender. Sharks were shown cruising the coast, making fishing impossible. Against these dangers Welles beautifully set the atmosphere of deep friendship and community suffering that bound the fishermen together, their construction of native huts to withstand the weather, the women making lace, the cooking of the fish in handmade ovens, the making of the rafts from five tree trunks lashed together. At the end of the episode Welles showed the tragic drowning of a young *jangadeiro* and the funeral that followed, with mourning women — in shots influenced by Flaherty — outlined against the sky, the rocks, and the sea. Not a foot of the negative of this episode appears to survive.

His work in Fortaleza finished, Welles returned, after a brief visit to Buenos Aires, to New York in August. Meanwhile, on July 1, the Mercury Production Unit had been summarily ordered to get off the RKO lot within forty-eight hours to make room for a Tarzan picture crew, and all had been struck from the studio payroll. Jack Moss and Herbert Drake, vice president of Mercury and director of its publicity, issued a joint statement to the press which might — apart from its faulty grammar — have been penned by Welles himself: "We are Leonardo da Vinci, evicted from his draughty garret." They took with them the Mercury files, a mimeograph machine, and some few possessions, taking refuge until their final disbanding at the home of Herbert Drake, where they could receive Mercury telephone calls. They also removed from RKO — in a characteristic Mercury joking mood — the bronze outlet to Welles's steam room, where many Mercury conferences were held and which was now being used without invitation by the RKO executives. Bronze was unavailable due to wartime restrictions, the outlet could not be replaced, and Koerner never forgave them.

The Mercury remnants worked with a capital of $200 and were more or less sustained by the consolation of a telephone call from Welles in which he said, "We're just passing a bad Koerner."

Throughout the last six months of 1942, Welles, on good terms with Nelson Rockefeller in spite of everything, enlisted the aid of Rockefeller's office to try and salvage the footage shot in Rio. In July, 1943, the House Committee on Appropriations held a closed budget session to investigate the facts. Nelson Rockefeller and Francis Alstock, now new director of the CIAA's motion picture division (in place of John Hay Whitney, who was in the Army) told the committee bluntly that the CIAA was no longer responsible for the $300,000 it had promised RKO against loss on completion.

That, of course, was the end. The material shot at Fortaleza was not even printed from the negative, and of the remaining *jangadeiros* material, only the final arrival of the *jangadeiros* into Rio exists. The color footage of the carnival was shown to Preston Sturges at Paramount for possible use as stock footage in a comedy *(Carnival in Rio)* that was never made. There was some discussion of using it for shorts, and the CIAA considered buying it for use in Pan-American relations one-reel illustrative films. All these schemes were abandoned, and in January 1945, a duplicate negative was handed over to Welles, who for tax purposes lodged it in a vault in Salt Lake City; when Welles was unable to find funds to cut it himself, it was returned to RKO. The rest, both color and black-and-white negative, was retained, together with the *jangadeiros* material, in the RKO vault.

In 1946, when *The Stranger* was being finished, Russell Metty — shocked when Welles burst into tears and said he was broke and had no future plans — offered to assemble the whole of RKO's *It's All True* positive into some rough shape to show to a group of possible financiers. These men were interested in having Welles act as a go-between. They would buy the film from RKO, which distributed *The Stranger,* Welles would explain the film to the audience in an introductory talk, recut it in its entirety, and provide a coherent narrative. But he did not turn up at a screening that could have saved his film. "The son of a bitch was in New York," the still astonished Metty says today. "He had completely forgotten about the screening." [3]

The *It's All True* affair had a curious aftermath. In February 1957 Nassour Studio in Hollywood sued RKO and the King Brothers for $750,000, charging that their script for *The Brave One,* a Mexican bullfight story identical with *My Friend Bonito,* was based on one rejected by RKO in 1951 and filmed by Nassour as *Emilio and the Bull.* Next month, one Robert Rich won the Oscar for the script of *The Brave One,* released in mid-March.

[3]Interview with Russell Metty, Universal City, 1969.

On March 31 Robert Rich told *The New York Times* that he was not the story's author at all, but was in fact a nephew of Frank King of King Brothers, famous production team, who had posed as the author in order to obtain two free tickets to the Academy Awards. Rich claimed that he had met the real author in Germany, but would not name him.

Shortly after that, Paul Radar, director of film productions at WGBH-TV, Boston's educational television station, claimed that the film was based on his script

Ring Around Saturn, which he had written for Nassour and sold to them in October 1957. Then, on April 3, Fred Zinnemann in a joint statement to the Academy of Motion Picture Arts and Sciences and *The New York Times* disclosed that the story was precisely the same as one that Flaherty had shown him in 1931. Mrs. Frances Flaherty, Flaherty's widow, said that she still owned the original manuscript of the story, written in 1928 and called *Benito* [sic] *The Bull* (her misspelling has been followed by numerous Welles critics, including Peter Noble and Peter Cowie).

The King Brothers pointed out that the story was a legend in the public domain, and that Tom Lea, author of *The Brave Bulls,* had also written a version of it. It later emerged that Fred Zinnemann had tried to buy the story from the Flahertys in 1936, but that Welles

had already acquired an option. Welles himself wrote from Europe to reveal the price he had paid for it. Finally, the King Brothers settled with Nassour for the full $750,000 out of court. The author of the screenplay using the name of the King Brothers' nephew was in fact Dalton Trumbo, hiding under a pseudonym because of the blacklist.

What became of the footage of *It's All True?* In 1958 RKO was acquired by Desilu. When Paramount took over Desilu several years later, Hazel Marshall, Paramount film librarian, was given orders by the fire department to junk every foot of film in one vault as it had decomposed to the danger point. She had it shipped out to sea and dumped in the Pacific.

Of the remainder, Miss Marshall, afraid of copyright problems when clearances seemed not to have been

filed on the principal figure, Grande Otelo, cut and destroyed every foot of the film in which he appeared gaily dancing through and binding together the story of the Samba. The rest was trimmed from hundreds of outtakes to a continuity of dances and street scenes by her assistant Tony Pellegrino, who worked doggedly for

several months to fit together from negative and positive a working continuity. What he has produced is a condensation of hundreds of takes amounting to just over 30,000 feet.

By an incredible coincidence, the day I telephoned Paramount from Santa Cruz, where I was teaching, to ask the material's present whereabouts (Welles, in Hollywood after a sojourn to Mexico, was also seeking the footage), Miss Marshall told me she had just finished cataloging the material the day before. She had no idea what it signified, or what *It's All True* was. She called it "the Welles Mardi Gras material." It was the moment of a lifetime for a cinéaste. I flew at once from Santa Cruz that night, unable to sleep, and the next morning I saw the Carnival footage. Months later, after a hiatus caused by Miss Marshall's agonized concern that Paramount might have no right to show the material at all, a series of complicated coast-to-coast negotiations (involving seemingly half the attorneys of Paramount Gulf and Western Industries) resulted in my seeing what was left of *My Friend Bonito* and *Jangadeiros.*

I shall endeavor to describe exactly what I saw, though I cannot unfortunately share my precise feelings as I viewed the footage on a Moviola. I examined about 11,000 feet, all that remains of *My Friend Bonito* and *Jangadeiros,* mixed together out of sequence, brittle and often faded on twelve separate reels, and 7,000 feet of *Samba.* The remaining black-and-white negative still in condition to be printed amounts to about twenty reels. What I have seen is detailed below (all silent, black-and-white 35mm, except for two isolated Technicolor shots of the *jangadeiros'* raft being lifted by crane to the Rio wharves).

To take the earliest filmed material first, *My Friend Bonito* consists very largely of unedited takes, with numerous slates showing. Reel One features a religious procession: figures with candles, others dressed as angels with paper wings, others still carrying crosses. Above them, as they wind in packed procession through the narrow streets, the Virgin Mary in effigy is carried proudly high. These are religious devotees on their way to the blessing of the bulls. The second reel shows a church, with bells ringing, palms, and a baroque exterior; more of the procession, with one splendid below-eye-level tilted camera shot of the Virgin outlined against a tower, all against great escarpments of cumulus cloud.

The third reel consists of tests of Chico asleep, nodding, or leaning head on hand in a great sombrero. Then we see numerous takes of the animals being brought by children to be blessed, endless shots of a priest touching the nose of the bull with a flower, the boy laughing, and the dog, geese, goats, sheep, and cattle of the young people brought for the benediction, in rinsed, sunlit images of rich beauty.

Later, in Reel Four, the boy plays with the bull in a great meadow, pulls its tail, teasingly "bullfights" it around trees, and runs after it, until the bull in its turn butts him. All the time an old man, the local grandee, smilingly looks on against dramatically clouded skies.

Reel Five, to be discussed presently, is from *Jangadeiros*. Reel Six is devoted to a superb sequence of two men (picadors) testing and teasing the young bull. Out of a glittering sky, the two men on horseback swoop in parabolas, while the bull moves in humped and determined counterpoint, all observed in a huge and wonderfully sustained take lasting several minutes. The camera retreats, darts forward, hurtles across the plain with breathtaking freedom and ease. And the ritual has a legendary quality, perfectly formalized and poetic.

Reel Seven shows the preparations for the great corrida at the end of the picture. This is at first more routine: a picador straps heavy metal plates to his legs, and we see numerous takes of a matador advancing beyond the protecting wooden wall with a cape. There is, though, one stunning shot at the end of this reel: the boy runs at breakneck speed through a moldering township then bursts out of cool shadows into a sudden blaze of sunlight, framed in a long shot of an archway as he emerges, scattering a flock of geese. Their white wings dazzle in a whirl of sundrenched feathers against a pale sky as he moves across a plain to a smoky horizon.

Reel Eight is again *Jangadeiros*. Reel Nine is routine: bulls at feeding time, training of the bull, fragments of the animal blessing. But with Reel Ten we are in a ciné-

aste's paradise: this is magnificent, fully cut and assembled footage,[4] testimony to the talents of everyone concerned with it.

Brilliantly edited by Joe Noriega, Welles's trusted Mexican cutter, this thrilling reel — marked "Reel 99" on the original leader — remains one of the high-water marks of lost cinema. The shots flash by in incredibly rapid succession, drenched in light, expertly stylized and pointed, with photography by Floyd Crosby of startling, characteristic vividness. Here the whole lost film in miniature is seen: the testing by the picadors, the boy scattering geese as he runs to the old ranch owner and seeks permission to take the bull to be blessed, the love he has of the bull, its coaxing, teasing, and roping, the wonderful blessing of the animals, with faces outlined in groups, pairs and single shots against the sky, the flowers, the bells, the approach of a hundred figures with their pet creatures, and all the time one boy with a donkey chapleted with flowers easing it forward, while Chico delightedly laughs at Bonito's uncomfortable receipt of the benison. Ribbons flutter against clouds; we gaze through a bell tower as dust rises up from hooves and paws; a girl lifts a pig for the flowers. At last, in ironical counterpoint to the blessing, the bull is branded; it has become blooded; it is ready to face death in the afternoon. In the final scene of this great reel the boy watches tenderly and sadly as the bull, marked forever, trots glumly from the meshes of wire around the enclosure, on, on into the blazing afternoon until Bonito is only a smudge of darkness against the horizon. The remaining two reels, consisting of further out-takes, are inevitably anticlimactic after this.

My Friend Bonito, as it stands, is notable for its vivid compressed sunlit energy, its Eisensteinian sharpness of detail, and its warm, unsentimental response to the faces and rituals of the Mexican poor. It is, even in this fragmentary version, worthy to stand beside *Que Viva Mexico,* though some might complain that the story and its final premise (though based on a true in-

[4]It was prepared by Floyd Crosby to show to Robert Rossen when Rossen was planning *The Brave Bulls.*

cident) are fundamentally banal. The boy unquestionably was a "natural," spontaneous, unpretty, and direct.

The material from *Jangadeiros* is in some ways even more striking, though all that is left — in positive film at least — is the great final entry in triumph of the raft fishermen into Rio harbor. Here one has a very sharp glimpse of Welles's genius. Roughly cut though it is, the sequence has an extraordinary momentum and rhythm. It is opened and closed by the shot of a plane flying low over Sugarloaf Mountain, symbol of release. At first, the approaching *jangado* raft is seen at a great distance across a seemingly endless expanse of Atlantic Ocean. Then, one by one, the local small craft begin

to respond to the word of the heroes' arrival. A forest of arms starts — in an electrifying moment — to wave. More arms wave; a superb image as they sprout from masts like the arms of plants. Ropes snake across the compositions of pressing sails, climbing bodies, and sequined sea — Welles the romantic at full stretch. The pace builds more and more exhilaratingly as the camera retreats at incredible speed before the boats, which seem to bear down on us like a threatening navy. Now the excitement is almost overwhelming as row upon row of boats curve and scud in a spanking breeze, the crowd dances on the wharf, the air explodes with sails, arms, ropes, bursts of clouds, and lancing sunbeams. At the

last moment the spectator becomes a pilot seeing it all from the air (the camera crew literally hung out of the side doors of a bomber to shoot this), swoops like a bird low over the great flotilla, and skims out across the ocean until the whole image is filled with nothing but a thousand sparkling waves.

Unfortunately, the carnival footage emerges less satisfactorily. It is, at least in its present form — and one cannot blame Tony Pellegrino, who worked devotedly on its restoration — a rather scrappy assembly of travelogue shots, printed black and white from a color negative. Nevertheless, the material often fascinates, and it won't be easy to forget the moment when it first flickered onto the Moviola at Paramount, breaking a mystery that had remained inviolate to all save a handful of movie people for twenty-seven years.

Crowds swarm below the balconies of a theater, all festooned in a thousand streamers, the men in white tuxedoes and the women in fantastic costumes and headdresses, filmed by Welles in the Municipal Theater in scenes specially staged. Bands and opulently dressed people samba along the cobbled streets and sunlit waterfront areas of Rio in answer to the rhythms; a few shots of Grande Otelo are mysteriously left in, the camera tracking past stalls as he dances; enormous floats pass by with women on boats or elephants, in *Cleopatra*-like tableaux or surrounded by revolving pillars, girls smile on a gigantic barge; we see a donkey, gigantic and covered in sequins; one float represents the Greek principle of democracy, with a book and a helmeted head; lanterns are carried high above the crowd, in wreaths on the tips of spears; and all this magnificence is lit with vivid flares against the swarming night. One can see here at least the baroque imagination responding.

In the later scenes the intensity of the response to the material notably increases: for here the crowds swarming past Copacabana and under the shadow of Corcovado are in a state of ferocious hysteria. Welles and his camera crew in some overhead shots succeed in creating a feeling of extraordinary frenzy and exultation, with people rushing at each other from all directions, and Grande Otelo glimpsed briefly in their midst.

The images are glistening, opulent, and rich, interrupted by the marvelous shot of the Christ statue with the moon behind it, shot by ferry from the bay.

Many of the scenes showing the villages where the Samba originated do survive. These second-unit sequences are very ordinary. So, too, are the shots of the *favelas,* and of Rio itself. Nevertheless, one hopes that this material, variable though it is, will be saved by somebody; that it will not, like so much of this most fabulous of lost collectors' items, wind up at the bottom of the Pacific Ocean.

6. THE STRANGER

By 1945 Welles, with three financially unsuccessful films and an unfinished fiasco behind him, was a black name in Hollywood. He appeared in, and almost certainly influenced, *Jane Eyre;* he worked in radio, exploring some South American themes based on his Brazilian experiences; he starred in the indifferent *Tomorrow is Forever,* with Claudette Colbert. Then, after four years in the wilderness, he at last obtained the opportunity to make another feature: *The Stranger. The Stranger* came about because Sam Spiegel, producer of *Tales of Manhattan* (which as we know inspired *It's All True),* deeply admired *Citizen Kane* and for many years had wanted to work with Welles. Victor Trivas sold Sam Spiegel the story in 1946: it was the account of a Nazi official who escapes from Germany at the end of the war, slips through Argentina and Mexico, and finally takes refuge in a small university town in Connecticut. Spiegel engaged John Huston and Anthony Veiller to develop the story, and Spiegel, knowing Welles's interest in the theme of power, decided to approach Welles to play the leading role. At that time Spiegel hadn't intended to ask Welles to direct; Huston, in fact, was to have done it himself. But Welles asked Spiegel pointblank if he could direct it, and Spiegel realized that if he refused he would lose Welles's cooperation entirely and would not be able to cast him. After discussions with his associate William Goetz, Spiegel decided to risk hiring Welles to direct the picture, to be released through RKO. To keep him tightly to budget and on an even keel, he hired Ernest Nims, an editor of great skill, to provide within the script a completely pre-planned pattern of editing. He then told Welles that both script and editing schedule must be followed to the letter. He also stipulated that if Welles reneged on this agreement he would be dismissed as director but must remain on as star.

Surprisingly, Welles accepted these conditions. He even agreed to let the studio cast Edward G. Robinson instead of Agnes Moorehead, whom he had wanted as the War Crimes Commissioner. Perry Ferguson, who had designed *Kane,* expertly reconstructed a Connecticut village for the picture. His greatest achievement was in building the highest set built in Hollywood since *Intolerance*: the 124-foot clock tower which forms a nucleus of the action. Welles found the clock, which prior to 1922 had been in the Los Angeles County Courthouse; when that building was torn down it had been placed in the cellar of the Los Angeles County Museum. Welles had it hoisted by 150-foot cranes in two sections, and then reassembled it in the imitation tower. (It was not, as the script said, a "Hobrecht of Strasbourg."

For the photographer, Russell Metty, there were few special problems in a high-key subject. The greatest challenge was in the scene in the woods — shot in a huge single take that absorbed a full day's shooting — and in the clock-tower sequence: the tower was boxed in on all four sides, the walls were not removable, and there were very few places to hide the lights. Scenes from the top of the ladder had to be done by building a series of parallels which were miraculously kept out of camera view. The shots of the exterior of the tower were not faked; Welles risked his life by teetering eighty feet above the ground without a net, and Loretta Young also hung above space when she slipped from the ladder during a tense moment in the action. The tracks on the tower had to be specially greased so that the various moving Strasbourg clock figures could be shown in action with Welles in the same shot, and this still further increased the crew's danger on their precarious perch. But neither Welles nor Metty would use back projection, a fact which ensured the film's impressive realism. Welles made Russell Metty wait up night after night to get a shot of the moon peeping round the clock tower for the death fall of Charles Rankin, the fascist central figure. This was finally achieved at 4:30 one morning, and cast and crew were hastily assembled for the shot, which sprang from Welles's recollection of the effect achieved in Rio: the moon behind the Christus statue.

Apart from this realism, however, the film is visually unremarkable. Its qualities are largely interior: they are not chiefly observable in the images. For this reason, in dealing with the film I have not exhaustively examined those images. There are far too few compositions with any personal quality, and the handling is for the most part strictly "Hollywood." Nothing could be more futile than describing a multiplicity of "average" set-ups, medium shots, standard close-ups, and commonplace locations. Dramatically absorbing, *The Stranger* is — after the opening scenes — a cinematically conventional film.

Not a single event marked the thirty-five day shooting of the film; it was brought in under budget and under schedule, the precutting was followed most carefully, and for once the sound recording was done simultaneously. The film made money — it was indeed the only one of Welles's pictures that could be called very profitable — and helped him get the opportunity to make *Lady from Shanghai.*

• • •

The film opens with conventional romantic-menacing music, characteristic of the composer, Bronislau Kaper. Wilson, the War Crimes Commissioner, is in Marktkirch, Germany, surrounded by a tight little knot of people:

"Leave the cell door open. That's all there is to it. Let him escape!" Pompous demurrers: "It's all very irregular" from one man, complaints in a French accent from another. Wilson: "Blast all this discussion! What good are words? I'm sick of words! Hang the repercussions and the responsibility! If I fail, I'm responsible! Leave the cell door open! Let him escape. Let him! It's our only chance! If they were to threaten me with the bottom pits of hell [Wilson's pipe stem snaps as he utters these fateful words] still I insist! This obscenity must be destroyed! *Do you hear me, destroyed!"*

It is a powerful opening. A war criminal, Meinike, is deliberately released in order to lead Commissioner Wilson and his team to discover the criminal's former colleague, Franz Kindler.

Meinike (Konstantin Shayne) leaves the *S.S. Simon Bolivar*[1] and passes through the shadowy levels of a Latin American port, repeating over and over, "I am traveling for my health, I am traveling for my health." The presence of Wilson, dogging him everywhere, is shown only through his smoking pipe, which acts as a continual symbol of the pursuer. (This technique is a development from *Heart of Darkness;* see Chapter 2.)

At the passport check-in Meinike declares that he comes from Poland; after checking into the Hotel Nacional, he goes to find a photographer's studio. All of this has a powerful Kafka-esque horror, as the fleeing man moves like a hunted creature through the stone corridors, which seem claustrophobically to entrap him, emphasizing the impossibility of his escape from his conscience, and the memory of the people he has murdered in the concentration camps. A dark woman, Senora Marvales, the wife of an agent, follows him through the swarming shadows like a figure of doom. When Marvales puts through his report to Wilson by local telephone, Wilson is seen in a brief cut-in handling a copy of *The Clock Book,* by Wallace Nutting: this clever device at once discloses that Wilson has discovered Kindler's obsession with clocks and presages the film's climax in the clock tower.

[1]Evidently he changed ships for North America as his towels later bear the name *S.S. Cristobal.*

We cut to the photographer's studio. As the rubber bulb is pressed and the flash taken, the fugitive's face is framed in the lens of the passport camera, while the photographer looms to the right and the music burps. Meinike asks where Franz Kindler is:

PHOTOGRAPHER: There is no Franz Kindler! Franz Kindler is dead, and cremated!
MEINIKE: I have a message for Franz Kindler — from the All Highest!
PHOTOGRAPHER: It is forbidden!
MEINIKE: I command you in the name of that authority!

The photographer tells him that Kindler is living in Harper, Connecticut, under the assumed name of Rankin — believing that the "All-Highest" means Hitler *redivivus,* not realizing that Meinike, a religious fanatic, means God.

The music changes from menacing brass to a tripping theme on the strings, and we cut to a postcard of the quiet country town and its clock tower, which comes to

life as Meinike turns it sideways to examine it, spelling out the unfamiliar word "Connecticut." He is drawing into the neat central square of Harper in a bus.

In the local store the storekeeper is listening to the patter of a radio stand-up comedian who is describing something that took place at Lake Arrowhead; it is almost inaudible, but fully scripted; "The hotel room was so small every time I closed the door the knob got into

bed with me. You know how cold brass doorknobs are on a winter night." Over this bedroom anecdote the storekeeper welcomes the new arrival, Wilson; and the anecdote continues. "About seven o'clock in the morning the house detective knocks at the door and says is there a maid in your room? I said no, so he pushed one in." The storekeeper Potter's laughter echoes over the audio image. Meinike leaves his suitcase in Potter's charge.

Wilson follows Meinike into the Harper School for Boys; he pursues him through the complex gymnasium set, but Meinike doubles back on his tracks and stuns Wilson with a blow from a practice ring.[2] Then Meinike calls at Charles Rankin's house; he is out, but Meinike meets Mary Longstreet (Loretta Young), who tells him that she is to marry Charles Rankin that afternoon. ("I know it's most unconventional, my being here today, but I want to get these curtains up.") Already, Welles and the writers have established an effective contrast between a quiet, pleasant suburban American existence and the horror of Europe; between Meinike's fear and the threatening presence of Kindler, and Mary Longstreet's simple desire to hang curtains.

Meinike meets Rankin in the street after leaving the house. Rankin, saying that they mustn't be seen talking together, tells him that he will meet him in the woods. A group of boys from the school are tracking towards the woods in a paper-chase, cajoling him in the process, "You ought to be running the trail, Mr. Rankin. Take a little off that waistline." While the youths' happy parabolas act as a cheerful counterpoint, Meinike and Rankin have a grim conversation in the bright sunshine and the sparkling leaves of the forest.

Rankin tells Meinike that he is about to marry the daughter of Judge Longstreet, a justice of the Supreme Court and a famous liberal. He points out that his camouflage is perfect: "Who would think to look for the

[2]On the Walls, in a typical Welles joke, are pennants reading "Harper vs. Todd" — the name of Welles's own school. After Meinike stuns Wilson he leaves by a door which Welles has fixed up with the sign "Use this apparatus at your own risk."

notorious Franz Kindler in the sacred precincts of the Harper School, surrounded by the sons of America's first families?" Meinike tells Rankin that all their former colleagues have been hanged and that he alone has escaped. He confides that the cause of this is an act of God; he has been converted to the Christian faith by the mere fact that the cell door was left open, that his escape from prison was facilitated. But Rankin knows that Meinike's freedom proves only one thing: that he is being used to reach Rankin. "They freed you so you'd lead them to me." Meinike begs Rankin to come to salvation, to confess his sins; to proclaim his guilt to the world. He asks him to kneel, and Rankin strangles him in the midst of their prayers, all the time glancing to see if he is observed by the boys.

At the marriage of Rankin and Mary Longstreet, the simple and beautiful words of the ceremony make a bitterly ironical contrast with the confession called for by Meinike just a short time earlier in his fanatical ravings before death. Meanwhile, Wilson is in the store, having a disjointed conversation with Potter, talking about aspirins and coffee, discovering details of the Rankin-Longstreet marriage, settling down for checkers at twenty-five cents a game.

Over the play Wilson, posing as an antique dealer, probes Potter further. (Potter knows everybody around town through his two jobs as storekeeper and town clerk, and probes Wilson in his turn.) At the post-wedding party, Rankin can't be found; he has slipped out to bury Meinike in the woods. Now Wilson establishes through Mary Longstreet's brother that Rankin is an expert in clocks: he is about to repair the Strasbourg clock in the Harper School's tower.

Wilson insinuates himself into the family for the homecoming dinner. "Mr. Wilson," Judge Longstreet says, "is compiling a catalogue of Paul Revere silver." Noah, Longstreet's son, adds: "He's also an authority on clocks." The conversation gets round to Germany, and Wilson deliberately keeps the ball bouncing.

WILSON: Do you know Germany, Mr. Rankin?
RANKIN: I'm sorry, I have a way of making enemies when I'm on that subject. Pretty unpopular.

WILSON (ironically): Well, we should get the objective opinion of an objective historian.
RANKIN: Historian? A psychiatrist could explain it better. The German sees himself as the innocent victim of world envy and hatred, conspired against, set upon by inferior peoples, inferior nations. He cannot admit to error, much less to wrong-doing — not the German. We chose to ignore Ethiopia and Spain. But we learned from our casualty lists the price of looking the other way. Men of truth everywhere have come to know for whom the bell tolls. But not the German. No, he still follows his warrior Gods, marching to Wagnerian strains, his eyes still fixed upon the fiery sword of Siegfried. And in those subterranean meeting places that you don't believe in, the German's dream world comes alive, and he takes his place in shining armor beneath the banners of the Teutonic knights. Mankind is waiting for the Messiah, but for the German the Messiah is not the Prince of Peace. He's another Barbarossa. Another Hitler.
WILSON: Well then, you have no faith in the reforms that egalité, fraternité," but in Germany. . . .
RANKIN: I don't know, Mr. Wilson, I can't believe that people can be reformed, except from within. The basic principles of equality and freedom never have, never will take root in Germany. The will to freedom has been voiced in every other tongue. "All men are created equal," "liberté, egalité, fraternité," but in Germany. . . .
NOAH: There's Marx, "Proletarians unite, you have nothing to lose but your chains."
RANKIN: But Marx wasn't a German, Marx was a Jew. (Significant closeup.)

Wilson concludes the scene by refusing an invitation of Mary's to a faculty tea; he is leaving Harper the next day.

After this dinner party — perhaps the best-directed scene in the film — Rankin, understandably restless, takes the dog for a walk; later, Wilson calls Washington, telling his bosses that they were right about Rankin being innocent: "He's above suspicion." But he has second thoughts: "Who but a Nazi would deny that Karl Marx was a German because he was a Jew? I think I'll stick around for a while."

In the Rankins' bedroom, Mary wakes terrified from a dream about Meinike, whom she remembers from his call at the house: "That little man was walking all by himself, across a deserted city square . . . Wherever he moved, he threw a shadow . . . but when he moved away,

Charles, the shadow stayed there behind him and spread out just like a carpet. . . . Wish you could think who it might have been." It is a powerful image, poetic and charged, and at the precisely correct dramatic moment in the film it reinforces the sense of nightmare, of a world of horror from the past closing in on the guilty Kindler and the innocent Mary. "You're overtired," he tells Mary. The frantic whimperings of her dog, which might lead police to the murder spot, echo up from the cellar where he has locked it: "Charles, I don't believe in dogs being treated like prisoners."

Wilson goes fishing with Mary's brother, Noah, in a fresh, sunlit scene; he discovers from him that Rankin spends most of his time working on the clock, and *never* goes fishing. "Why don't you like him, Noah?" He tells Noah, after the noncommittal reply, that he is a war crimes commissioner who suspects that Noah's brother-in-law is a war criminal. "I hope I'm wrong, Noah, but that's the way it is. People can't help who they fall in love with."

Back in the store Potter asks Wilson: "Hear Professor Rankin's aimin' to fix the clock, figure it'll tell the time rightly? And will the angel circle around the belfry? Is that a man or woman angel, Mr. Wilson? Well, don't reckon it makes much a difference among angels." Wilson notes that Meinike "never did pick up his suitcase" and he encourages Potter in his desire to open it and see what's inside it: "soiled linen, sweater, soap and a razor wrapped in a towel with *S.S. Cristobal* written across it, a pair of old shoes, nothing but religious pamphlets."

Rankin arrives with Mary, and Wilson points out that he has been examining the luggage in the hope of provoking Rankin; but he does not succeed. Outside he tells Noah: "One thing is certain — [Mary] knows nothing now. Nothing at all. Except that he didn't want her to admit having seen someone she did see. I'd give something to know what explanation he's making right now." The audience is more fortunate. We see Rankin telling Mary in church:

RANKIN: I was a student in Geneva. There was a girl. The night before I was to leave we went out on the lake together. She told me unless I promised to marry her she'd never re-turn to shore. Oh, I thought, she was joking, naturally, but she wasn't. Before I could stop her she stood up in the boat, and . . . Well, I dived in after her; it was too late, she was gone. Only one person knew we were on the lake together: her brother. He knew I hadn't murdered her but he told me he'd be willing to call it an accident for a — a . . . compensation. I gave him all I had, and left Switzerland. As the years went by, I allowed myself to believe that the dead past really was dead . . . and then, *on our wedding day*, Mary, he appeared again, her brother . . . the little man. I gave him all the money I had in the world, and he went away again.

MARY: Darling, you should have told me . . . Why didn't he go back for his things?

RANKIN: Well, I suppose once he had money, he could afford better. Darling, I'm terribly nervous, I think I'll work up in the clock.

A shot of the Longstreets' dead dog is accompanied by someone saying: "He must have just crawled here and died." Potter, fatuous as ever, remarks: "Looks like he's dead to me. Take him up to Dr. Lawrence's office." Wilson asks Lawrence: "How long could the dog have lived with that amount of poison in him?" And from the answer he begins to deduce that Rankin must have killed the dog, who must have been digging in the woods for Meinike's body.

In Potter's shop Rankin ("One hears so little news up in the clock tower") hears of the search for Meinike. At home, packing, questioned by Mary, Rankin admits he killed the dog. "Murder can be a chain, Mary, one link leading to another until it circles your neck. Red was digging at the grave of the man I killed. Yes. Your little man." The reason Rankin gives is that Meinike planned to blackmail not only him but also Judge Longstreet. He expertly throws himself on her maternal mercy: "Oh Mary, I should have gone away and lost myself in a world where you could never find me, but, I loved you. . . . " And she offers to become an accessory to his guilt, because "I'm already a part of it, because I'm a part of you."

We cut to Potter in the woods with the found body, making a typical remark: "He's changed some: being buried in the earth does it." And Wilson tells Noah: "I think your sister should be ready to hear the truth," while back at the house Mary has to discuss arrangements for the faculty tea with the family maid.

That night in Judge Longstreet's study, Wilson questions Mary, asking her if she met the dead man. She denies it, and he says he suspects her of hiding something. He shows her a picture of Konrad Mcinikc, "commander in charge of one of the more 'efficient' concentration camps," and then shows her films of the gas chambers, a lime pit where hundreds were buried alive. "All this you're seeing, it's all the product of one mind, the mind of a man called Franz Kindler. He was the most brilliant of the younger minds in the Nazi Party." In a rather weird account of the Nazi "final solution," he goes on:

WILSON: It was Kindler who conceived the theory of genocide, mass killing of the populations of conquered countries, so that regardless of who won the war Germany would emerge the strongest nation in Western Europe. Biologically speaking. Unlike Goebbels, Himmler and the rest of them, Kindler had a passion for anonymity. The newspapers carried no picture of him. Oh no. And just before he disappeared, he destroyed every evidence that might link him with his past, down to the last fingerprint. There's no clue to the identity of Franz Kindler, except one little thing: he has a hobby that almost amounts to a mania: clocks.

In prison, in Czechoslovakia, a war criminal was waiting execution: this was Konrad Meinike, one-time executive officer for Franz Kindler. He was an obscenity on the face of the earth. The stench of burning flesh was in his clothes. But we gave him his freedom on the chance that he might lead me to Kindler. He led me here, Mrs. Rankin, and here I lost him, until yesterday. Your dog, Red, found him for me.

And, as the terrible images of starvation flicker and fade from the wall, and Mary and Wilson are shown in close-ups by the flickering projector light, Mary starts back, startled by the sudden slapping of the end-leader against the projector. "My Charles is not a Nazi!" She still tries to protect her husband; and she leaves the room hysterical with anger and repressed fear.

But Judge Longstreet follows her, and tries to convince her of her husband's guilt. Wilson says: "She has the facts now, but she won't accept them. They're too horrible for her to acknowledge. . . . but we have one ally. Her subconscious. It knows what the truth is, and is struggling to be heard. The will to truth in your daughter is much too strong to be denied." And he warns Longstreet that Rankin may attempt to kill his daughter.

A moment after that, the clock in the tower strikes: a powerful symbolic reminder of Rankin's presence in the town and his threat to his wife's existence. Mary tells Rankin: "Mr. Wilson was there. He tried to tell me that you were a Nazi." Small-town excitement prevails in the square over the restoration of the clock, as we have a typical comment from Potter: "What I want to know is, if it's going to chime all night long, how is anybody going to get any sleep? Them chickens o' yours is goin' to be on and off the roost every fifteen minutes!"

At the faculty tea the chatter is about murder. A woman asks eagerly: "Were you able to see when they opened the grave, Mr. Randall? Was it too horrible?" Someone else says: "What was that Frenchman's name?" "Landru." Someone asks Rankin if he knows the quotation from Emerson: "Commit a crime, and the earth is made of glass." Wilson beautifully continues the quotation (looking all the time meaningfully at Rankin): "Commit a crime, and it seems as if a coat of snow fell on the ground. Such as reveals in the woods the track of every partridge and fox and squirrel and mole. You cannot recall the spoken word. You cannot wipe out the foot-track. You cannot draw up the ladder so as to leave no inlet or clue." A silly woman tells Wilson she has heard he is the chief suspect; that the crime was committed "to gain possession of some priceless antiques."

After the tea, Mary, questioned closely by Rankin about the presence of Wilson at the party, collapses, and in another part of the house, Wilson, hearing of her desperate crying, says: "The flood gates have opened. Her subconscious has almost won." From now on, Longstreet and Wilson decide, she is in mortal danger: a slippery sidewalk, a speeding car, anything available could be used by her husband to cause her "accidental death." And we see Rankin sawing through a rung of the ladder in the tower. A moment later, the

bells chime, accompanied by the incredibly high-pitched echoing of Kaper's strings (a notably unsettling effect on the sound track, brilliantly achieved by Welles): the tension now is becoming unbearably tight.

After Rankin saws through the rung, we see him teaching class (making a joking reference to the full name of Frederick the Great.) He arranges for Mary to be sent to the tower where she will step on the sawed-through rung and plunge to her death. Then he goes to the store to play checkers with Potter to establish an alibi.

The housekeeper has strict instructions from Wilson to see that Mary does not leave the house; she first becomes temperamental, then even fakes a heart attack. Noah goes instead to the tower, and he and Wilson discover the sawed ladder rung.

By now, it is clear to us that Rankin's plan to kill his wife has failed. As he plays checkers, the bell rings, and he goes out as Potter — so often chorus to the action — says, "It's coming up for snow." Rankin walks into snow: this is a visual allusion to the Emerson quotation ("Commit a crime and it is as if a coat of snow fell on the ground. . . .").

Back in his house, Rankin is horrified to see that Mary is still alive. Finally, he tells her his plot. She begs him to kill her, handing him the poker by the fireplace, as she cannot endure to live with the knowledge of his guilt. Noah and Judge Longstreet come in with Wilson, and Rankin runs out.

The pursuit is on. That night, Mary sets out to kill her husband. Knowing he is hidden in the tower, she climbs the ladder to destroy him. She tells him what she is going to do; that she knew he was hiding there. He informs her proudly: "They searched the woods. I watched them. Like God, looking at little ants." But Rankin is trapped; Wilson is concealed below. The lights of the search team blaze brightly. Rankin screams, in words that presage Eichmann's: "I only followed orders. I only did my duty. I'm not a criminal." In the subsequent struggle Rankin is impaled by the avenging angel figure revolving on the clock tower. The disease is stamped out; the obscenity is destroyed. But we must not be complacent: Wilson's last words to Mary carry a hint of irony and warning: "Pleasant dreams."

• • •

The Stranger's script is a triumph of dramatic concision and irony, and the direction, although at times a trifle too forced and overemphatic, drives home its points with considerable strength. The handling, greatly assisted by the camerawork of Russell Metty, is always functional and even, its pace perfectly controlled.

From the arrival of Wilson and Meinike in Harper we have a continuing series of ironic contrasts: Potter chuckling over the tawdry bedroom jokes of the radio comedian while hunter and quarry pursue each other through a deserted school gymnasium; the simple domestic calm of Mary Rankin's existence — antique-decorated house, school teas, quiet family dinners, the hanging of new drapes for the marital house — continually threatened by dreadful hints of the European past, Meinike dying during the bright circlings of the paper-chase through the woods close by.

Once again, Welles is concerned with showing us a particular kind of American innocence that can vanish as quickly as the snow from the Rosebud sled when the heat of reality — the knowledge of pain, misery, and cruelty — scorches away illusion.

The characters are observed with precision. Charles Rankin/Franz Kindler is one of the American cinema's few convincing portraits of a fascist, a man who had become obsessed with the idea of genocide, who pretends only to have taken orders but who has betrayed human decency for the stench and squalor of the concentration camps, who can still move among bourgeois Americans without suspicion, whose smoothly convincing voice and manner only occasionally betray the arrogance and heartlessness of the Nazi. His attitude to Mary is nicely ambiguous: he is in love, not so much with her, but (as he makes clear to Meinike before he kills him) with the idea that he, Franz Kindler, can get away with marrying a pretty American girl, the daughter of a Supreme Court justice. It appeals to his sense of humor (as it does, for dramatic reasons, to Welles's), and the delineation of their relationship fascinates because of the two levels on which it moves: it is a portrait of an apparently respectable and controlled mutual passion which conceals from her the fact that he is using her to acquire safety and respectability. She is deeply trusting and warm, *Redbook's* idea of a perfect wife given verisimilitude by the intelligent and understanding writing.

Because Rankin's tensions are powerfully established in the opening stages — because we are made to feel the deep desire of the guilty ones of the world to find a refuge in the bosom of convention and decency and security — we are deeply engaged in the matter of his fate. As the net closes in, as we know for certain that he is doomed by justice and the avenging angel personi-

fied by Wilson, we are inextricably involved. Only at the very end, when the script turns the ironic screws too tight and insists that Rankin be impaled on the actual avenging angel on his own favorite clock, can the film be said to betray its mood of firmness.

Welles's performance is ideal: he can make convincing the character's intelligence and attractiveness, the qualities that draw the Longstreets to him and made Wilson temporarily doubt his guilt, yet he can also from the first suggest the feeling of a man haunted. The body may be well-fed and comfortable-looking, the hands steady and strong, the posture relaxed and assured, and the jokes delivered without strain, but the eyes are brilliant with cruelty and distress. From a stained soul they speak out to us continually while he indulges in badinage with his students, while he delivers the honeyed words of love to Mary Longstreet Rankin, while he teases the sorority women and flatters the townsfolk. And in the brief comments when his nature really shows through — in the murder of his old prison commandant inferior while they are praying, in the sudden speech about Marx as a Jew at Longstreet's dinner table — Welles the actor conveys with consummate authority the look of a man who is used to commanding millions of deaths.

By contrast, Mary Longstreet Rankin is a portrait of practical American goodness, decency, and strength. Once she has become involved with her husband, she braves the successive disclosures of his guilt with considerable fortitude; only her subconscious mind fights to release its pain. She is haunted by dreams, and one of the film's most effective passages is the one in which she recalls the ghost of Meinike, throwing a shadow (as her husband's shadow is upon her) "and when he moved away, Charles, the shadow stayed behind him. . . . " From the first moment we meet her, as Meinike arrives at the house, we see her caught up in a web of deceit and tension.

And later, she is involved in another dream, Rankin's fake story about the girl who drowned on Lake Geneva. Her whole life is caught up in a condition in which reality has become a nightmare, and everything she has taken for granted — security, the love of a husband for his wife, the comforts of provincial America — is eroded away until at last she walks through a cold Emersonian snow symbolizing truth and climbs a ladder to kill her husband for his guilt. Perhaps her most agonizing moment is when the films of the concentration camp shine grimly on her father's wall, and she cannot allow herself to see that the tweedy all-American who drew her into marriage can be the monster who fed these walking skeletons into the gas ovens, who heaped them in piles and buried them alive.

Loretta Young's performance altogether fulfills the script's purposes, although at times her expression of wide-eyed fright and breathlessness of tone is overdone. But she is an actress whose innocent surface has always contained an inner toughness and resilience, and her suggested simplicity about life in the wicked world combined with the ability to cope with hellfire when it comes is ideally suitable in the context.

As Wilson, Edward G. Robinson plays with dogged concentration a part in which there is only one keynote: a hunter's determination. Here is a man dedicated to bringing to earth a dangerous and elusive quarry, and to shattering the illusions of the man's wife, brother-in-law, and father-in-law. Wilson's is a process of exposing nerves in a cozy world that knows nothing of brutality, and at the end his is the cold triumph of the undeceived.

The other characters — Noah and Judge Longstreet, the townsfolk, the silly women at the faculty tea — are of necessity mere sketches, but two characters in the supporting cast emerge in bold colors. Konrad Meinike is a character of whom Graham Greene would not have been ashamed: haunted by guilt after his evil doings, his long and black record of running the camps, he has become a zealot, obsessed with confession, and sufficiently unhinged to believe that he has been released from prison by an act of God. His case, stuffed with religious pamphlets and left behind in the Harper store, is proof positive of a person who has not, like Kindler, left reality deliberately behind, but who has been driven from it by fear. His death in the woods while kneeling to pray is a classic execution of poetic justice. And Konstantin Shayne's brilliant performance of the part cannot be overpraised.

Potter, too, is a powerful creation, a William Saroyan character rewritten by Montherlant. Massive, ugly, and stupid, obsessed with his radio and checkers games used to wheedle information, and, finally, hunting eagerly for the body of Meinike, he makes inane remarks at every key moment of the action, from the discovery of the body to the key dramatic moment when, after Wilson tells Longstreet that Rankin may kill his daughter, the clock significantly strikes. Potter is, like Grisby in *The Lady from Shanghai* and Bernstein in *Citizen Kane,* Welles's reminder to us that we must always contend with the dumb crudities of people. The writing of the group scenes, and the group playing of all these characters, are perfectly realized: the family tensions around Rankin and the unwitting Mary, even the brief scene in school when Rankin makes a joke about Frederick the Great, itself an ironic comment on his own delusions of grandeur which can lead him, at the very end of the film, to liken himself, looking down from the clock tower and the Strasbourg clock, to God, looking at little ants. As in all Welles's films, the wicked destroy themselves, and Wilson and the Longstreets, cleansed of the disease that was Charles Rankin, are free to enjoy peace and happiness, and perhaps to sleep deeply, without evil dreams.

7. THE LADY FROM SHANGHAI

The Lady from Shanghai, directed by Welles in the last months of 1946, came about through a characteristic Welles predicament. Welles needed money desperately (the exact amount varied no less than seventeen times in my taped interviews), chiefly to extricate the costumes for his stage show *Around the World* from a New York firm which had refused to release them. He telephoned Harry Cohn, who had vowed earlier that Welles would never work with him after Welles had married the studio's reigning female star, Rita Hayworth, thereby supposedly damaging her sex-symbol appeal. We do not know the exact reason why Welles picked on Cohn. It may have been because Cohn knew Sam Spiegel, who would certainly protect his own choice of director if Cohn should ask about Welles's work on *The Stranger.* In any case, after talking to Spiegel, Cohn sent the money to Welles immediately — with the proviso that Welles direct a film for Columbia free of charge. The story of how Welles chose the subject of the movie he was to make for Columbia has been told in half a dozen different versions. Welles claims that while on the telephone to Cohn, he saw beside him a copy of an Inner Sanctum paperback, Sherwood King's *If I Die Before I Wake* (1938), in either the ticket office of a theater or a cinema or at a separate newsstand. Richard Wilson claims that Columbia owned the rights to the book at the time, and that William Castle (director of a film Welles admired, *When Strangers Marry*) had signed to produce and direct the film on a low budget. Welles, talking it over with Castle, appropriated it for himself,

hiring Castle as associate producer for the picture. The book is set in Long Island: it is a simple, well-constructed thriller about the murder of a millionaire attorney; it is not so different from the film as is sometimes claimed.

Welles decided to make the film in the manner of Louis de Rochemont, producer of *The March of Time,* who had just introduced a type of narrated semidocumentary thriller, which actually owed much to Welles. Welles had intended to star the attractive French actress Barbara Laage, but Cohn wanted Rita Hayworth to star, so the budget escalated. Welles began constructing a matchstick Eiffel Tower of a plot that nobody — including Welles — really understood.

The actors found it nerve-wracking to work with Welles, because they often arrived on the set with their lines memorized only to find Welles sitting in the director's chair smoking a cigar and rewriting every line they would utter during the day. Sometimes he deliberately upset them to make them give nervous, uneasy performances. He would even force them to forget their lines so that they would improvise new ones. Erskine Sanford, as a judge in a brawl in his chambers, cries out, "This isn't a football game!" The line was made up on the spot because Sanford couldn't recall what he was supposed to say. Glenn Anders, who played the lawyer Grisby, was constantly bullied by Welles until he was so distraught that the unit dubbed him "Glenn Anguish."

Shooting began in the late fall of 1946. It continued for more than thirty-five days in Acapulco where Errol

Flynn's yacht and crew were used. The opening scene in Central Park was shot later, with a carriage bought in Mexico. The scene in a New York garage entrance was shot in a downtown Los Angeles area while striking technicians picketed and tried to stop shooting by drowning out the sound track. Shooting in Mexico began in early November, at the Hotel Papagayo, Acapulco, where two men high on a parapet talk about murder, and on the river estuary at Green Hell nearby. Insects, financial problems, and endless studio emissaries, cables and memoranda made shooting a nightmare. At night, millions of poisonous insects swarmed over the arc lights, blotting them out. Welles was more than usually capricious. Everett Sloane, who played a lawyer, was impossible to get on with and shunned everyone. Welles never saw rushes, either projected or on a Moviola. When Viola Lawrence received the rushes, which had to be shipped to and from Hollywood daily, she was horrified to discover that Welles had not shot a single close-up, essential to a "star" film. She flew in a fury to Cohn, who ordered Welles to make some. Welles at first ignored the order, but finally obeyed it in Hollywood on his return in January, having an ironical last laugh by making the close-ups of Rita Hayworth the most banal and emptily glossy things in the film. (The reason he avoided close-ups of her was that he was sickened by the slow preparations of her make-up men and hair stylists brought along on the expedition.)

In Hollywood Welles also had to reshoot much of his Mexican footage, either because he hated the way it appeared as Viola Lawrence had cut it, or because he had filmed it so clumsily that it would not cut. He had to match in shots of Hayworth with a stand-in, who had to have her long tresses shorn and bleached and was paid $500 for the privilege. Shots of Hayworth running down an Acapulco colonnade were done at the Twentieth Century-Fox ranch. The hall of mirrors was designed with the aid of the special effects man Lawrence Butler, who had made carpets fly and a genie emerge from a bottle in Korda's *Thief of Bagdad*. (Only the last shot of this sequence, when Welles walks out into the sunlight at Playland on the San Francisco oceanfront, was shot on location.)

Welles had had long conferences before the film started with the cameraman, Charles Lawton, Jr. They decided to use low-key interior lighting and natural light sources, with comparatively few reflectors for exterior scenes (this information comes from Herbert A. Lightman's *American Cinematographer analysis of the* film, published in June 1948). Transitions from indoor to outdoor sequences were achieved without too many violent contrasts because carefully filtered skies were used for the exteriors. By using natural light in exteriors, with stark contrasts, some dramatic modeling of facial features was possible. For example, in the scene in Acapulco when the sailor and the lawyer talk about murder, Welles was deliberately dressed in a white linen suit to make his face look dark and somber, while the lawyer wore gray clothes to make his complexion look dark and sticky.

Wide-angle lenses were used for close-ups to achieve the deliberate distortion characteristic of the director's style. In the Aquarium scene the lights came from sources simulating those in the tanks, while in fact the tanks were shot separately and matted in after enlargement to give a more striking effect. Welles, through this device, could match selected creatures to the character's thoughts. As Mrs. Bannister describes the murder scene, a shark glides behind her face; as she mentions the lawyer, a slimy conger eel writhes past her.

Shooting aboard the yacht presented Lawton with highly specialized problems. These were turned to good effect by having extremely cramped compositions in every shot. But the crew still encountered difficulties. While shooting at sea, they could not depend on their usual light-meter readings. Reflections from the water's surface kicked up more intensity than the meter recorded, causing over-exposure. A whole series of experimental tests had to be made before the problem was solved by rule-of-thumb techniques.

Studio scenes also had their photographic problems. In the Central Park sequence, Welles planned the longest dolly shot that had ever been filmed: (with a close runner-up in his own Lucy/George carriage ride in *Ambersons*). Lawton, with his camera on a twenty-two foot crane, kept Welles and Rita Hayworth in focus as they rode three-quarters of a mile along the backlot in a horse-drawn open victoria. Huge arc lights, a sound boom, and the camera crane rolled the full length. (The sequence was later expertly cut by Viola Lawrence, but the single-take effect was lost.)

For the fun-house sequence, originally a reel long, Welles himself painted, and Stephen Goosson constructed, sliding doors, distorting mirrors, and a 125-foot zigzag slide which began at the roof of the studio sound stage and ended up in a pit eighty feet long (it was forty feet wide and twenty feet deep). Halfway down was a thirty-foot-high dragon's mouth. In one shot Lawton and his operator, Irving Klein, slid on their stomachs down the 125-foot slide with the camera on a mat, to give the subjective view of Welles sliding down. The mirror maze contained 2,912 square feet of glass. Eighty plate-glass mirrors were used, each seven by four feet, and twenty-four distorting mirrors as well. Some of the mirrors had a "two-way" construction so that the cameraman could shoot through them, or holes drilled in the glass. Welles spent night after night working on this bizarre fun fair, nearly all of which was cut by the studio. And all the time he and his colleagues were working on possible versions of *Carmen* and *Salome* for Rita Hayworth—which were later made by other directors.

Harry Cohn was appalled when he saw the film and could not understand it. Virginia Van Upp and others of his production staff wanted to reconstruct the whole

work within the framework of the trial scene, flashing back to the main events and explaining them through additional dialogue. Cohn rejected this plan. Virginia Van Upp and Welles, who disliked the picture anyway and was thoroughly bored with it by now, spread the cutting continuity all over her office floor and reworked it piece by piece on hands and knees.

Re-edited, re-scored and re-dubbed, the film was previewed to the public; Welles nervously held tight to Viola Lawrence's hand at the preview and did not always look at the screen.[1] More work was done after the audience proved restless and wrote damaging remarks on their report cards. Finally the film, a patchwork of retakes, old and new dubbing, and Mexican and American scenes, found its way to the circuits—and sank without a trace.

The theme of *The Lady from Shanghai* links directly with Welles's other important themes: the misery of the rich, and the survival of the innocent. Just as Kane died imbedded in his own selfishness, alone in his dead castle, just as the Ambersons faded away in proud shadows, their great mansion an obscure boardinghouse in the

[1]Interview with Viola Lawrence, Hollywood, 1969.

midst of an industrial city which has greedily absorbed it, so the creatures of *The Lady from Shanghai* rot from within. Just as Kane's image is reflected in an eternity of mirrors at Xanadu, so Elsa Bannister and her husband, gorgon and evil mate, face a hall of mirrors before they die, seeing their truth reflected over and over again. Elsa Bannister is *La belle dame sans merci* who recurs in the history of cinema and especially in the Hollywood of the forties. Mario Praz in *The Romantic Agony* has traced the history of these figures, from Althea through Scylla and Clytemnestra to the present day. In literature they have tended to be women of violent passions, like Monk Lewis's fatal and erotic Matilda, Flaubert's voluptuous Salammbô, Merimée's Carmen, and Pierre Louys's Conchita. It is significant that the last two figures have been played on the American screen by Rita Hayworth and Marlene Dietrich. Their screen sisters—Joan Fontaine in *Ivy,* Ann Todd in *So Evil My Love*, Gene Tierney in *Leave Her to Heaven,* even Louise Brooks in *Lulu*—have had a hard implacability far removed from the heaving temperament of the nineteenth century's *femme fatales.*

Rita Hayworth in *The Lady from Shanghai* is used plastically. She is a Medusa for the screen, as coldly monstrous as the writhing figures of the Aquarium. And in common with Joan Fontaine's Ivy Lexton or Ann Todd's Olivia Sacret she is driven by a fate she cannot understand but must obey. Fate uses her beauty to allure and destroy, and she accepts its power: "Those who follow their nature keep their original nature in the end." Her face hard and blank, her eyes full of fear, her voice pitched in the tone of someone breathless and pursued, she is a woman unable to control what fate has laid down for her. She is momentarily drawn to her victim, Michael, but she must still try to send him to his death. She hates her life ("Who would want to live around us?"). She is trapped by her husband in a marriage she doesn't want, but must have: for money, since greed is the spur that drives her on. She wants to murder Bannister and his partner and have Michael die to conceal her guilt. Her determination and coldness are oriental, and it is not insignificant that she was born

in China and speaks fluent Chinese, that a childhood of misery has left her with an iron determination to survive in a world she believes to be altogether bad: "You've got to deal with it, make terms."

Michael has retained a fundamental innocence, a wry acceptance of the world's evil that his humor keeps at bay. He knows he is a fool, but he also knows that his folly gives him a kind of protection and freedom; he does not know the iron in the souls of the calculating. He does not accept Elsa's fatalism, but believes in following something better than one's original nature; and he is contemptuous of the cruelty of the whole group who employs him, symbolized in the story of the sharks. Yet he cannot resist Elsa's suggestion that he sail off with her into the sunrise in an escapist image that is perfectly Hollywood. Welles draws the character well, only erring by making him too intelligent to be believable, a sophisticate improbably placed below decks, typing a book even in the hiring hall.

Bannister and Grisby, though played brilliantly by Everett Sloane and Glenn Anders, are less well drawn—caricatures rather than characters. Their effect on us is achieved solely by the application of a dazzling array of surface mannerisms. Bannister as the most famous trial lawyer in America is not convincing, but one thread does hold together what there is of his personality: the reality of his pain. This is a human being for whom pain is the central fact of existence—the pain of his inability to have a proper relationship with his wife, the pain of his wracked body gone over and over again by surgeons in endless operations, the pain of knowing that only money has saved him from total paralysis, that he is the intended victim of a murder plan. For him, death in the hall of mirrors comes, one feels, as a release.

Grisby is the American hick incarnate: vicious but naive, sweating constantly, giggling and inept, a voyeur and a fall guy, whom Elsa uses to assist her in her attempt to murder her husband, then plans to dispose of. His involved and absurd scheme for disappearing with Elsa inevitably results in his death. Michael O'Hara, the Irish sailor who stumbles into this nest of vipers, is another variety of the American hick. Tough and cynical on the surface, "a notorious waterfront agitator," he is fundamentally innocent and is used with ease by Grisby and Elsa in their murder plan. But at the end he walks out of the place where the Bannisters have died and experiences the clean taste of a San Francisco morning. For the simple and decent ones of the world, Welles is telling us, there is always a chance of renewal, of a rediscovery of childhood happiness. If anything were needed, after Kane and Amberson, to convince us of Welles's fundamental romanticism, then this is it.

Welles's attitude to the minor characters again has the affectionate cruelty, the caricaturing irony, of a Dickens. The judge who presides at the trial is a feeble-minded, fussy old man (*The Inquirer*'s editor *redivivus*) who plays chess with himself, hums when alone, and is completely unable to control what is going on in his own courtroom. The officers of the law are boobies, outwitted by Michael when he breaks out of the hall of justice (in a scene notable for its comic unreality). The jury is a collection of typical Welles hicks—scuffling, sneezing, coughing, and erupting—made up of petty businessmen and housewives. The crew on the Bannister's yacht and the sailors in the hiring hall at New York are cheerful clowns, randy and self-conscious. The schoolteacher who discovers the lovers in the Aquarium is an inquisitive, darting old spinster whose last flickers of erotic feeling are expressed at the trial in the combined outrage and desperation of "Oh, I just want to look at her!" The range of faces in the film astonishes, and no other Welles film has explored his own country with such precision, such ruthlessness. His conclusion is morally idealist: the evil destroy themselves, the good find their own way through. The final image of Michael walking free across a wharf wet with morning rain is a poetically exact metaphor of release, the joy of the innocent American who lives his life physically.

• • •

The opening scene of the film is set in Central Park, where Elsa Bannister is riding in a horse-drawn carriage. A gang of toughs grab her and pull her into the neighboring bushes, but O'Hara (who has been trying to pick her up) rescues her, and they continue on their nocturnal journey. She, with face and hair steely, settles back against the intense blackness of the carriage hood, talking about her past in China (she was born in Chifu), her eyes suggesting a lifetime of high-class prostitution and compromise in tones of disillusionment and exhaustion. (Rita Hayworth's beautiful voice is at all times perfectly used, whether here or in the breathless, nervous tone it assumes later on.)

Michael, wandering along beside the carriage or riding in it, is whimsical as he talks about his travels ("the nicest jails are in Australia"). Beautifully unacademic cutting and the elliptical nature of the conversation, the rolling of the carriage and Michael's lolling gait accompany the discovery by Michael that he is attracted and Elsa's certain knowledge that she can seduce him. Later, she asks her husband to hire him for a yacht cruise to San Francisco via the Panama Canal.

The crippled husband's entrance into the hiring hall to sign up Michael (and others) for the cruise is cruelly observed: first we see his knotted canes like extensions of his twisted limbs, then we observe him crawling like

a broken spider. The image, grayly lit by Lawton, is harshly realistic; the brilliantly used hiring-hall set conveys heat, boredom, and an underlying animal vitality as the sailors gather round, one carrying a monkey, to watch the warped phenomenon in their midst. In a bar where he has taken Michael and two other sailors, the lawyer's misery and imposing drunkenness are contrasted with the jaunty, healthy, empty-headed sailors and the cheerful American symbol, the jukebox.

As Michael arrives at the yacht, which is significantly named *Circe,* Elsa's pet dachshund yaps and circles, and Elsa's face has a stark blankness under a yachtsman's cap. On the boat she uses sexual innuendos to tease him, to hook his interest. Asking him for a cigarette she says, meaningfully, "I've learned to smoke now. Ever since that night in the park, I've been getting the habit." He knows what she's up to (even though he can't resist her physical attraction): "Do all rich women play games like this?" Now she turns girlish, seeking out his protective masculinity: "Oh, Michael, what are we scared of?" He bites the hook, and embraces her warmly; Grisby, who supposedly has been watching them kiss, calls out to them, "So long kiddies!" from a speedboat. As we learn later, Grisby's partner in crime, Elsa, has achieved the first part of a murder plan: he and Elsa are to murder Bannister for a share of his money, using Michael as the fall guy.

After Elsa's fake passion, appealing to Michael by making him feel she is sexually neglected (whereas in fact she is as sexually lifeless as her husband), her feelings towards him are ironically underlined by the knowing commercialism of a hair-oil commercial, played to a Latin American beat.

> *Glosso-Lusto in your hair*
> *Keeps it Glosso-Lusto bright,*
> *Glosso-Lusto - G - L - O - S - S - O*
> *L - U - S - T - O - is right!*

So remember ladies, use Glosso-Lusto, pleases your hair, pleases the man you love.

Later, there is a romantic, "Hollywood" image—Elsa with her hair caught in the wind as the boat moves through a sparkling ocean. Mike asks her: "Love. Do you believe in love at all, Mrs. Bannister?"

ELSA: I was taught to think about love in Chinese.
MIKE: The way a Frenchman thinks about laughter in French?
ELSA: The Chinese say, it is difficult for love to last long. Therefore one who loves passionately is cured of love, in the end.
MIKE: Sure, that's a hard way of thinking.
ELSA: There's more to the proverb: Human nature is eternal. Therefore, one who follows his nature keeps his original nature, in the end.

Here Welles is having a joke at the audience's expense: the unwary would probably take it that Elsa was erudite, perhaps referring to Confucius, that she has intellectual or semi-intellectual interests—whereas in fact the quotation comes from that very American bestseller *The Wisdom of China* by Lin Yutang!

We are in Mexico now, at a monstrous picnic or-

ganized by Bannister. The picnic is introduced by a laconic voice-over by Michael: "It was no more a picnic than Bannister was a man." Down the river the little party is towed, location footage expertly matched as snakes and alligators slither into the water and flamingos flash through the liana roots. As torches spread out across an inlet, men wade through black water, and Heinz Roemheld's arrangement of "Baia" echoes from far away. Elsa is anxiously telling Michael about the role of the yacht's steward, Broome:

ELSA: He isn't really a steward. He's a detective. My husband hires him to watch me. He wants to fix it so I'll be able to divorce him. He'll cut me off without a cent.
MICHAEL: Does that matter, I shouldn't think it would?
ELSA: I told you, sweet, you don't know anything about the world.

And shortly before, Bannister, told by his chauffeur that he is to be the victim of a murder plot, reveals that he knows all about it. Bannister, Grisby, and Elsa swing in hammocks, exhausted by the heat, exchanging smart remarks.

BANNISTER: You're a stupid fool, George. I don't mind a bit if Michael's in love with my wife. He's young, she's young. He's strong. She's beautiful.

The suggestion is made that Michael wants to leave the cruise, and Elsa expresses a private agony as she says: "Why should anybody want to live around us?" Michael is called over and sees the rich in their Scott Fitzgerald traps, Grisby serving "Grisby specials" from a cocktail shaker; he learns that Bannister blackmailed Elsa into marrying him.

Michael's comment is bitter: "Is this what you folks do for amusement in the evenings, sit around toasting marshmallows and calling each other names? If you're so anxious for me to join the game I'd be glad to. I can think of a few names I'd like to be calling you myself."

BANNISTER: You should hear how Elsa got to be my wife. Then you'd really be calling me names.
ELSA: Do you want me to tell him what you've got on me, Arthur?

Sadistically (and rather stuffily) Michael tells them the story of a pack of sharks off Brazil, and what became of them:

Do you know, once off the hump of Brazil, I saw the ocean so darkened with blood it was black, and the sun fadin' away over the lip of the sky. We put in at Fortaleza.[2] A few of us had lines out for a bit of idle fishin'. It was me had the first strike. A shark it was, and then there was another, and another shark again, till all about the sea was made of sharks, and more sharks still, and the water tall. My shark had torn himself away from the hook, and the scent, or maybe the stain it was, and him bleedin' his life away, drove the rest of them mad. Then the beasts took to eatin' each other; in their frenzy, they ate at themselves.

[2]This was, of course, the location for the final shooting of *Jangadeiros* in *It's All True* and the shark reference echoes the circumstances of Jacaré's death.

You could feel the lust of murder like a wind stingin' your eyes, and you could smell the death, reekin' up out of the sea. I never saw anything worse, until this little picnic tonight. And you know, there wasn't one of them sharks in the whole crazy pack that survived?

And as Michael walks off Bannister wheezes: "George, that's the first time anybody ever thought enough of you to call you a shark. If you were a good lawyer you'd be flattered!"

Details of the cruise have been vividly sketched in: Elsa swimming or perched on a rock watched by Grisby through binoculars, Elsa singing a torch song flat on her back on deck while the servants sit restlessly below and Grisby and Bannister exchange decadent wisecracks ("That's good, Arthur!" "That's good, George!"). Acapulco provides a brief pause in the journey, a location which gives Mike / Welles a chance, looking down from the parapets above the harbor, to comment on Mexican (and Western) society: "There's a fair face to the land, but you can't hide the hunger and the guilt." A moment later a gigolo says to his off-screen companion: "Darling, of course you pay me!"

Along the cliffs above the shining bay Michael and Grisby walk together, their faces held in huge closeups, at times seeming to be vertiginously poised in a shimmering void. Grisby, sweating and grotesque, expresses his wish to escape his wife and fear of Armageddon in the shape of the atom bomb (the film was made at the time of Hiroshima) with the words: "First, the big cities, then maybe even this!" Grisby asks Michael to fake his murder: for $5,000 he is to pretend to murder him so that, thought dead, Grisby can escape to a South Seas island away from the menace of the bomb.

That night, in the dark streets of Acapulco, Michael tells Elsa about Grisby's proposal, about his fear that the world would explode; and she tells him of her suicidal impulses.

Broome pops up in the middle of the conversation, lasciviously threatening: "I'd hate to have to report you to the lady's husband." Michael knocks him out; and in the flurry that follows, Elsa runs away in fear. Michael catches up with her, and once more assumes a protective pose: "Sure, I'm going to take you where there are no spies." By now he's thoroughly hooked. She expresses her philosophy: there is no escape from life's pain, the pain of being alive; they are in a far place now, far from the centers of civilization, and there is still suffering: "Everything's bad, Michael, everything. You can't escape it or fight it. You've got to get along with it. Deal with it, make terms. . . . You're big and strong, but you just don't know how to take care of yourself. So how could you take care of me?"

In early October the yacht *Circe* drops anchor in Sausalito, near San Francisco, much to Michael's relief. His commenting voice is dry: "Living on a hook takes away your appetite." He asks Elsa: "Would you have to take in washing on five thousand dollars?" Already he has decided to leave with her, to live on a desert island, and we know that he has decided to accept Grisby's scheme.

Over a beer Grisby starts to lay down the details of the murder plan: "The firm of Bannister and Grisby is insured against the death of either partner. That means if one of us dies the other stands to get a lot of money."

Bannister calls Grisby away, and Elsa's Chinese servant tells Michael she will meet him in the San Francisco Aquarium at nine the next morning. That night Grisby provides Michael with a fake confession at his office: "The state of California will say I'm dead, officially dead, if somebody will say they murdered me. There's no such thing as homicide without a body. It isn't murder unless they can produce a corpse."

The Aquarium: in silhouette against the writhings of squids, octopuses, and groper fish, Elsa reads the fake confession. "I, Michael O'Hara, do freely make the following confession. . . . We arrived at the boat landing at approximately 10:20, Mr. Grisby said he heard a sound, something suspicious, he said he was frightened of a hold-up, he asked me to get the gun out of the side pocket of the car just in case. I reached in and got hold of the gun, but I had hardly got hold of it when the gun went off by accident in my hand . . . and I saw that Mr. Grisby was covered with blood. It took me a minute to realize that Mr. Grisby was dead, to realize that I, Michael O'Hara had killed him." Elsa tells Michael she is convinced her husband wrote the confession and got Michael to sign it in order to murder Grisby; but the deliberately foolish suggestion is only intended to confuse Michael still further.

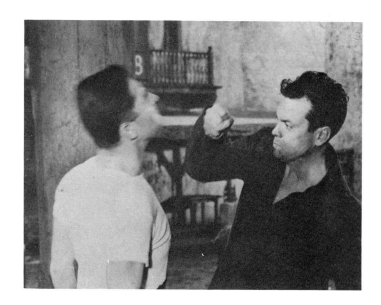

The next few scenes are telegraphed vividly: Broome tells Grisby at the Bannisters' house that he knows the details of the murder plan and wants to be paid for his silence; Grisby shoots Broome. Elsa finds Broome shot, and he tells her about a plot to kill Bannister, of which she pretends to know nothing. Cut to Grisby's car: he arranges a collision with a truck, smearing the seat with blood from the cuts caused by flying glass, explaining to Michael: "It's perfect. If you shot me there *would* be blood." There is a background of a solo piano from a bar; a vivid impression of a waterside town alive with people; the sound of shots; and men and women run

out in the midst of a general hubbub, led by a fat saloon keeper: "Hey, what are you doing with that gun?" And Michael says: "I was just doin' a little target practice."

Michael now rings the Bannister house at San Rafael, and the dying Broome says that Grisby is on his way to the Grisby and Bannister office on Montgomery Street to kill Bannister. But Grisby is carried down Montgomery Street dead instead—shot by Bannister, presumably—and Michael is arrested because Grisby is holding Michael's cap in his hand (despite the fact—a Welles cheat—that the confession included a statement that the corpse had been thrown into San Francisco Bay.)

Sitting outside the courtroom, observed in one of the longest and slowest forward dolly shots on record, the Bannisters conduct a weird conversation:

BANNISTER: If I defend Michael, any jury is going to think that I have reason to believe Michael is innocent. . . . I hear that Galloway is going to say that Michael took George's corpse into the city in our speedboat.

ELSA: But he didn't. We can prove that.

BANNISTER: Prove? But George couldn't have taken it in himself. How could he get back?

ELSA: Back where?

BANNISTER: The yacht, naturally! The speedboat couldn't have driven itself. Maybe it was George's ghost. Maybe the boat just drifted back. No, lover. Michael has got to plead justifiable homicide.

ELSA: And you can prove he didn't do it with his gun. They already know it wasn't Michael's gun that killed George.

BANNISTER: The gun that did kill George can't be found, lover. So we can't prove that Michael didn't shoot him. And it was Michael's gun that killed Broome.

ELSA: You want to make sure he doesn't get off, don't you?

BANNISTER: I've never lost a case, remember? Besides, my wife might think he's a martyr. I've got to defend him. I haven't any choice. And neither have you.

Elsa visits Michael in jail: she tells him to trust her husband.

In the trial scene, with the coughing crowd in a huge, dusty courtroom, Arthur Bannister is drawing laughs with a typical crack: "I object! The question calls for the operation of the officer's mind!" ("Sustained!")

D.A. (cross-examining police witness): Very well! In the interests of saving time, we will proceed! As I'm sure Officer Peters is most anxious to get home to his wife and family, before returning to duty. Now then, Officer Peters. Except for the blood, the clothes were dry. Yet the defendant stated in his confession that he threw the body in the bay.

BANNISTER: Your honor, the District Attorney isn't cross-examining, he's making speeches.

D.A.: That simply isn't so!

BANNISTER: I move that a declaration of mistrial be brought on the grounds that the jury is being prejudiced.

D.A.: These are some of the great Bannister's "trial tactics." In an appeal for sympathy . . .

BANNISTER: The D.A. is beginning to get vicious.

JUDGE: When you two gentlemen get over your argument, tell me who won. Then I'll decide on the objection. (Laughter in court.)

A moment later Bannister discredits the prosecution's witness, Officer Peters, by showing that the District Attorney's concern ("I'm sure Officer Peters is most anxious to go home to his wife and family") is faked: Officer Peters has no wife and family.

It is soon made painfully clear that Bannister is turning the trial into a farce, deliberately throwing away his client's case. As two Chinese girls chatter about the case in their own tongue (one of them concluding with "You ain't kidding!"), Bannister takes the stand to be cross-examined; questioned on Michael's activities, he doesn't answer the points one by one but accuses the prosecutor of making speeches and drawing conclusions, and finally calls again for a mistrial; later, he cross-examines himself, reasserting Michael's virtues in order to discredit his own case. No single defense of the prisoner makes sense; inevitably, the case collapses. Elsa suggests by a glance that Michael take an overdose of her husband's pain-killing tablets, after Bannister says, "This is one case I've enjoyed losing." He adds, "I'm going to come and see you in the death house, Michael. Every day I'm going to ask for a stay of execution. And

I hope it will be granted. I want you to live as long as possible before you die." Taken into the judge's chambers to walk off the effects of the pills, Michael escapes just before the verdict is announced. Elsa finds Michael in a Chinatown opera theater, the actors' eyes darting in ratlike fear through their make-up, the sound track ticking and scraping with the sound of oriental instruments.

Kidnapped by Elsa's servants, Michael plunges down

a slippery dip at a fun fair through gaping papier-maché mouths while his sound-track voice gives a concise account of Elsa's murder plan. There he meets Elsa, who confesses to him; a moment later, in a hall of mirrors, Bannister arrives, his image multiplied with its gnarled sticks in layers and layers of glass panes. ("I knew I'd find you together. If I hadn't, Elsa, I might have gone on playing it your way.")

Elsa shoots him down, and he shoots her, their aim confused by the mirrors. The mirrors smash, the figures lurch in cavernous holes of splintered glass. Bannister's last remark is typical: "For a smart girl, you make a lot of mistakes. You should have let me live. You're going to need a good lawyer." Elsa hisses: "*He* and *George,* and now *me!*" As she falls to the floor, Michael says: "Like the sharks, mad with their own blood. Chewing away at their own selves." He adds: "You said the world's bad, you can't run away from the badness, and you're right there. But you said we can't fight it, we must deal with it, make terms. And then the badness will deal with you, and make its own terms, in the end, surely." Elsa reminds him, "You can fight but what good is it? We can't win," and he says, "We can't lose either. Only if we quit." With expressions of terror as she lies on the floor, the camera at floor level, she utters a brief, sentimental farewell: "Give my love to the sunrise!" and her last cry is a cliché: "I don't want to die!" Michael walks out. The harsh, deliberate rattle of the exit gate terminates their relationship. As the camera swings up to take in Michael's last walk across the pier to call the police, he says: "Well, everybody is somebody's fool. The only way to stay out of trouble is to grow old. So I guess I'll concentrate on that. Maybe I'll live so long that I'll forget her. Maybe I'll die, trying." He will, we know, be exonerated by a letter that Bannister has left with the D.A.

• • •

More than any other Welles film, *The Lady from Shanghai* is a work of energy and freedom. The opening sequence is perfectly constructed: close-ups of Elsa in the carriage shimmer with an extraordinary intensity, the light on her face even harder than William Daniels's

arcs fixed on Garbo's, the hair bleached white, the cheekbones highly polished. The intercut shots of Elsa attacked by thugs have the casual, brutal look of a newsreel. Against this, Michael's lolling walk and the shaky movement of the carriage are matched in tracking shots so as to appear jerky, disconnected.

The scene in which Bannister hires Michael is excitingly staged, cutting from elaborately grouped shots of the sailors in the hiring hall (an excellent set) to the single advancing figure of Bannister.

Aboard the yacht the treatment is extraordinarily mock-casual, the images often looking like those of some inspired home movie or a gifted amateur's travel documentary covering a voyage at sea. Shaky and grainy, often using bad light and inappropriate times of day, they are done with unerring skill: and Viola Lawrence's much-maligned cutting sometimes manages the transitions in a style that captures Welles's intention — an elliptical, off-key tone. The opening scene on the yacht, featuring a close-up of Elsa's dachshund, rich close-ups of her face with the lips waiting for a kiss, the eyes fluttering shut, then a longer shot of her at the wheel, the wind blowing her hair as the radio commercial mocks her falsity: all this is expertly pointed and condensed.

The scene in which Elsa lies on her back singing while Bannister and Grisby lurk exchanging wisecracks (and the servants restlessly toss in the heat below), is one of the film's high points. The camera observes Elsa from directly overhead, her hair forming an aureole around her face, her black swimsuit setting off her pale limbs. Bannister and Grisby are taken mostly in medium shot, although the camera moves in brutally when Bannister describes how only money has saved him from a lifetime flat on his back in a county hospital. The scene in which Elsa, imitating the siren Circe after whom the yacht is named, perches on a rock is an ironical use of "Hollywood" techniques to establish a visual point about her phony allure, which is in fact drawing Michael onto the reefs of death.

At Acapulco the camera tracks restlessly above the "bright guilty world" of the rich in their playground, capturing the bays, the cliffs, the bustle of tourists. The picnic, held upriver, is a chiaroscuro of torches flaring against black water, men wading through the sparkling and flashing depths, the Bannisters and Grisby in their hammocks in a shimmering oasis that seems to glow with the effulgence of decay, and Michael, poised against a background of fishing nets and ocean that evokes the Brazilian locale where he saw the sharks destroy each other.

The oceanic image recurs later, first in the light-filled, sparkling impressionist shots of Sausalito, with bright beams striking through the windows of a bar and a suggestion of salt, sun, and wind, and then in the Aquarium, its echoing halls filled with the rippling light of the tanks, the shadowy figures of octopuses, a snake and a groper fish ominously drifting through the powerfully lit squares of glass, while the lovers in silhouette move against them, each section of the confession read breathlessly by Elsa Bannister and marked by a cut to a new section of the glass panes, accompanied by an eerie chamber arrangement for woodwind.

The faked murder of Grisby at the pier is by contrast harsh and jagged, achieved through staccato editing and the startling effect of the pier people running toward the camera — led by a fat man in an apron, a scene altogether different in tone to the ironic-poetic mode of the Aquarium episode. The discovery of Grisby's body is jerkily handled, with swooping shots giving an oddly unsettling feeling to the audience as the stretcher is taken out of the office building: a strange, affecting scene. The trial, despite the liberties it takes with legal process, is a masterpiece of cutting, so complex that a whole chapter could be dedicated to it alone (some images last only a few second on the screen), and the set is authentic. Welles cuts from Bannister looming in freckled closeup to Elsa perched elegantly in the witness box, from the babbling audience and the coughing and sneezing jury to the dim-witted judge, from the strident district attorney to the whole court. The scene's final effect, with the pills in the foreground and Elsa in the background indicating that Michael should take them, recalls the composition of the attempted suicide in *Citizen Kane*.

Rapid cutting also distinguishes the tense scene in the Chinese theater; the strange shifts of tone in the Chinese music are accompanied by the bizarre effects achieved by the lighting. The mirror scene is extraordinary: the husband's canes repeated over and over again in a series of vertical panels, then his face, and Elsa's — full-length figures alternated with distorted close-ups, an episode as poetic and unreal as the Aquarium scene. At the end comes the shock of reality as the panes are blasted away and the husband and wife are seen facing each other across a desolate waste of shattered glass, mortally injured and bleeding, illusion splintered into a thousand pieces — their guilt, misery, and knowledge of the futility of greed staring them in the face. The film ends on a contrast: the camera is at floor level, sinking as far as it can go, to record the death agony of Elsa Bannister, then it cranes up high and free to record Michael's walk across the sparkling pier to freedom, to a release in the clean life of the sea.

8. MACBETH

I'm doubtful about Shakespeare for the movies. For while the movies do most everything better than the stage, they don't do verse better. But MACBETH *and its gloomy moors might be grand. A perfect cross between* WUTHERING HEIGHTS *and* THE BRIDE OF FRANKENSTEIN. —Welles interview, *Modern Screen,* April 1940.

Rain, fog, sun, and snow; fall, summer, and winter; these are the weathers and seasons of Welles's Shakespearean trilogy, which follows Verdi in adapting in identical sequence three works: *Macbeth, Othello,* and (encompassing a whole group of plays) *Chimes at Midnight.* Rain and fog, and the dark colors of the dying year figure in *Macbeth;* the blazing sun of Cyprus beating on white stone in *Othello;* the still winter snows, the cold glitter of December sunlight on the rocks, the turrets, the doomed crown of Henry IV in *Chimes at Midnight* (called *Falstaff* in many countries). Through the seasons Welles transmutes emotion into universal symbols: Macbeth's stormy soul, shrouded in despair, Othello's brave and desperate spirit, filled with the white fire of the Mediterranean, Falstaff's and his king's stricken hopes, buried deep in the bitter snows of England. No artist of the cinema has moved us as deeply as this, has more thoughtfully addressed us on the subject of mortality, the death of commoners and kings.

Through the trilogy or triptych, many themes are knotted together, but no theme is greater than that one which dominates all Welles's work: the destructive effect of power. Kane died desperately alone; the Ambersons perished in the dust of a machine age already doomed by instant rust and wear; the creatures of *The Lady from Shanghai* consumed each other with their greed and lust. Shakespeare himself understood this theme most deeply, and Welles has taken it up and sung it with the camera, in images ruined or perfect, in visions stricken by his own weakness or elevated by his own sense of order and beauty. Impatient as we may be with the deficiencies of *Macbeth,* the deep flaws of *Othello,* the slackening of energy in *Chimes at Midnight,* yet we cannot deny their creator the final accolade, the acknowledgement that in images of darkness, of sun and bitter cold, he has made Shakespeare live again and flourish in the twentieth century's most potent medium of art.

• • •

The offer to make *Macbeth* came, astonishingly, from Republic, home of cheap B-westerns and Vera Hruba Ralston. Welles promised Republic's production chief Herbert Yates that he would shoot the film in three weeks, and he came in on schedule, at a cost roughly equivalent to other Ralston films — $800,000. The film succeeded surprisingly well (according to Yates); but it was Welles's last American picture for almost a decade. Filming was first announced in April 1947, with a proposed budget of $700,000. According to *Variety,* Republic restricted the budget on the grounds that Shakespeare might not "sell," but Welles, according to others, deliberately cut costs to prove that good films could be made cheaply.

Among the economies he imposed was cheeseparing on

sets. These were surprisingly spare; a *New York Times* correspondent described them as "fragmentary staff-and-frame pieces," of which there were a total of eight on the same sound stage. (They looked strikingly solid on screen.) All were of the same color: a dirty slate gray suggesting weather-beaten rock, with backgrounds of a clifflike appearance twenty-eight feet high. Many of the sections were movable and could be combined with others, as in Welles's previous films.

The ghost of Banquo was achieved without distortion or the use of mirrors: the make-up expert Roman Freulich took a piece of clear optical glass twelve inches square and placed it on a stand in front of the camera, about fourteen to sixteen inches away. Then he smeared

Vaseline around the edges of the glass for his ghost effects.

Several actresses, including Tallulah Bankhead, turned down the part of Lady Macbeth, partly on the ground that Welles wanted it played with a Scottish accent. Finally, Welles cast Jeanette Nolan, a friend who had appeared with him in "March of Time," "Suspense," and other radio programs, including "Snow White and the Seven Dwarfs," in which she played the witch.

Macbeth — which Welles had originally wanted to make ahead of *Citizen Kane* — was tried out by being first produced on the stage at the Utah Centennial Festival in Salt Lake City. Welles designed the sets and costumes and produced some startling effects: bagpipe players emerging from pitch darkness, marching through the audience and out into the street, phosphorescent lights exploding in a blue blaze from the pit to the ceiling, and the witches with weird faces seemingly floating above the audience.

The film performance, though omitting these touches, was much the same as the stage performance, except that to economize, and because he believed that actors declaiming their lines "live" would disconcert audiences, Welles had the entire sound track recorded in advance after two weeks of aural rehearsal, involving the cast in drastic problems of lip synchronizing.

Disastrously, the track was recorded three times in three accents: one Scottish, one British, and one half-American, half-British. Then portions of the three tracks were melded together, producing a hopelessly confused result. Once again, Welles made the fatal mistake of leaving the picture before it was cut; he was in Italy playing Cagliostro in *Black Magic,* abandoning the film just when it needed him. "His cutter tried to do everything Orson wanted from cabled instructions," Jeanette Nolan has said.[1] "But he was in a state of total confusion. Even the British and the British-American re-recordings weren't touched by Welles."

Because of the different actions required for the camera, the lip movements often could not be made to match these crude and jumbled prerecordings; in one place Macbeth was on the battlements delivering a speech that should come in a courtyard.

"On the day we began shooting," Miss Nolan said, "there was not a man for Orson. We finished the first take of the murder scene of the grooms at five minutes after midnight. There were sixty camera moves in one day, and everyone on the crew had said they could not be done. But he won everyone over with his camera brilliance; he held the crew spellbound."

Nevertheless, the struggle of the actors to match in with words blasted from loudspeakers was appalling, and it affected the quality of their performances. To make matters worse, bits and pieces (of the sleepwalking

[1] Interview with Jeanette Nolan, Sydney, Australia, 1968.

lines spoken by omitted minor characters) in dramatic contrast with the evil of the three witches (whom he renamed "The Three" and turned into Druidic sorceresses who hated the encroachment of the future). He even dared to alter the sleepwalking scene, so that Lady Macbeth, instead of returning to bed, is wakened by Macbeth's kiss. Her suicide over a cliff — reported by Malcolm in the play — is shown as vividly as Tosca's, and the Verdian parallel is clearly deliberate. The Scots burr that proves so maddeningly distracting on the sound track was intended by Welles to slow the actors' tempo and permit an unlettered audience to grasp Shakespeare spoken naturally in dialect. (The result, of course, was disastrous.) The cast was asked to play as naturalistically as possible.

As in *The Magnificent Ambersons,* Welles used more than one unit to make the film, dashing from one part of the set to the other to supervise shooting, using three cameras at once in the siege of Dunsinane. Members of the crew worked in antique armor, with their backs to the camera, using hand-held cameras (Eyemos) to catch details of the action that could later be intercut with the overall long shots. The multipurpose set was an extension of that used in his own stage production of *Julius Caesar,* which in its turn was based on Greek models. The whole concept had been a dream of Welles's since he had presented a Negro *Macbeth* at the Federal Theatre in New York twelve years before.

Shooting began in the last third of June 1947, with some changes in the originally planned casting: John McIntire, Jeanette Nolan's husband, was to have been the Holy Father finally played by Alan Napier, Everett Sloane was originally to have been Banquo, and Erskine Sanford, Duncan; Dan O'Herlihy of the Abbey Theatre and Roddy McDowall, formerly condemned to a love affair with Lassie, were added to the cast. The witches were played by Brainerd Duffield in drag and two Goldwyn girls with long, blonde wigs. "It was," said Duffield, "very dangerous up on those crags."

Completed in July 1947, *Macbeth* was released — after more redubbing by Welles in the summer of 1948 — in October 1948 in Boston, Minneapolis, Salt Lake

scene, for instance) were recorded live in contrast with the rest.

The film was severely reduced in editing (partly because Welles was not present) including many episodes with Lady Macduff.

Welles's intention in making Macbeth as a compact, engrossing melodrama at a cheap studio was to bring the play to the world of the small town, the half-educated suburbanites and out-of-towners of the American hinterland (an extension of his own theories of making Shakespeare accessible to the masses, exemplified in his specially prepared *Everybody's Shakespeare* editions published many years before). He cut the script to ribbons, added the character of a "Holy Father" (who was given

City (where the stage production had taken place), and Seattle. After a bad press, the film was withdrawn and still further re-recording was done under the supervision of Richard Wilson. For nine months the work continued, making nonsense of Welles's previous attempts. Welles himself, busy in Europe, had to recreate his own vocal performance in London, and Wilson had the unenviable job of intercutting his tapes with the others in Hollywood. Then, finally, in 1949, the film was premiered not less disastrously, in Los Angeles, Portland, Oregon, Minneapolis, and New York.

• • •

High-pitched strings introduce "A Mercury Production by Orson Welles." Against heavy fog, Welles speaks the introduction: "Ancient Scotland . . . lost in the mist that hangs between recorded history and the time of legend." He outlines the existence of black magicians, hellish priests, and sorcerers, who are plotting against the forces of law and order, while a massive stone cross fades in over the white and swirling fog. We dissolve to three witches with streaming white hair; the commentary records the facts of Macbeth's life and death. Images of dissolution are followed by the thorn branch that sym-

bolizes Macbeth's doom to pain, a close-up of gnarled hand plunging into a boiling cauldron that seems, like the marshy landscape itself, to be brimful of mist, as the witches' speeches echo, with heavy Scots burrs, in our ears. They take a clay shape and mold it slowly in the white clouds, their fingers kneading it until the fatal word "Macbeth!" is uttered, and we see the grim face of the clay image.

During the next few minutes the irony is strong; Macbeth embraces his wife passionately, while the captive Thane of Cawdor is dragged to the execution block. Eisensteinian figures hold barbaric crosses high. Close shots show a drummer beating powerfully, the fall of the axe, the cessation of the drums; then there is silence. Not one sound colors the track as the figure of another victim of Macbeth's fate dangles from a gibbet in the background. As Lady Macbeth utters the words, "Look like the innocent flower, but be the serpent under it," we see Duncan, the object of her murderous plans, arriving along a mountain road with the harsh thudding of Ibert's march theme accompanying him.

As Duncan arrives at Dunsinane, the Holy Father gives a service in the mist, Welles adding new dialogue to Shakespeare; the effects of high poles piercing the near-darkness, the bizarre shots of preacher and congregation, the shot of the head of the murdered Thane of Cawdor on a pole, all carry a flavor of *Ivan the Terrible*.

Duncan's penetration of Dunsinane's stone labyrinth is counterpointed by the eaglelike hoverings of Lady Macbeth, high in the black rocks that tower among the battlements, which have seemingly been hewn out of a mountainside.

Macbeth's first soliloquy is spoken over his sweating face, the lips not moving at all. As he greets Lady Macbeth, in fierce whispers she suggests killing Duncan, unguarded in his bed. She climbs a great stone ramp, returning to her position of controlling daemon of her husband's murderous career, goes through a stone corridor and picks up a knife from a drugged groom; dissolve to the figure of Duncan on his bed; as her shadow advances across Duncan's bed, threatening his death later that night, we see Macbeth's clay image, with a knife across its eyes, while Macbeth utters the "Is this a dagger," speech in anguish: the witches' prophecy is fulfilled. Macbeth reaches out for the phantom dagger as the camera moves in to his agonized face. Lady Macbeth brings the groom's dagger still poised above him — an evil presence driving him on against his will. As he says, faltering in his resolution, "If we should fail?" thunder echoes threateningly in the background, and a bell rings the fatal hour; Lady Macbeth has her rigid back to the camera, expressing an inexorable will.

Once more a shadow advances across Duncan's bed: this time it is Macbeth's. As the knife (off screen) thrusts home, Lady Macbeth starts back, shocked by the hoot and flutter of an owl from the battlements.

The dialogue between the Macbeths following the murder of Duncan is conducted with the camera stationary, the figures moving in front of it to give visual variety, and as Lady Macbeth takes the daggers to smear the sleeping grooms with blood, we see her brooding in a below eye-level shot, all observed in an enormous, long take that lasts for eight minutes on the screen. By not breaking the flow with a single cut, even to the floor where the knocks are being delivered, an extraordinary intensity is achieved, but the technique of directing the performance on a monotonous and unchanging note of charged and oppressive grimness works against the accomplished technique. Even the flurry of action that follows the discovery of Duncan's body does not quite dissipate the constipating effect of so much verse delivered without a trace of light and shade. A flourish of torches, cries in the darkness, swarming figures: the effect here is confusion rather than the dynamic outbreak of energy that presages the funerary procession held for the body of Duncan is carried across the battlements — in a shot that presages the funerary procession held for the body of Othello — the effect is not nearly so moving as it should have been because of the muddle surrounding it.

The next scenes are insufferably handled, with the direction collapsing into a leaden pace and the performances peculiarly lifeless. The "Macbeth has murdered sleep" speech is completely thrown away.

We return to the witches with their melting figure of

Macbeth. The crown is placed on its head, and we see it in the distorting mirror of a gong, dissolving into Macbeth's own face in a mirror, putting it on. As Macbeth looms over the court in a fur cloak, he might well be Cherkassov's Ivan; once again, Eisenstein has cast a deep influence over the direction. The pouncing of the first and second murderers on the victim Banquo is routinely done, their beautiful introductory conversation ruined by indifferent recording.

Macbeth arrives at the banquet through a dark labyrinth of stone, and there is a series of rapid cuts between him and his wife, establishing a strong sense of tension. A shadow comes over his face as it changes to an expression of terror, and this is the presence of Banquo. The others at the table do not see the ghost, and when Macbeth sees it the table is absolutely empty. In a brilliant effect we follow the shadow of Macbeth's finger subjectively, moving with it down the table to Banquo's blood-dappled form. At times we see the table from Banquo's subjective camera position: a cleverly original idea.

The scene following — the murder of the Macduff children — is less interestingly done (although specialists may note the presence as a nurse of the old lady in the Aquarium in *The Lady from Shanghai*). Even Macbeth's visit to the witches at this stage in the action is unexciting, marred by crudely obvious studio thunder-and-lightning and some wretched recording of the score, and relieved only by the effective moment when the witches are altogether blanketed by pitch darkness, their voices echoing out of what seems to be a bottomless pit: "Beware Macbeth!" The scene concludes with a very slow dolly shot in which Macbeth's face is like a glowing firefly in the remote blackness, then grows to the size of a moon and finally comes into full close-up: an idea that, incongruous as it may sound, may well have come from Welles having seen a similar effect in *Gold Diggers of 1935.*

The next section of the film is directed without a trace of skill; it is perhaps the worst passage, outside of *The Trial,* in the whole of Welles's repertoire. Even the "All my pretty ones" speech, moving as it is, goes for absolutely nothing, and Dan O'Herlihy's delivery of it could not be more boring. The appearance of the Holy Father at the announcement of the killing is wholly ludicrous; Alan Napier in the part looks like a cross between Boris Karloff and Heidi.

We return to the witches at once, a background of mountains and lakes, and in the middle-distance the galloping figures of the Thane of Glamis and his companions. The horses rise up; the crown is fixed on the clay image, prophesying Macbeth's future elevation to the throne of Scotland; thunder rattles in the background.

The Holy Father emerges to greet the travelers; and we see through the mists the castle of Dunsinane looming in the distance (incidentally quite unlike the real one, and more like Xanadu, a pile in the remote mists). We see Lady Macbeth reading her husband's letter, her breasts heaving theatrically as she lies on a bed heaped with furs. She rises and goes to the window as she speaks the lines about milk changing to gall, and there is a powerfully effective shot of the fog beyond her room, an overhead shot of Macbeth galloping towards her, like a creature impelled helplessly by fate, the threatening shape of Dunsinane a bleak and towering magnet on the skyline.

As Macbeth's party arrives at the castle, there is a strong effect of damp, of pigs and goats swarming through courtyards, scattered by the horses' hooves, against a background of thudding, threatening drums.

Eisensteinian effects show tall staves with crosses as the army of Macduff advances towards Dunsinane, and Macbeth talks on the battlements, the mist heavier than ever now, patches of damp on the stone, shadows cast by the soldiers on the glistening battlements, Macbeth calling to his dwarfish, half-mad servant Seyton for his armor and the saddling up of his horses.

Lady Macbeth is intercut in this scene framed between armor and iron spikes, lying in bed in anguish, as Macbeth remembers the prophecy about Birnam Wood and we see the enemy troops marching down a mountain pass: the end is coming near. There is a vivid flourish in Ibert's music as the soldiers receive their instructions to cut down the branches of the forest and use it as camouflage: this is splendidly staged. From this action, designed to destroy Macbeth, we dissolve to a black, bleak skyline, with a few puffs of smoke, cloud, mist, and the forest moves forward slowly through it. The serving woman and the physician talk about Lady Macbeth in whispers at the bottom of the frame as she emerges at its very top, teetering above an immense flight of steps in her sleepwalking pose.

She carries a candle high, screams, drops it, and lurches into medium close-up: all this is most carefully staged, but unhappily here Jeanette Nolan's performance is at its least adequate, the figure bending to and fro and keening, the tears all too theatrical and forced, the Scots burr introduced (where so often elsewhere it is neglected) with an incongruously heavy emphasis. A moment later she is a Milwaukee virago, crudely American and vulgar. The branches of the enemy army thrust forward through the darkness, and Lady Macbeth throws herself down the battlements to lie, a broken figure, at their foot. The "Tomorrow and tomorrow" speech which follows is spoken against an effective shapeless swirling of mists, symbolizing the insignificance of life, its hopeless drifting and lack of organization, which the speech emphasizes.

In the next scene Macbeth is seen wearing a crown, an exact copy of the one fixed on his clay likeness by the witches. A figure hangs from a bell, as in a series of shots from high above Macbeth is seen making ready to sound the alarm that the advancing troops evoke. Macbeth looms in the corner for the "Blow winds, come wrack!" speech, and with a blaze of trumpets and a roar of excitement the enemy pounds its battering ram against the gates: this is enterprisingly staged in the Curtix manner, vividly pointed and composed.

The fight on the battlements is quite strikingly managed, torches flickering as Macbeth enters the death struggle and his head is slashed from his body and raised on a pole before the multitude, as the Thane of Cawdor's had been at the beginning. The music accompanying the duel has a Stravinskian power, and drums throb tremendously as wild cheers greet the display of Macbeth's head. Like *Kane,* the film concludes with a long retreating shot from the Disneyish castle, and in the now subsided mists the three witches sit in silhouette, Y-forked sticks held high, brooding with their backs to us over the ghastly fulfillment of their prophecy.

Like Kurosawa in *Throne of Blood,* Welles ignores the tragedy of a great man fallen that Shakespeare clearly intended: an imaginative, conscience-stricken figure whose wife is the destructive force which drives him to murder and death. Instead, Macbeth is here from the beginning a doomed, driven being, and his wife is as trapped as he is in the web of fate. No free will here, no virtue brought low by ambition, but rather an obedience to compulsion, to the doom which is sealed at the very outset of the film by the fashioning of Macbeth's face by the witches, dark symbol of his end even at this stage. In its crumbling, decaying, but at the same time formatory shapelessness, the face is at once a mirror and a death mask.

The military side of Macbeth's character, so powerfully emphasized by Kurosawa, is here altogether lost, and at the end he faces the advancing human forest of Birnam alone and undefended. His loneliness and introspection, his feeling of being haunted, overpowered by the crow wings of darkness, are emphasized very heavily. This is a film of interior observation; the whole black, labyrinthine, mist-wreathed pile of Dunsinane sweating

with dew is a precise reflection of Macbeth's tortured mind and soul.

Even the political ramifications of the play, crude though these are, have been shorn away, so that Macbeth's precise motives for killing Duncan and Banquo are obscured in the action. The slight subterranean hint — initiated by Banquo — that the witches may have been caught in the mesh of evil by whetting his ambition and thereby forcing him to fulfill the prophecy has also been suppressed. Banquo is no longer a figure of sensibility and goodness, but an obscure figure whose death does not disturb us emotionally. Duncan, too, is scarcely glimpsed — and not brought to life — before he is murdered: we feel nothing, because we have not been given the picture of venerable dignity and decency that Shakespeare gave us. But it is not Welles's purpose to move us with these deaths. Banquo and Duncan are simply skittles which Macbeth cannot help knocking over, and the tragedy is reduced to the melodrama of fate.

Lady Macbeth is the implement used by fate to insure that the witches' prophecy is carried out, that both she and her husband act precisely in accordance with their mutual necessity. Her thin, writhing, serpentine form, tossing on a fur-covered bed or looming in almost every composition above her husband, twining into his limbs for an anacondalike embrace, is warped by its destiny. Her eyes are fixed, and her voice is vibrant with a repressed hysteria which in itself contains a note of acceptance. When her shadow advances across the bed where Duncan sleeps his last living sleep, it presages the shadow of Macbeth's finger that points towards the figure of Banquo, the camera following it darkly along a wall. Shadows lead us on through the film, as do the endless labyrinthine corridors and the winding paths up the battlements, into the convolutions of a diseased brain. Like Banquo, Macduff emerges not as a human being of probity and goodness, but rather as yet another figment of Macbeth's imaginings. When Birnam Wood advances, when Lady Macbeth plunges to her death, and when Macbeth's head is slashed from his body, we are still trapped in Macbeth's dream.

The concept is powerful, and it is unfortunate that

because of hasty shooting, the restrictions of Republic Studios, and his own occasional lapses of style, Welles made this one of his unhappiest films. His own performance, played on one note of grimacing misery, entirely fails to capture the feeling of a man who has become the quarry of the hounds of hell. The outward appearance is correct — the desperate eye, the sweating brow — but the inward responsiveness to his own interpretation of the role's implications does not emerge.

Again, Lady Macbeth as played by Jeanette Nolan is outwardly accurate within the film's highly personal terms of reference. She suffers more than anyone else from the endless re-recordings — made to hiss away like Elsa Bannister in a hushed and desperate monotone, her voice works against the character's complexities, reducing them to colorlessness. Only her sleepwalking scene, well handled, conveys her doom-laden predicament.

The other players are uniformly feeble, with the arguable exception of Edgar Barrier's Banquo; and it was an absurdity to introduce one character not in Shakespeare and give Shakespearean pastiches to utter: the Holy Father.

Visually, the film is often impressive, with its beautifully realized dankness and blackness photographed by John L. Russell, who later shot *Psycho* in much the same style; and Ibert's score is magnificently brassy, resplendently martial. But the cutting is lamentably confusing, and the sound track ruinously bad, reducing many of the verbal points to a swamp of incoherent sounds punctuated by imitation accents and a nerve-racking multiplicity of noises off screen. It is impossible to deny that *Macbeth* is a failure; but its concept was a noble one. It remains an authentic *film maudit,* worth re-seeing today.

9. OTHELLO

What, precisely, was lost in 1947 when, with many disillusioned and impatient things to say about Hollywood, and even about the cinema itself, Welles fled to Rome and then all over Europe, and finally became a European? Most importantly, he lost something which the cinema itself was soon to lose: the black-and-white, infinitely intricate world created by the superb miniaturist technicians of the Hollywood system. The strength of his best American films lay to a great extent in their interlocking, Chinese puzzle structure, each separate section carved and polished by master craftsmen in order to convey his vision unflawed. In *Kane,* when a dissolve to a sled is accomplished by a train whistle and falling snow, we know that the cutters, the special effects men and the sound recordists have conspired to make a matchless single, overwhelming poet's image of loss. Moments of technical virtuosity, like that supreme one in the same film when the camera sees rain blurring a glass nightclub skylight and a dissolve simultaneously admits us to an enclosed world, no longer occur in Welles's European films. We cannot imagine Europe providing the wizardry of that shimmering effect in *The Lady from Shanghai* in which fish tanks are enlarged and arranged so that the creatures in them reflect and echo a murderess' thoughts. In America the interior of Welles's films is as intricate as that of a prize-winning watch; in Europe the springs hang out.

It is not merely American money that Welles has missed in his last two decades in Europe. He has missed the small screen. He wrote in *The New Statesman* (London, May 24, 1958), "The old camera permits of a range of visual conventions as removed from 'realism' as grand opera. This is a language, not a bag of tricks. It is now a dead language." He has mourned that language, and the fellow speakers of it that he once worked with across the Atlantic.

In return for the loss of Hollywood's magic box, Welles in the looser and freer atmosphere of Europe has developed the poetic talent that in California was always slightly constrained. This talent illuminates *Othello, Chimes at Midnight,* and *The Immortal Story* with an exquisite effulgence; Europe has brought a new tenderness and softness, a new maturity and elegance to the *Wunderkind.* The greatest films of his latest period may excite us less, but they more often move us. Technically imperfect, they bring us, more and more persuasively, that bold, unmistakable voice.

• • •

The story of the shooting of Welles's first European work in 1948-52 is a confusing one, already the subject of an entire book, *Put Money in Thy Purse,* by Micheál MacLiammoir.[1] Welles began work on the film when he arrived in Rome to appear in a film called *Black Magic;* he spent almost three years shooting it, scraping together sums of money as he went along, sometimes directing with ferocious intensity, at others dodging schedules and failing to turn up when required for a scene, often vanishing to some unknown destination in search of funds.

[1]London: Methuen, 1952.

In the looser atmosphere of Europe his always shaky personal discipline collapsed. Without the strictness of Hollywood he became gigantically disorganized, quirky, and confused, living in an agony of indecision, muddle, and frustration as he dashed from one exotic location to another.

No film has been recast in both senses as often as *Othello:* Welles is known to have engaged — and dismissed — three Desdemonas, four Iagos, two Ludovicos, three Cassios, and countless bit players as he moved across the continent appearing in other people's dreadful films (only Carol Reed's *The Third Man,* though now heavily dated, gave him a decent opportunity), and announcing grandiose projects for Alexander Korda — including *War and Peace*, with Merle Oberon as Natasha(!) and Laurence Olivier as Andrei, and *Around the World in 80 Days.*

He sacked his first Desdemona, Lea Padovani, and drove his second, Cecile Aubry, literally off the set. The third Desdemona, Betsy Blair, came and went in a matter of weeks. Only Suzanne Cloutier, a little-known and tough French actress dubbed by Welles "the iron butterfly," could endure his intransigence, and stayed to play the part.

MacLiammoir was also loyal: a brilliant Irish actor, who had been partly responsible for Welles's hiring in Dublin theater in the thirties, he was prepared to rearrange his schedules constantly to suit the master's shifting plans.

In Paris in February 1949 the scattered but hastily reassembled unit suddenly heard from the director (in London) that it was to go to Morocco, where he had just signed a contract to star in *The Black Rose*. Commandeering half the costumes in that bizarre epic about Genghis Khan, Welles shot more sequences in Mogador, mainly in its fifteenth-century fortress, engaged hundreds of local citizens as extras, and raged at, flattered, and infuriated his players and technicians as he shot all day and then gave lavish parties that lasted all night.

Experts in history and costuming drifted in and out; secretaries came and went, sometimes only lasting hours; and Welles followed his usual custom of shooting se-

quences forty times over. When he had exhausted what was left of his money and most of his cast, Welles had to break up the whole unit. Then after persuading an unfortunate financier in Casablanca to put up more cash he continued shooting in Venice, had a nervous breakdown in Rome, began selling costumes and props, and drove the cast into doing other productions to help prop up the budget.

Shooting finished in Mogador, but in the meantime whole sequences shot elsewhere were cut. In 1950 Welles starred as Harry Lime in a London radio series based on *The Third Man* characters, and thereby paid for *Othello's* editing and scoring. At the end of this work he an-

nounced to the press that he was going to make a film called *Love Life,* about sex; a chase film with Akim Tamiroff; a version of *Salomé,* and a giant *Odyssey;* a story about the flood; and *Don Quixote.* He worked on all these projects, while playing on the air, editing at night, and junketing incessantly in every nightclub in London. Finally, he rushed *Othello* into the Venice Film Festival in 1951, withdrew it for more work, hesitantly showed it at Cannes in 1952 — and won the Grand Prix.

In Welles's version of Shakespeare's tragedy Othello is a noble human being doomed by his involvement with the repressed homosexual Iago. Welles intended that the character of Iago should express an envious impotence, like Arthur Bannister. As MacLiammoir observed in his diary:

No single trace of the Mephistophelian Iago is to be used; no conscious villainy; a common man, clever as a waggon-

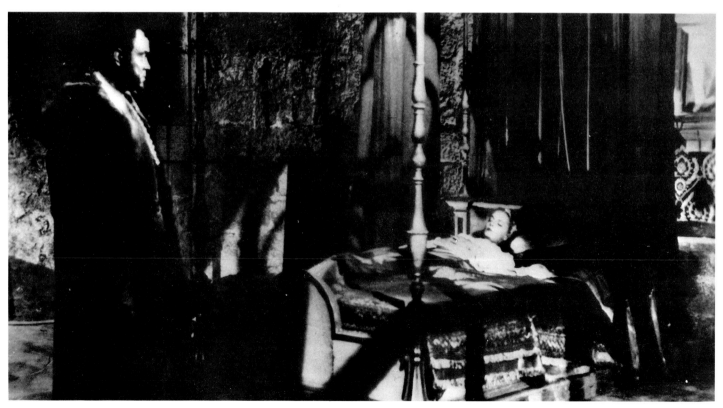

attention to focus with unbearable sharpness upon the two central protagonists: the virile lion and the cold adder which writhes at his feet, destroying him in the end. This observation and interpretation of character is vivid and apt, making sense of the Iago-Othello relationship as few productions have done. As in so many of Welles's films the theme is the destructiveness of ambition, of lust for power, and it is persuasively conveyed in images that impress with their naked, savage kinesthetic force.

Physically, while *Macbeth* is a film of dark interiors, of a cramped and rain-swept world of crags and man-made stone labyrinths, *Othello* is its opposite: full of sun-drenched, wind-lashed exteriors, of settings that are extravaganzas of baroque, a chiaroscuro of whipping flags, sky-piercing turrets, bristling spears, and lashing foam, a world in which the sea and the clouds are eternally present. A ship arrives from an expedition against the Turks, and the screen is filled with an incomparable blaze of maritime images, of taut rigging, bellying sails, and the strained bodies of sailors. A murder is attempted, and the setting is a Turkish bath, with sweating muscles and white towels, walls smattered with crudely chalked hearts, steam rising in thick clouds, and a sword thrust desperately through the boards of the floor. And along with these charged images — as electric as any Welles has given us — there are always the haunted figures he has made his own. Othello, like Macbeth a damned soul driven into desperate action by an evil familiar, is a victim of predestination, while Iago — the very portrait of destructive ambition seeking finally the absolute extinction of the man he secretly lusted for — is as consummate a symbol of the power of fate as Elsa Bannister, or Hank Quinlan in *Touch of Evil*. All obey their destiny, and Desdemona in this version seems merely to be a passive accepter of the destiny they bring her. Cool, detached, and static, at the end she lies down with eyes closed to wait for the thrust of her husband's penis or the thrust of his knife: she seems resigned to either possibility. She is an ideal occupant of Welles's universe because she knows that nothing can shake the inexorable march of destiny.

load of monkeys, his thought never on the present moment but always on the move after the move after next: a business man dealing in destruction with neatness, method, and a proper pleasure in his work: the honest honest Iago reputation is accepted because it has almost become the truth . . . Monotony may perhaps be avoided by remembering the underlying sickness of the mind, the immemorial hatred of life, the secret isolation of impotence under the soldier's muscles, the flabby solitude gnawing at the groins, the eye's untiring calculation.

Welles intended to show how Othello depends more and more on Iago's presence, "the merging of the two men into one murderous image like a pattern of lovely shadows welded." (MacLiammoir.) Welles's dignified performance was expertly contrasted with MacLiammoir's flabby, mean, serpentine playing of his devilish familiar.

The other parts are more conventionally observed. Desdemona is cool and remote. Cassio is played as a rather cold and unpleasant figure, while Bianca is radiantly good and kind. Emilia becomes a whining and tiresome woman in the accomplished playing of Fay Compton. But everything is played down to allow the

Despite the vagaries of shooting I have described, *Othello* is a film of perfect unity, balance, and order, marred only slightly by the technical shortcomings of indifferent dubbing. The score, with its pounding chords for the clavier and its thrumming strings, is a masterly accompaniment to the continually bold, florid, and dashing images. The very tone of the period is recaptured aurally and visually, and the verse is splendidly spoken: Welles's thunder, Micheál MacLiammoir's silky, gelded cat's purr, and the actress dubbing Suzanne Cloutier's cool servile precision are faultlessly countered and contrasted.

The film opens with an image presaging the commencement of *The Trial*: the face of Othello, dead and still, taken from the back of the head; the camera rises high above the bier to show the Moor laid out in state, hands folded, clanging chords and mourning choruses providing a resplendent accompaniment as the bier is lifted toward us and carried by pallbearers toward a line of soldiers outlined against the horizon.

A great cross is borne high; we see battlements, crags, a vast luminous sky full of mountains of cloud; and Desdemona's body, still under a transparent veil of black silk, is carried to its last resting place. Their two biers converge diagonally, making the same path toward interment.

Monks walk, men with halberds stand at attention; Iago is drawn in chains through an avenue in a mocking crowd, a haunted, terrified animal. He is hurled into a cage to the frantic clanging of bells, hoisted on creaking chains, spinning above the crowd, seeing the dead bodies whose end he has brought about, the camera taking his captured eagle's eye view, the ground and the monks swaying from a subjective angle, Iago's eyes wide with horror. It is a scene that conscripts Welles's baroque skills, his sense of tragic doom and the fate that pursues the wicked, into an unforgettable unity.

The whole of this sequence has preceded the credits. The opening titles are simple; they are printed over a wall as the camera swoops down, blotting out the image of the mourners. As in Macbeth, Welles has found it necessary to provide a synopsis of the first scenes in verbal narrative at the outset: the plot is given a simple rendering, from Desdemona's escape from her father to marriage with Othello, to the machinations of the ensign Iago. We see Roderigo (Robert Coote) and Iago brooding from balconies in Venice as Othello and Desdemona make trysts below: Iago threatens to destroy the Moor, to "poison his delight," and the pair draws the attention of Desdemona's father Brabantio to her affair with "the lascivious Moor." As Othello and Desdemona move past in a gondola, Brabantio rushes from his rooms in a nearby palace, crying "Thief! Raise my kindred!" A blaze of torches illuminates the palatial corridors as they come to investigate the apparent abduction of the girl. Brabantio's "The sooty bosom of such a thing as that!" is followed by a shot of the Moor himself, handsomely passionate and committed: there is no doubt about Welles's sympathies.

In his speech to the senate Othello's heroic stature is powerfully established. The impact of this scene is reduced only by the lack of intensity in Suzanne Cloutier's playing of Desdemona, her confession of divided loyalty delivered with a correctness that eliminates feeling. The Eisensteinian compositions have a glowing splendor, reflecting the nobility of Othello's own nature. His form towers over the weak body of Brabantio as the old man is stricken with a mortal disease and carried away by retainers.

It is at this stage in the action that Iago's burning obsession to eliminate Othello's lieutenant, Cassio, is disclosed in a series of powerful duologues with Roderigo — counterpointed with Othello's passionate love-making with Desdemona. Thunder and lightning break loose, bells ring, and against the storm-swept battlements of Cyprus, the Turkish fleet swoops down, attacked by a great broadside of cannon: here Welles's gift for barbaric spectacle is in magnificent display. Wind whirls, Othello's ship arrives, its shadow cast ahead on the white wharf, and we have a shot from below the huge sail, the poetry of arrival dashingly conveyed as the gale whips cloaks and flags under a brilliantly sunlit sky.

The combination of bells, wordless chorus, ship's rigging straining in the wind, Othello marching up the steps, grand in his victory, has an overpowering visual and aural impact, one of the half-dozen finest scenes Welles has given us.

Othello's embrace of Desdemona, his discovery of her fair haven after the storm and blast of war, is accompanied by a fanfare of trumpets, a whirling of banners, as Iago pretends to Roderigo that Desdemona is in love with Cassio. As Iago tries to make Cassio drunk, wild dancing and revelry swamps the background, and at each mention of Othello and his wife we see their tower room illuminated, a square of light in a vertical cylinder of stone, reminiscent of a similar scene in *Jane Eyre*.

The revelry increases, with people laughing, Roderigo tumbling clownishly, the whole port swarming with kicking, punching, leering, and wenching soldiery, carousing in vividly condensed images of animal greed and pleasure. A duel is fought through pillars; prisoners rush to the bars; and Othello rises from his bed to quell the duel between Roderigo and Cassio which has been encouraged by Iago.

Shocked to see Cassio degrading himself by being in-

volved in a night brawl, Othello dismisses Cassio as his lieutenant. On Iago's advice Cassio seeks the aid of Desdemona in reconstituting him to office, thereby ensuring that Othello will believe her to be unfaithful, and bring about both her doom and Cassio's. All this scheming is expertly handled by director and players, its successive stages made sharp and clear by visual pointing of gesture and expression.

On the battlements, above the foam and waving flags, Desdemona greets Cassio and promises him help; in a corridor whipped by wind, she begs Othello's assistance to restore him to his position, but he refuses. As Iago continues to poison Othello's mind against Cassio the

Now we are in a street full of a Sternbergian complex of shadows — of nets and ropes from the sea — and crammed with laughing and carousing people while Othello tests Desdemona in conversation, trying to gauge her faithfulness, but maddened by her pressure on him to restore Cassio to his position. As he begs for the handkerchief, the music is plaintive, agonized. And as Othello spies on Cassio through a gap in the castle wall, the screaming and swooping of gulls mirror his growing distress. As Othello cries in his distress ("Oh, the pity of it!") cannons sound and a ship arrives, the camera whirls like an eagle up the walls, goats are driven past, and we are made aware that, while Othello's private grief grows by the minute, the affairs of the world roll indifferently on. As he walks away from Iago, the screen is full of a multiplicity of wooden struts, images of his mortal prison, foreshadowing the scene in the painter Titorelli's claustrophobic birdcage studio in *The Trial*.

Gulls wheel and scream again, and Othello lies transfixed on the rocks, gazing upward at their predatory swoopings, thinking of his cuckold's plight. He is laid open to the heaven like a corpse waiting for the attack of vultures. Against a shimmering, cool sky, he speaks the speech "Farewell the tranquil mind!" as the rigging of ships dissolves and dissolves again in a dazzlingly complex sequence of images. An intense white light blazes about his face, as though he is speaking out of the very heart of the sun: "Farewell! Othello's occupation's gone!" At the end of the speech, a sail swells with wind, and the sun beats more fiercely down.

Unfortunately, the next scene is almost ruined by Suzanne Cloutier's performance; when Othello charges her with infidelity, calling her a "foul weed" only "as summer flies are in the shambles" she might as well have been told she has a speck on her cheek. But Welles's own intensity saves the scene from ruin. And the final shot is powerful, as the crushed and bewildered Desdemona is seen from overhead, a glittering insect darting across a vast tesselated courtyard, the camera rushing toward Othello as he stares down at her from behind a pillar, asking Iago for the poison to destroy her with, hearing with approval that he should strangle her in the very bed she has supposedly contaminated.

camera tracks with them in long sweeping shots on the battlements, emphasizing the doggedness of the deceiver's attempt. The conversation continues in Othello's rooms, with the Moor framed in a mirror, his anguished face haunted by Iago's behind him.

After Iago's distorted reflection, we see Desdemona's stricken with anguish. From Emilia Iago snatches the handkerchief which he believes will incriminate Desdemona; it is to seem to have been a token of her passion for Cassio. When Othello challenges Iago to prove her a whore, he threatens Iago on the battlements, seeming almost to be about to hurl him to the rocks below, the two figures as vertiginously poised as Michael and Grisby at Acapulco. Iago shrinks backward, looking down in terror at the shore that might in a minute dash him to pieces.

There follows one of the most powerful scenes in Welles's whole *oeuvre*: a boy plays a lute in a Turkish bath, and almost nude figures muscularly gleam through the swirl of rising steam. The thick, twanging notes of the lute tremble through the sweating room as Roderigo looks stupified, staring transfixed at a candle spinning on a string. Roderigo makes a flabby and effeminate attempt to end Cassio's life, encouraged by Iago's promise that he shall soon enjoy Desdemona's flesh. The lute grows more frantic every minute as we invade a forest of bodies and towels, an avalanche of water tumbling down, steam and wooden slats. An indecisive whirl of action is followed by the thrusts of a sword through floorboards — Iago pursuing Roderigo.

A wind whistles around the walls as Othello's shadow moves powerfully on the walls of the nuptial bed chamber. Emilia delivers her speech about the plight of womanhood and moves away. Othello remains — an ever more threatening presence. The screen is full of shadows, and it becomes superbly pitch-black at the moment when Othello utters the words, "It is the cause, it is the cause my soul." There is a clang of iron doors accom-

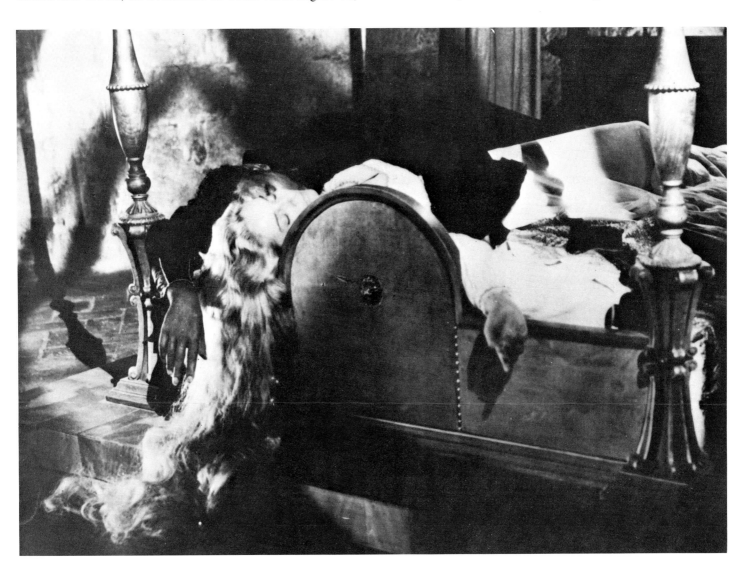

panying the speech (the music indicated in the screen-play was not used) and, as Othello moves toward the bed for the first time wordless singing wells up. A forest of pillars fills the frame; Desdemona moves nervously and lies down as he snuffs out the candles at the altar; he looms over us, and sweeps aside the curtains. Her eyes are closed; she lies stiff and waiting.

As he instructs her to make confession, he seems to swell with muscle and potency, virility turned to a grim purpose. When he cries "Strumpet!" his voice resounds in an echo chamber; he puts a scarf over her face, tightening it so that it seems already a death mask. Her face becomes a shapeless blur as he kisses her, stifling her. Bells, whirling smoke, agonized cries outside as retainers race through balustrades: the explosion of violent action is brilliantly contrasted with the still horror of the preceding murder.

As Othello turns at Emilia's knock, Desdemona's body rolls off the bed and crashes to the floor in a tangle of sheets. Her dead body, as Emilia hovers in anguish over it, blurs and freezes into a still, a stunning, utterly Wellesian idea.

Emilia discloses finally the truth of Desdemona's statement and is stabbed to death by Iago; her death is shot from floor level, like the death of Elsa Bannister. Othello stabs himself and learns that he is stripped of his power and Cassio is now ruler of Cyprus; his death is seen subjectively, the ceiling whirling round as he experiences an attack of vertigo, the choir shrilling, windows spinning, the bed now the focus of the composition as witnesses peer down from a hole in the ceiling and Othello carries Desdemona's body to the bed. His face is isolated in complete darkness as he delivers his final speech, and as he falls, the camera swoops down on the two bodies, and the door concealing the hole is slammed shut. We return to the funeral procession, the bodies loom against the skyline, and the work is over. The end titles are printed over reflections of rigging, flickering light, ships in water — images of Othello's lost career at sea. Despite all the vagaries of shooting, Welles never made a more coherent and beautiful film; the lucid, dashing, vibrant style has seldom been so perfectly wedded to its subject.

10. MR. ARKADIN
or CONFIDENTIAL REPORT

There is little of interest to be said about the shooting of *Mr. Arkadin,* which remains one of Welles's few fiascoes. He began work on it in 1951 while appearing on British radio to pay the heavy bills on *Othello.* Further preparation was done while he appeared in a stage production of *King Lear* for Peter Brook in 1953. He evidently wanted to recapture and duplicate the success of *Citizen Kane* in the story of a European tycoon resembling Kruger, the match king. (Welles was also said to have been haunted by the character of the armaments manufacturer Sir Basil Zaharoff since playing a similar role in *Ten Million Ghosts.)*

In 1954 he finally succeeded in a miracle: a group of Swiss and Spanish backers found the money to support him in his new film. He shot over eight months, in all weathers, with a scratch crew, often using hotel furniture, on location in Spain, Germany, and France. Patricia Medina, the wife of his old friend Joseph Cotten, was cast as the heroine; Robert Arden, an indifferent actor Welles had met while appearing in the Harry Lime radio series in London two years earlier, appeared as the bewildered hero (he was bought out of the cast of *Guys and Dolls* for the part).

The film was shown in London late in 1955 and received mysteriously good reviews.[1] Welles always claims it was ruined by the distributor — vandalously recut and rearranged. One only hopes that he is right.

Mr. Arkadin[2] is, together with *The Trial,* Welles's least satisfactory film, so fragmentary and ruinous that we need not dwell on it in painful detail. The writing is abominable; and the character of Arkadin is a mere joke, a creature of fancy rather than the tremendous creation that Kane is.

Nevertheless, portions of the film have power. As Van Stratten, a shoddy adventurer typical of Welles's unglamorous heroes, trudges through the snows of Germany or threads his way through the nightclubs and palmlined streets of the French Riviera in search of the truth about the mysterious Arkadin, he encounters some impressive grotesques. We remember, after we have forgotten the bumptious comedy drama of the rest, the top-hatted skeletal flea-circus proprietor played by Mischa Auer, the ferocious gangleader of Katina Paxinou and her flabby mate, a corrupt Mexican hero; the world-weary aristocrat of Suzanne Flon, and above all Akim Tamiroff's hopeless relic Jakob longing for a last meal of goose livers. Exaggerated, weird, childishly comical, these figures still exert a potently repulsive appeal.

And the film fascinates as a record of an obsession. Underneath all the bad recording, the jumble of accents, and the disconcerting sound of Welles's own voice cropping up to dub character after character, there is a strong narrative thread. Van Stratten may be wretchedly played by Robert Arden, but as he probes into the dark labyrinth of Gregori Arkadin's past, we follow him with the

[1]The facts in this introduction are based on Peter Noble, *The Fabulous Orson Welles* (London: Hutchinson, 1956).

[2]Welles has disowned authorship of the novel.

fascination of visitors to a great cave. The maze goes on, the line we follow is teased out, until we are inextricably involved in the quest.

The basic thesis is intriguing. A man dies suddenly amid the looming crates of a Naples freight yard, blurting out information that leads Van Stratten to a meeting with the fabulous Arkadin, who wants every detail of his unsavory past rediscovered and — by means of a series of murders — blotted out. The purpose is to conceal Arkadin's own wickedness from his daughter. It is the story of a search and its thwarting by the quarry who started it, told with maddening, eccentric weirdness.

• • •

The film opens with simple, mysterious typed words: "A certain great and powerful king said to a poet 'What can I give you of all that I have?' He wisely replied, 'Anything, sir . . . except your secret.'" A plane is seen flying across a threatening sky above a desolate landscape, like the surface of the moon. The music accompanying this powerful image is harsh and strident. Welles as narrator says: "On December 25 an airplane was sighted off the coast of Barcelona. It was flying empty. Investigation of this case reached into the highest circles. And the scandal was very nearly responsible for the fall of at least one European government. This motion picture is a fictionalized reconstruction of the events leading up to the murder, and to the appearance, last Christmas morning, of the empty plane."[3]

The main title of the film is made up from a collage of newspaper clippings dealing with the death of Arkadin, a great tycoon of the Kane stamp. The cast, in order of appearance, is shown in film clips, as in early sound films.

As the final credits unfold, Van Stratten is seen walking across a desolate, wintry square (a shot taken from a later part of the film). The opening sequence is as bizarre as any Welles has given us. In a freight yard of

[3] A typical Welles red herring. Since the victim, Mr. Arkadin, was alone in the plane, it could only have been a suicide. And why should his death threaten an entire government?

long vistas framed by enormous unmarked crates, figures run about, casting flickering shadows, precursors of the ghostly shapes that loom in the opening of *Touch of Evil.* A man called Bracco, dying (like the character in Hitchcock's *The Man Who Knew Too Much)*, leaves a message in the ear of Van Stratten's woman, Mily, whose lover may be accused of Bracco's murder. Lying in a position like that taken by Elsa Bannister in *Lady From Shanghai,* Bracco indicates that Arkadin has been responsible for his death.

Van Stratten, determined to discover the secret of Arkadin that preoccupied the man at the moment of death, questions Mily in a cheap Riviera nightclub (the setting, seedy and palm-fringed, is well captured). He also becomes acquainted with Arkadin's daughter, Raina, played by Paola Mori, after temporarily distracting her British boyfriend, the Marquis of Rutleigh, by a fake telephone call at the nightclub where they are dining.

Arkadin's power is cleverly suggested in a lowering shot of his car as he waits outside the nightclub where Van Stratten has met Raina. A short, explicit instruction greets Van Stratten and Raina: Mr. Arkadin says that it is getting late. She disappears into the car, but not before Van Stratten has wangled an invitation to her father's party. He hitches a ride to it with Raina.

The party scene is splendidly introduced. To the high, shrill notes of a flamenco, a fairy-tale castle is seen on the horizon, "the castle," to quote from the novel, "of the magician or wicked ogre." At San Tirso, where the castle stands, the flamenco changes to a penitential chant as hooded figures with flickering candles held before them straggle through the night. In a whirl of winding pilgrims, peasants, and penitents Van Stratten finds his way to the castle, where most of the guests are dressed in bizarre, Goya-esque costumes with masks.

Here, in a room beyond the bizarre masked figures, there is a splendidly terse exchange. Arkadin, sinisterly masked, interviews Van Stratten. He is obviously convinced that the adventurer's designs on his daughter are dishonorable, and is driven to protectiveness by his own fierce desire for her, a desire he dare not and can never consummate. Across a massive bed, symbolically empty

— for Arkadin, despite his power to buy anyone he wishes, is still lonely and unfulfilled — Arkadin's bearded figure looms, as he hears Van Stratten threaten to expose him, to prepare a dossier on him. Arkadin decides — after his initial fury — to make use of the younger man. When Van Stratten returns to his hotel, Arkadin has his minions recall him.

The handling here is powerful: Arkadin's tension, the suggestion of wicked, bought assistants, the insolence (finally made usable) of Van Stratten. When Van Stratten returns, close to dawn, the party is still in full swing, and Arkadin is telling a story to a fascinated group of guests: the story of the frog and the scorpion. The scorpion wanted to cross a river by riding on a frog's back. "No," said the frog, "no thank you. If I let you on my back you will sting me, and everyone knows it is fatal to be stung by a scorpion." "Don't be silly," said the scorpion. "If I sting you, I'll die." The frog was forced to admit the logic of this and let the scorpion ride on his back. But just in the middle of the river, the frog felt a terrible pain. The scorpion had stung him. As it sank taking the scorpion with it, the frog cried: "Is that logic?" "No," the scorpion replied. "But I can't help it. It's my character." A few moments later, Arkadin shows his character by seeking from Van Stratten the means whereby he can obliterate his own past, and Van Stratten follows his own nature . . . in the end by following the trail across Europe.

An extraordinary sequence follows. The camera prowls along the outside of a row of portholes, and suddenly we are in the cabin of a ship, observed for once with awful realism as it swings and swags like a pendulum in the heavy waves of an ocean swell. A drunken Mily and a gloomy Van Stratten desperately discuss the quest for Arkadin's past; Mily reveals that Arkadin helped the Nazis during the war, organizing the escape of several to South America, a direct reference back to the time of *It's All True*.

In Copenhagen, where Arkadin was a poverty-stricken youth, Van Stratten finds "The Greatest Flea Circus on Earth." In a tiny room, under a single lamp powerful enough to illuminate the exhibits for the curious spectator, Mischa Auer brilliantly sketches in the character of "The Professor," top-hatted and cadaverous, whose fleas are his pets and only friends. Through him Van Stratten tries to trace Sophie, Arkadin's former mistress, who holds most of his secrets. A flea perched on a thin arm for feeding time; an eye seen through a huge magnifying glass; the scene has a wonderful weirdness. Van Stratten is led, though, only to tracing Trebitsch, a feeble antique dealer played by Michael Redgrave. Nervous, introspective, pottering about in a shabby dressing gown with a filthy hair net on his head, Trebitsch tells Van Stratten Sophie's surname, all the time caressing his kittens with the ferocity the professor reserved for his fleas. And, after being coaxed with a bribe, he discloses the name of the Baroness, a special policewoman who had tracked down the infamous dealings of Sophie and Arkadin years before. The Baroness, intriguingly played by Suzanne Flon, proves equally useless in giving Van Stratten what he needs. Working at a fashion house, she turns out to be dining with Arkadin himself. But she tells Arkadin about Sophie's present life: married to a retired general, in Acapulco.

In Mexico, amid a shimmer of sunlight, glittering umbrellas, and flat blue sea, Van Stratten and Arkadin converge on this ferocious woman — superbly played, with mannered, grotesque vindictiveness, evil and gross, by Katina Paxinou. This was the woman who ran the biggest gang in Central Europe, now she lives off her massive fortune, with her husband, a former hero of Mexico. Dealing cards as though she were dealing in human lives, a Russian cigarette hanging from the corner of her mouth, she is directed and played with consummate ruthlessness.

Later follows the most remarkable passage in the film, directed with a tortured intensity, wintry and violent. In the deep snows of Munich, Van Sratten tracks the one man who can turn the last key in Arkadin's past: Jacob Zouk (Akim Tamiroff), a grubby, unshaven beggar, reduced to wretched circumstances, sitting in a shabby room staring blankly ahead of him. And by now, Van

Stratten learns, Mily and Sophie and many of his other contacts have been murdered; his mission has been to locate the potential victims of Arkadin's knives.

Here, in the winter streets of Munich, as Jacob Zouk is questioned by Van Stratten, as the old man feebly seeks goose livers in return for the information he alone can give, the film briefly reaches a high level. Arkadin helps Van Stratten get Zouk's dinner of goose liver, traps Zouk and organizes a meal for Zouk himself, the figures of waiters rushing out through the icy night with dishes under hot covers, while Arkadin has made plans to murder the recipient of the meal.

And when Zouk is murdered, the truth at last dawns on Van Stratten: that he, too, must die, because he might tell Raina what he knows. He dashes to the airport ahead of his millionaire pursuer, boarding a plane which will take him to Raina and a revelation of the truth. Arkadin's army of secretaries try to get him on the plane but it is useless; it is fully booked. Arkadin, in a splendid sequence, goes to the barrier, offering any passenger a fortune if they will give him a seat on the plane. But his pleas are useless, he is mistaken for a madman and laughed at; and the plane flies off. The whir of propellers drowns his last words, and he is forced to take to the skies in a private plane.

Hovering in space, the tycoon is utterly done at last. He telephones Raina from the air, to the control tower at Barcelona airport, begging her not to listen to what Van Stratten may tell her. But it is too late. So Arkadin plunges to his doom, and we see the empty plane stalling and spiraling; the last thing this captain of empires sees in his lifetime is a forest of controls in a tiny, second-rate aircraft. It is a powerful close to the work, the plane hovering in a washed-out sky, Arkadin's body off-screen plunging to the earth, and Raina, frantic in the control tower, realizes that she has killed her father with her words. But this is still a patchwork film, a parody of *Kane,* and we cannot deny its failure.

11. TOUCH OF EVIL

In 1956 Welles returned to America after an almost unbroken sojourn of eight years abroad. He appeared in his own Broadway stage production of *King Lear,* playing it in a wheelchair when he broke his ankle, a mishap that had also occurred in the middle of shooting *Citizen Kane.*

The next year Welles had word that Albert Zugsmith, famous producer of the crudest melodramas in Hollywood, wanted him for a part in a film. This was the role of Hank Quinlan, police chief of a small American city. Hard up as ever, Welles agreed to play it. Charlton Heston, also cast, told Zugsmith he assumed Welles would be directing as well. Zugsmith — unwilling to annoy a famous star — shelved his plans to have the film directed by a routine Universal craftsman, and allowed Welles to take over the whole production and rewrite the script. Heston, an admirer of Welles, was delighted.

Shooting took place in the cold and depressing winter of 1957-1958 in Venice, a suburb of Los Angeles which a Kane-like millionaire had once converted into an imitation of the Italian city. Welles switched the script's setting from San Diego because he liked the idea of fixing the whole film in the squalid ambience of a Mexican border town, and Venice, called Los Robles in the film, with its oil wells and disused canals and Spanish architecture, was ideally appropriate. The whole area was relit and converted into a reflection of Welles's vision.

The cameraman was, as on *The Stranger* and on parts of *Ambersons,* Russell Metty — himself physically a Wellesian figure, but incomparably more pragmatic, taci-turn, and tough. Chewing away at a cigar of Wellesian proportions, he would listen to Welles's instructions quizzically, then immediately and coolly solve the most enormous technical problems. When Welles wanted the whole of the opening sequence of three minutes to be shot from a twenty-two-foot crane in one take, starting with a close-up of a time bomb dial, Metty unhesitatingly complied. In one scene he dollied from the exterior of a building to an interior, into a tiny elevator, up five floors with several people in the elevator and his operator crouched in the corner, the lights and the top of his head one-half inch out of frame, to show as the doors slid open a perfectly timed shot of Charlton Heston greeting his colleagues after taking the stairs.

Metty broke new ground, too, by avoiding back projections in a scene of a car driving through the Los Robles streets. To convey the feeling of being carried at a great speed, he fixed the camera on the hood facing two men, and placed the batteries and wires in the back seat. Artificial light was completely avoided in the daytime scenes, an unheard-of procedure in Hollywood.

Welles cut the picture completely with Virgil Vogel, then grew impatient and recut it from beginning to end with Aaron Stell, another Universal editor. He constantly recast the editing sequence, providing different interpretations of whole scenes by transpositions, frequently disrupting the continuity. Still he wasn't satisfied, and at the end of work began to become "ill, depressed and unhappy with the studio's impatience" (Stell). Characteristically, he left before final cutting, terminating his work

with the suggestion that the gunshot which kills the sheriff at the end of the film should be eliminated from the sound track. Stell could not understand why, and Welles finally left the gunshot in. Welles never saw a finished cut or even a rough cut; he obviously could not bear to do so. The one partial cut that Stell ran for him he did not look at; he looked at Stell, to study his reactions, instead.[1]

Touch of Evil barely received any American exhibition (it was not even listed in the *Motion Picture Almanac* or *Film Yearbook)* but it did gain a critical reputation in Europe and won a prize at the 1958 Brussels

Fair. Today it is frequently shown in specialized American theaters. But its total failure at the box office finished forever Welles's chances of an American comeback. His statement that it was wrecked by the studio cannot be taken seriously. Allowing for their problems, the studio cutters did a very good job on the film, and Russell Metty among others confirms that Welles's concept was followed to the letter.

Charlton Heston told me that the scenes added by the studio were directed by Harry Keller, a television director under contract with Universal. He said:

The scenes Keller made were shot in less than half a day. Contrary to rumor, the footage does not replace any mysterious material shot by Orson, but is merely structural cement

[1]Interview with Aaron Stell, Hollywood, 1969.

to clarify what the studio felt to be unnecessarily ambiguous sequences in Orson's version of the film, explaining time and place and whatnot. For today's audiences, Orson's staccato editing and ambiguities of time and place are not at all disturbing, I think. Twelve years ago this may not have been true.

Heston confirms that the studio made only slight adjustments to the film during editing, and did not interfere at all during the shooting. "The picture," he concludes, "is very close to Orson's original intent."

Touch of Evil shares with the best of Welles's films the evocation of a fully enclosed world of the imagination. Like Macbeth's Dunsinane, its setting is not intended to be a specific place but rather a universalized microcosm of corruption. Los Robles is a town consumed by wickedness, in its physical self wholly wicked, its very stones, its cramped rooms and winding streets and prowling cars, its ceaselessly flashing seedy electric signs, expressing, almost breathing the moral sickness of our age.

Paradoxically as ever, Welles relished his horrible creation. The film proves that he is as much in love with the contemporary world of violence, of thrown bombs and shrieking victims, of probing torches and rock 'n' roll's feral savagery, as he is devoted to the elegant past. This is a work of total passion, delivered at the volume of an ambulance siren.

The film's structure is serpentine, characteristically labyrinthine in its windings. Like *Kane* and *Arkadin,* it has a theme of search, but here the search is split up between the various characters. The audience's representative, occupying more vigorously than Thompson the role of investigator into a diseased world, a surgeon probing into a cancered brain, is Mike Vargas, a Mexican-American narcotics detective. He arrives in Los Robles to expose the Grandi gang, a pack of hoodlums peddling dope across the border, headed by a fat, greasy pater-familias who has amassed a fortune from various rackets. Simultaneously, Hank Quinlan, the corrupt local sheriff — representing everything Welles hates about back-slapping, venal American hicks — is seen in pursuit of the Grandis. The double chase is complicated by two drastic problems: Vargas and Quinlan clash con-

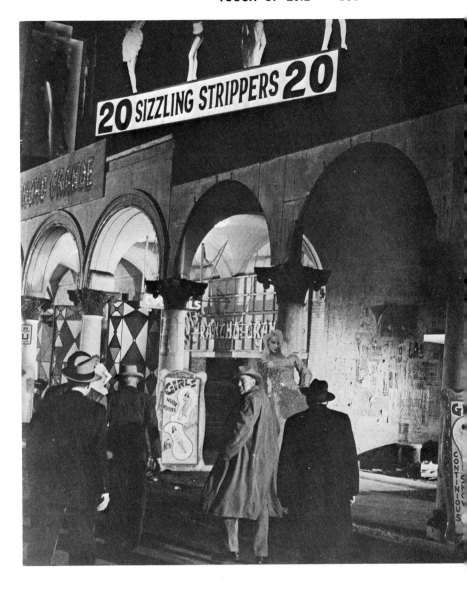

stantly, the local man bitterly resenting the encroachment on his exclusive authority, and a Los Robles tycoon, Rudi Linnekar, is blown up by the Grandis in his car, thus causing the searchers to reach for a further target: the killer.

Hank Quinlan is a very fully developed character, among the most persuasive Welles has given us. He is shown to us at first as gigantically genial, puffing at a vast cigar, one of the boys, up to his rheumy eyes in

warm, if gross, human sentiment. But within minutes we see the real man; and as the film develops, as he frames a witness and fakes evidence, we know that Welles is showing us that the law in America is as evil as the creatures of darkness it pursues.

In the end, like all Welles's evil men, Quinlan is destroyed. He becomes an extinct monster, a *Tyrannosaurus rex,* wallowing in the curd of oil that has been left in an abandoned "Venetian" canal. Yet, since Welles is portraying and creating him, he is not wholly despicable. Welles shows us his human side, the memory of his wife's murder which has made him hate Latins all his life, his sense of justice which, warped though it is, still winds like a frayed thread through his nature. And through the character of Tanya (Marlene Dietrich) the wise, infinitely worldly proprietress of the local brothel, and the devotion of his faithful lieutenant Menzies (Joseph Calleia), we see that he is capable of inspiring love, like Kane[2] — and equally incapable of giving it.

His enemy Vargas — intelligently played by Charlton Heston — is a man of tense, tortured integrity, doggedly seeking the truth, a more youthful and energetic replica of Wilson in *The Stranger.* His wife (Janet Leigh) is subjected to a series of agonizing indignities (her name, Susan, refers back directly to *Kane),* but she emerges at the end to the warmth and security of her life with her

[2]There is a deliberate parallel with Kane in one scene: Quinlan walks across a square and his voice booms, "The people of this county!" in exactly the same tone as Kane used.

husband. Like Mary Longstreet she, too, can sleep deeply without evil dreams.

These central figures persuade, and so does Grandi — an extraordinary portrait by Akim Tamiroff. Gross, vulgar, cowardly and obscene, hair slicked down conceitedly with grease, eye popping and jowls wobbling, he is like Quinlan in miniature, hunter and hunted almost identical, save for the important differences of Grandi's weakness and hysteria. Grandi's sons, tough, leather-jacketed, swarthily sexy, are the embodiments of brutal virility, symbols of youth out for murderous excitement, blood-kin to the Wild One.

Various supporting figures are introduced in almost a spirit of intramural joking: Joseph Cotten appears as a policeman, Zsa Zsa Gabor as (rudely) a whorehouse madam, Mercedes McCambridge as a mannish, strapping over-age female hoodlum. This curious element of high camp in the film exists also in several quarrel scenes, with everyone becoming shriller and shriller and cutting across each other's dialogue, and in the sequence in which Susan is followed in a dark room by the probing, almost phallic light of the Grandi boys' torches. This quirkish casting and handling has the effect of damaging the film's realistic mood of squalor. The frivolous exhibitionism that frequently emerges here shows Welles's worst side, his habit of running away from the finality of a serious statement to perpetrate some wild schoolboy joke.

Russell Metty's camerawork serves Welles's intentions superbly. The opening shot is breathtaking: beginning with a close-up of the time bomb set for the destruction of the Linnekar automobile, it swings on a gigantic crane past a series of houses covered in peeling posters and across a busy street, encompassing groups of people and the chief heroic protagonists (as well as the victims) in three minutes of almost incredible virtuosity, finally coming to its close as the car bursts into flames. The camera, everywhere mobile and free, whirls round the great square of Venice, sweeps through arches, pounces in as a bomb explodes with a smoky hiss against a wall, perches on a car hood as two men talk about murder, squats outside a window as men visit a quarry, one face

almost on top of the camera in gigantic profile, or pushes through swaying beaded curtains, rushing out of darkness into brilliant light to match the tension of a bar-room brawl. Physically, the last sequence is the most remarkable of all, Quinlan and Menzies wandering along a bridge while Vargas tapes their conversation with a portable recorder below them. Here the images are overpowering: oil pumps looming like grotesque praying mantises, derricks spread against the night sky, water flashing jet black around Vargas's legs, the conversation echoing as the end of Quinlan draws near. And after that there is the extraordinary climactic shot of Quinlan foundering like a stricken beast, swallowed up in oil waste.

· · ·

The film opens to the harsh brass and pounding bongo drums of Henry Mancini's admittedly commercial, but thoroughly effective score. The opening shot establishes in very rapid strokes that Rudi Linnekar and his girl friend, a blonde floozie played by Joi Lansing (later to star in *The Fountain of Youth*) are doomed from the outset of the action. The same shot introduces us to the cheerfully married Vargas couple, and a moment later we are conscious of Welles's black humor: arriving at the frontier, Linnekar and the border official completely ignore Linnekar's floozie when she complains she can hear ticking at the back of the vehicle in tones uncannily echoing those of Susan's whining in *Kane*. The note of black humor recurs when, just as Vargas says to his wife "Do you realize I haven't kissed you in over an hour?" the Linnekar car blows up.

The next scenes are brilliantly handled: police, witnesses, and criminals scurry like termites as the whole evil town is disturbed by the murder in its midst. Welles faultlessly evokes the sensation of accident or murder: he matches to the feverish emotions of the event the neurotic movements of Metty's camera, the flare of the fire that burns the couple, the eruption of figures from a local whorehouse, and, as his visual climax, Quinlan arriving, shot from below eye level, eyes squinting in a warp and woof of lines, the stomach bulging over the trousers, a cigar stuck crudely in the corner of his mouth as he struggles out of his car. Two voices "off" have the same chorus effect as the Chinese girls commenting on the trial in *The Lady From Shanghai* and the town women talking in *Ambersons*: "An hour ago Rudi Linnekar had this town in his pocket." "Now you could strain him through a sieve."

Identified by Linnekar's daughter ("I guess that's my father"), the tycoon's charred body, with its companion, spurs Quinlan on to discover the killer. He traps a boy who had been having an affair with the Linnekar girl by planting dynamite in his bathroom. The interrogation of the nervous youth is held in a tiny, cramped, suffocatingly claustrophobic room, crammed with police; the effect is to give us a concentrated picture of the horror of the third degree.

Here, the black humor continues, Quinlan saying to the boy, "An old lady on Main Street picked up a shoe. The shoe contained a foot. We're going to make you pay for that, boy."

Vargas is determined that the boy, whom he discovers immediately has been framed, should not be railroaded to the electric chair. Here Quinlan's first serious clash with Vargas takes place: Quinlan sees that he is in danger of having his skulduggery exposed by this man of impeccable integrity. Vargas, in fact, from now on is involved in a double hunt: to expose not only the Grandis but also Quinlan.

Meanwhile, the Grandis seize the opportunity of Vargas's absence from Susan's hotel to harrass her continually, the boys threatening to rape her, their father trying to intimidate her. For safety's sake, Vargas (in a scene directed by Harry Keller) tells her to cross into Mexico and take refuge in a motel there. She agrees, and shelters in a prefabricated monstrosity like an army camp in the middle of a desert. Her only "protection" there is a skinny manager terrified of women and certain the Grandis are going to swoop, which they do: first they tease Susan through the walls and play rock 'n' roll unbearably loudly, then they break into her room, led by a ferocious Mercedes McCambridge, and pump her full of drugs. The final shot of this electrifying sequence shows

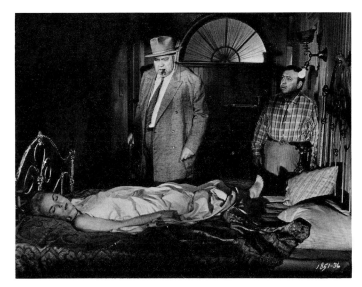

them crouched over the bed, some boys preparing to mount her while others stab her with needles.

Vargas follows Susan to the motel, and there is a tiresomely eccentric sequence, wrecking the mood of realism, when he cross-examines the manager, who twitters and jerks in terror against the night sky. Susan, meanwhile, has been returned to a hotel, moaning and almost unconscious. Quinlan, who has temporarily "befriended" Grandi to obtain help in framing Susan on a drug charge, realizes that Grandi, who is a coward, may give him away, and he decides to kill him now that he has served his purpose.

The death of Grandi is a fantastically violent episode even in this violent work: Quinlan and Grandi locked in a death struggle over the brass bed, electric lights from across the street jittery and distorted through the windows, Susan on the bed, the music whining, Grandi gurgling, and finally his killer's overwhelming bulk withdrawing to show the dead man's face horribly distorted against the wall. Moments later, Susan struggles almost naked onto the fire escape, while her husband, oblivious to her plight, plunges into a saloon the Grandis frequent and, followed by the camera as dogged as a bloodhound, smashes the place to pieces.

The final sequences of the film show Vargas's efforts

to clear his wife's name and destroy the Grandis and Hank Quinlan. He manages to persuade Quinlan's henchman, by producing evidence from the Los Robles Hall of Records, that Quinlan was guilty of attempting to frame both the lover of Linnekar's daughter and Susan (with the aid of the Grandis). The henchman agrees to walk with Quinlan on a bridge across the canals, where he can obtain the facts from Quinlan, and Vargas can record the confession. The plan comes off; and Quinlan is shot like an animal.

The film's last moment is utterly Wellesian. Coming by the canal, Tanya, perhaps the only woman who loved and understood Quinlan, looks wryly at the body, all Marlene Dietrich's worldly knowledge and laconic stoical honor showing in the humorous eyes, in the sardonic curl of the lips. She sums up the humanist argument that all along has saved the film's portrait of viciousness from being in itself vicious: "He was some kind of a man. What more can you say about people? *Adios!*"

12. THE TRIAL

The opportunity to make a film of Kafka's *The Trial* came in 1959, when Welles was acting in Abel Gance's *Austerlitz*. The producers of *Austerlitz,* the Salkind brothers, offered Welles a quite generous budget (650 million francs) and a choice of subject in the great works of literature; he settled on Kafka and decided to design every aspect of the film himself, creating an unsettling, Kafka-esque world of no particular time yet symbolic of the present, with offices and courtrooms and studio interconnecting, and the action taking place grayly indoors. Gradually, as K's plight became worse, the sets were to disintegrate, until he would be left pinned and helpless in his fate against a blank expanse, an image of death from which every last piece of set material had been removed.

Alas, Welles was not to be permitted to make the film he planned. The Salkinds ran short of money, forcing him to improvise drastically. He began shooting in Zagreb, still hoping that funds might be found to execute his conception at the Salkinds' hired studio in Paris (they were not). He had to transform real Zagreb streets into reflections of a Kafka-esque world. William Chappell wrote in *The Sunday Times* (London) on May 27, 1962:

"In the middle distance (of the scene Welles was shooting) stood a group of low, dilapidated houses with sagging, tiled roofs. Behind them towered a huge, unfinished block of new flats, gaunt, hideous, and somehow threatening. Nearby stood a gnarled tree dusted with a drift of blossom, a hag in a bridal veil." This was to be the scene of K's execution in the final scene, an abstract of an urban wasteland: the world we all inhabit.

After three weeks in Zagreb, Welles moved to Paris. Restless over the fact that he could not make the film he wanted, he stood sleepless at five one morning at the window of his hotel in Paris. Chappell wrote:

"He became half-hypnotized by the twin moons of the two great clocks that decorate the deserted and crumbling [station], that triumphantly florid example of the Belle Epoque that looms so splendidly across the trees of the Tuileries Gardens. He remembered he had once been offered the empty station [as a location] and his curiosity was aroused.

By 7:30 he had explored the lunatic edifice, vast as a cathedral: the great vulgar corpse of a building in a shroud of dust and damp, surrounded and held together by a maze of ruined rooms, stairways and corridors. He had discovered Kafka's world, with the genuine texture of pity and terror on its damp and scabrous walls, real claustrophobia in its mournful rooms; and also intricacies of shape and perspective on a scale that would have taken months and cost fortunes to build.

Another visitor, Eugene Archer, added in *The New York Times:*

The enormous latticed ceiling [of the Gare] emitted a dusky atmosphere entirely appropriate to Kafka's somber mood, while the acres of empty floor space gave Mr. Welles's indispensable tracks and cranes ample room for any effect he desired. For intimate scenes he had his set designer decorate the tiny cubicles lining the old station's walls, and cheerfully shifted his camera from one set to another guided only by his creative mood at the moment.

This was, of course, an extension of his technique in *Ambersons* and *Macbeth,* of using multipurpose sets. Welles and his cameraman Edmond Richard used only reflected light in the film, to create a gray, uniform effect, rather like that in the railway station scene in *Ambersons*. This, Welles felt, would make up for the lack of gray uniform sets he wanted. For a scene in which K runs from an artist's studio along a narrow corridor, Welles mounted the camera on a wheelchair and had it pushed by a champion Yugoslav runner. The purpose of the film was to use the Gare d'Orsay, as well as the locations in Zagreb, to show that every part of K's environment interconnected: courtroom, artist's studio, K's flat, the bomb site where he meets his end. Roads and corridors wind together to form a labyrinth, with K a futile moth beating about it, lost and blind but constantly seeking reassertion of his dignity as a living creature.

Welles's intention was to create a composite world, a microcosm of the totalitarian society. His own designs would probably have achieved this. But the converted station and the Zagreb locations had the effect of diffusing his vision. Their resplendent baroque quality, in the context, worked against his own concept: that human lives can be as ugly and cramped as those of insects.

Kafka's novel, icily gray, claustrophobically compressed, is a parable of the human condition; its central figure K, played tiresomely in the film by Anthony Perkins, scurries like a doomed rat around his mortal cage. He makes futile attempts to seduce his landlady, he becomes increasingly stifled as the hand of the law reaches out to flatten him. Welles reworks the story in the terms of his own vision, letting us see the dangers of the great

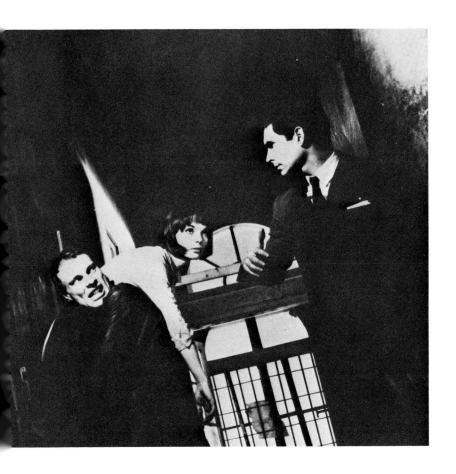

While the surface of the film is inappropriately baroque, its internal life is close to Kafka's yet paradoxically too faint and dimly seen. An artist in any medium, is, of course, free to alter any work he seizes on, to convert it in terms of his own vision. We have already noted how Welles has transmuted Shakespeare by his own talent, by seizing on Shakespearean themes of power and the ruin of power and carving off those elements in the plays which did not suit his central argument. The life of Hearst was justifiably distorted and simplified to provide a simple object lesson in the ruin of a man raised by a commercial organization and wrecked by a commercial world, while Tarkington was seized on and heightened to show the ruinous complacency of the old order. And in modernizing Kafka, Welles acidly intended us to see the power can also be invisible and all-pervading, that the vast machinery of world politics can crush a man like an insect.

He simply fluffs the film, and the reason lies, I think, in the very privacy of his vision, his muffled remoteness from the public. In most of his films this is counterbalanced by the other side of his genius: the promoter's punch and drive that can deliver even the most obscure artistic point with brilliant energy. In *The Trial*, however, he has withdrawn completely from us, so that we have to peer into his world through the narrowest of apertures. It might be argued that, in the context, this very narrowness is appropriate. But it is one thing to portray narrowness, and another to convey it narrowly.

There are certain artists — Antonioni among them — who can speak in a whisper yet, by the perfect enunciation of every syllable, make us understand an argument. The Welles of *The Trial* is not in that category. When he whispers, the details are slurred. Here, his visual ideas are not clearly conveyed in the physical presentation of the work. The photography, which should be subtly gray, is merely flat and textureless, wearing out the eye and numbing the brain. The sound track, which should be furtively resonant and subdued, is characteristically scrambled, a mess of inchoate sounds.

The result is, for me, an agonizing experience; there is no film I have seen which for me as totally defies the eye and mind. After seven viewings, I have continued to

anonymous powers which hang threateningly over us, finishing his film meaningfully on a shot of a mushroom cloud. In *The War of the Worlds* on radio he showed America the perils of complacency; in *Kane,* the perils of isolationism; in *Ambersons,* the perils of clinging to the past. In *The Trial* his admonition is that we must fight for our own identity before it is swallowed up in the giant international/totalitarian urban state we have created for ourselves.

It is a major theme, but it is, alas, delivered to us in a hoarse, exhausted whisper. The film's technical shortcomings, especially its appalling sound track, marred by wretched dubbing, and the second-rate playing of its cast — including Jeanne Moreau, abominable as Fraulein Bürstner, and Perkins, stiff and gauche in entirely the wrong way as K — are not its most important defects.

have the feeling of struggling through wads of cotton wool to reach the interior of the work; what follows is a record of what I have seen; it cannot convey the sense of concern at Welles's recessiveness that I have experienced on each occasion. For me, *The Trial* is a dead thing, like some tablet found among the dust of forgotten men, speaking a language that has much to say to us, but whose words have largely been rubbed away.

• • •

The plainly lettered credits unfold to the strains of Albinoni. Against a series of pin-screen drawings by Alexandre Alexeieff and his wife,[1] showing a prisoner trapped in a series of prison settings, Welles's voice reads the words: "Before the Law there stands a guard. A man comes from the country begging admittance to the Law. But the Guard cannot admit him." This is the narrative given in the book to a priest, and it is intended to summarize the film's theme: it is the story of a man who tries to bribe the Guard so as to obtain justice, and he waits for years, even getting to know "the fleas in the guard's fur collar." He ages, his sight is dimmed, but he still cannot get in, and he asks why no one else has sought admittance; the guard yells into his ear that the door is meant only for him — and now it is going to be closed. Welles adds: "It has been said that the logic of this story is the logic of a dream — or a nightmare." The whole film is dedicated to the idea of a man trying desperately and futilely to obtain justice before he is flung into a pit to die.

The film's opening is in intention powerful. We begin with a shot of K's face, taken from behind as he lies in bed, waking from a nightmare to a nightmare in reality. As in the opening of *Kane* a figure enters aslant a door: K sits up and realizes at once that he is in the grip of the anonymous police. The camera withdraws slowly, coldly

[1]This process involves a screen composed of thousands of pins which can be raised or depressed to create shadows or highlights; its painstaking results have previously been known through a number of short films, the most striking of which is *The Nose,* based on a story by Gogol.

observing the new arrival: a detective sent to interrogate him. The endless ticking of a clock runs right through the scene, reminding us, like the cold gray light, that this is only 6:14 A.M., an hour of vulnerability, of human weakness. K talks and talks desperately as he changes into his clothes, the camera observing him in a characteristically Wellesian long take, his elongated form frequently observed at full length, like a stick insect looming through the dawn light. The whole sequence is directed to suggest the queasy unbalanced feeling of a sudden awakening, a stark introduction to approaching death. The apartment's white walls and impersonal electrical equipment, the oppressively low ceilings, give a feeling of a coffin closing inexorably in.

The dialogue, unhappily, with its flat, level recording, negates almost the whole of the intended visual effect of the scene: A typical Welles exchange, based on mutual misunderstanding and involving the question of whether K will or will not dress in the hall, becomes merely aggravating in the context.

The dialogue is, in fact, excessively feeble throughout the scene: K says at one stage: "This could be a joke, I suppose. An elaborate practical joke by some of my friends in the office." At another, asked the nature of an

cussion about an "ovular shape" concealed under a rug, and about the site of a dental chair once screwed into the floor; Mrs. Grubach (K's landlady) makes some banal comments on the interrogation.

Fraulein Bürstner (Jeanne Moreau) arrives. She is a seedy cabaret entertainer who drives Mrs. Grubach to a puritanical remark: "She not only performs in *that place,* but there's drinking afterwards, with men." Jeanne Moreau is an exhausted figure in a white raincoat, who exerts a strong attraction for K, a long dolly shot from his apartment to hers echoing their mutually excited but aggravated state.

The scene which establishes K's feelings for her is handled with a tragic clumsiness, indicating how far Welles's talent had declined at the time. The dialogue is wretchedly inept, worthy of a B-picture: "You're not getting any funny ideas, are you, just because I knocked on your door?" And Moreau's performance, attempting all the world-weariness of a Dietrich merely looks tired. ("It's been a long hard night" now seems sadly comic, an echo of the Beatles.) Their half-hearted approach to lovemaking altogether lacks the pathos and irony called for. And the flat recording and toneless delivery again destroy the effect of K's confession that all his life he has been "sick with guilt."

The scenes in the huge office building that follow are better handled, though still seriously affected by the defects of the recording and photography: the office set is on a massive scale, even if the intended impression of a gigantic impersonal work force tapping at machines is conveyed with only a fraction of the force of Vidor's similar scenes in *The Crowd.* Outside a woman struggles with a trunk across an urban wasteland, a world of desolate grays. K offers to help her, but his offer is rejected petulantly. After that is the best moment in the film: as K enters the court the door bursts open and suddenly a gigantic crowd of people leaps to its feet accusingly. The contrast between the cold silence of the corridor outside, the thunderclap of the door, and the sudden rush of sound, of accusing voices, may not be Kafka, but it is splendid Welles.

K is asked if he is a house painter; answering in the

instrument (why?) in the corner, K says, "That's my pornograph, I mean my phonograph,"[2] and elaborate play is made of this error. There is an equally tiresome dis-

[2] If symbolism was intended here, it is indistinct in the action.

negative he hears a burst of laughter from the throng —
and one can only regret most bitterly here the lack of adequate sound recording: what a good recordist could have
done with the scene! K's defense is observed from high
overhead and from below eye level; meanwhile an attempted rape is taking place at the door in the middle of
the proceedings. Threading his way through the office that
forms parts of the same nightmare structure of which the
courtroom is a part, K discovers three of the detectives
crammed into a stifling room, two of them about to be
flogged by the third. As the struggling figures bang the
bare bulb of the ceiling light to and fro, K desperately

wrangling with the men, the victims stripped to the waist
as the whip descends, there is a sensation of meaningless
violence, the whip lashing the lamp as it beats down, the
bestial figures crammed tight, inextricably entangled in
a series of cuts done at express speed.

From there, in an echo of similar shock cuts in *Kane*
— but the echo is, alas, a faint one — a chandelier
blazes into view, a luxurious contrast with the wilderness
of stone that filled the preceding shot. K is in the stalls
of a theater, and there is a splendid effect — only slightly
marred by the tonelessness of the actual image — of the
shadows of the great curtains parting over the audience,

like dark wings on a thousand faces. K's uncle takes him to see the Advocate, Hassler, played by Welles himself, who may be able to defend him. Corrupt, bloated, the Advocate sits up in bed, interviewing K with barely concealed contempt amid flickering candles, surrounded by clouds of cigar smoke, as hopeless a representative of the law as Hank Quinlan. His Chief Clerk is a quivering neurotic wreck, trembling at Hassler's every word. The Advocate's nurse lures K into an attempted seduction among the Advocate's vast collection of records. He does not succeed, and the uncle warns that the Nurse is the Advocate's mistress — to become involved with her would alienate the Advocate.

Later, the nurse advises K to go to the court painter, Titorelli, who may be able to help him; the painter lives at the top of a flight of stairs behind the courthouse. The conversation with Titorelli is the most striking sequence in the film. K climbs a narrow staircase, surrounded by the darting, tittering forms of children, their eyes staring and their hands fluttering past him. Titorelli's studio is like a birdcage itself, and all through their conversation the eyes of the children flash past its wooden bars, and the hissing, rustling, and giggling goes on while K beats about like a trapped creature, gasping in this windowless enclosure for a breath of air.

The bizarre studio connects claustrophobically, K finds, with the great courthouse itself, and he runs down the long lines of the doomed, the faceless old who are waiting hopelessly for just one possible judgment. He rushes in terror down corridor after corridor, like Elsa Bannister in *The Lady from Shanghai,* observed in complex tracking shots, the children in a corridor parallel with his, screaming with laughter through the slats, the laughter blended with a musical accompaniment. His shadow looms ahead of him, seeming to be running backwards, as he pounds along a subterranean corridor, like Harry Lime in *The Third Man.*

Running into a great cathedral, K discovers there is no solace in religion. He rejects the priest's offer of help, and the booming voice of the Advocate pursues him until he knows there is nothing left except death, that neither religion nor the law can help. Marched off by

the two policemen who figured in the story earlier, K is taken to a quarry, where he refuses to take the suicide knife they gave him. Instead, he blows himself up with dynamite, and the image dissolves into a fatal mushroom cloud, followed by a laugh that evidently symbolizes K's final triumph — the triumph of humanity over the system. Kafka's ending is far more powerful. In his novel the arresting presences take off K's coat and waistcoat, place his head on a rock, and carve his chest open with a knife. He dies "like a dog."

Welles saw K as "a little bureaucrat, I consider him guilty."[3] He saw him also as Prometheus; but he is "something that represents evil . . . he is not guilty as accused, but he is guilty, all the same. He belongs to a guilty society, he collaborates with it." In Welles's original screenplay, the executioners stab K to death. Welles introduced a more positive climax because "That ending

[3]Interview with Juan Corbos, Miguel Rubio, and J. A. Pruneda, *Cahiers du Cinéma,* April, 1965.

didn't please me. I believe that in that case it is a question of a 'ballet' written by a pre-Hitler Jewish intellectual. After the death of six million Jews, Kafka would not have written that . . . I made K's character more active. I do not believe that passive characters are appropriate to drama."

I have referred earlier to the muffled effect the film has for me, its recessiveness, and in these last remarks of Welles's I detect another clue to the cause of my feeling of dissatisfaction with the work. Welles says that K is guilty, yet his treatment of the film suggests that K is nothing of the kind; his whole handling of Anthony Perkins's nervously vulnerable personality suggests a warm sympathy not only for the actor but for the character. Yet both treatment and playing seem to me, paradoxically, passive and numb. Therefore, I am not merely baffled by the presentation, but by the fact that the presentation is having an effect that Welles *does not intend*. It is as though a painter were not merely to blur his effects, but to plan them in bold colors and then execute them in the palest tempera. The effect is a cancelation of the artist's very self; a denial, not merely of Kafka, which we may perhaps tolerate, but of Welles himself.

13. CHIMES AT MIDNIGHT

Now that we come to Welles's last released feature at the time of writing, we may consider his position in Europe after the completion of *The Trial*. He had been there fourteen years, and they had been restless, disorganized, and exhausting years, punctuated as I have said earlier by sharp feelings of nostalgia for the cozy, intricately complex world of the Hollywood studio system. By 1951 that system itself had broken into pieces, shattered by the fatal action of the American government in severing the studios from the chains of theaters they owned. *Kane* and *Ambersons* had owed their beauty not only to Welles but to the exquisitely gifted artisans who, in a small, intimate "cottage" studio like RKO, could execute each idea with the skill of Japanese workers in ivory. These films had the "RKO look," as well as the Welles vision; his influence may, as everyone says, have spread through Hollywood at that time like a flashing stream, but poverty-stricken RKO, with its flawless composite and counterpoint of unsung talents, influenced him no less deeply, as, of course, did Gregg Toland.

In Europe he became more and more a "character," a public spectacle, freakish and unpredictable as a twisting tornado. He traveled constantly, as though, like Arkadin or Eric Ambler's Dimitrios, he wanted to kick up every spoor mark. Now he was in Rome, now Madrid, now London; his addresses seemed to change by the week or even the day; he had the knack, shared by Garbo, of attracting enormous publicity by spectacularly avoiding it. He would play seemingly any role, in a variety of false noses for which he appeared to have unnerving pre-dilection: he turned up on a ferry to Hong Kong, a Vienna Prater wheel, a Scottish moor in a size-fifty kilt, more booming, grotesque, and vaster by the month. The great, rheumy, haunted eyes in their cross-stitching of wrinkles seemed to be trumpeting for help, and then a gigantic geyser spout of laughter, apparently beginning at the boot heels, swelling up the great legs, bubbling through the gaseous stomach, and shooting like a jet through the tobacco-raw throat, would fly and engulf us. A moment later the laugh would subside, the shoulders hunch, and the rhino's eyes sink glumly in the flesh.

Images of Welles persist from that difficult European decade: the great shape ploughing and snorting through a Madrid street with Kenneth Tynan, attenuated Laurel to his Hardy, in attendance on Welles's whims with Boswellian notebook and *Observer* or *Playboy* or *Holiday* expense account; desultory television appearances, trudging knee-deep through lines of marshmallow consistency, relieved — if that is the word — by one brief comic appearance across the Atlantic in *I Love Lucy;* the voice booming hollowly on the sound track of an eye-splitting Cinerama travelogue set in the South Pacific, bringing laughs to laconic Sydney audiences as it darkly thundered the words, "Australia, the sleeping giant." Freakish sports were indulged: a wallowing venture into Ionesco *(Rhinoceros),* a BBC visitor's guide to the Black Museum at Scotland Yard, the voice dwelling lushly over garotte or deadly blade; a bizarre play about Hollywood written in French and staged in Paris, with an imitation art film in its midst, *The Unthinking Lobster;* dogged safaris

through Africa in *The Roots of Heaven* and *The Southern Star;* turns as Benjamin Franklin in *Lafayette,* a parodied Korda in *The VIPS,* a self-parody in *Rogopag.*

Miraculously, through the scrappy jobs, the bits and pieces of work desperately picked up, with more and more noses affixed and more and more lines dug up from the compost heap of better days, Welles the artist somehow has managed to survive. In 1960 the foreshadowing of a new film occurred, when he directed a condensed version of *Five Kings,* a compendium of the Falstaff plays, in Belfast and Dublin with Hilton Edwards, who had so perceptively taken him on more than a quarter of a century before. He became obsessed, between other obsessions, with filming a work which, in its longer form,

had pressed him into service in Hollywood. The wheel swung full circle; the creation that had forced him into a designing a masterpiece almost became one itself.

Financing it with an astonishingly scattered range of sources, he began in the early sixties to put *Chimes at Midnight* or *Falstaff* together. Finally, he shot it, strugling to finish it over weeks that dragged into months, in the flashing winter snows of the Spanish sierra in 1964. Castles, few of them appropriate, reminiscent often of Arkadin's, were made to serve for English ones. Cathedrals were invaded: Henry IV, whose relationship with the church was never easy, would have been astonished to find himself, incarnated by John Gielgud, holding court in the resplendent Catholic apse of Cordova.

English actors and actresses flew in and out for brief appearances. Then came Welles's dread: the cutting. Threatening a nervous breakdown with every puffing minute, he started to have the film scored by Lavagnino (who had so marvelously handled the music for *Othello*), and to dub it, changing his mind all the time. (He flew Shirley Cameron, co-star of the Irish production, to Madrid to dub Jeanne Moreau, then decided to use Miss Moreau herself instead.) An extraordinary episode, recounted to me by the film writer Barrie Pattison, occurred in London. One of Welles's tracks was being cut in a tiny studio there; yet the room's door was so small that Welles could not get through it to see what was happening.

Welles recorded his own dialogue separately from the Shakespearean players', fearing that his American intonations would fit badly with theirs, thereby drastically reducing the film's aural flow. Matching of lip movements to words became more and more haphazard. Welles can never have more keenly missed the attention of his *Kane* and *Ambersons* recording experts, James G. Stewart and Bailey Fesler, as he sweated it out for months with technicians across Europe.

Simultaneously, he was working on and off on *Don Quixote,* at one stage call *Don Quixote's Trip to the Moon.* The filming had begun as early as 1955, starring the Mexican actor Francisco Rieguera as Quixote, and Akim Tamiroff as Sancho Panza. Modern in setting, shot over ten years, the film became progressively stranger as fashions in clothing altered over a decade. Peter Cowie has noted that one scene showed Don Quixote in a cinema, rushing to the aid of a screen heroine menaced by villains, only to split the screen: a combination of Don Quixote's fight with the Moors and *Too Much Johnson.* The famous windmill becomes a power shovel that sucks Quixote into churning mud; at the end, unlike K, the Don and his companion survive the atom bomb. For years, characteristically, Welles avoided the film's completion. Then, early in 1969, came the inevitable Wellesian tragic conclusion: Francisco Rieguera died. One doubts if this work, apparently a self-portrait of a man trying to be an individualist in an increasingly im-

personal world, and perhaps intended to link with *The Trial* as part of a possible trilogy on a theme of man against the machines, will ever be released.

• • •

In adapting the Falstaff story for the screen, Welles stripped away much of the comedy to show the encroaching tragedy ahead, so that even in the early scenes, when the fat knight and his gadfly friend are jollying in the inn, there are premonitions of their friendship's dissolution.

In this interpretation Falstaff becomes a doomed figure of wholesome humanity, of sensual strength. "His goodness," Welles has said, "is like bread and wine." The film is a long lament for Merrie England, symbolized by Falstaff himself.

In order to tighten the film, to give it coherence, Welles not only reduced Shakespeare's text but his own as well: he removed an opening sequence of the murder of Richard II and Henry Bolingbroke's debarkation. Although the film breaks no new ground technically, it is often expert in its use of crane shots and editing; in the battle scene each shot is cut so as to show a blow, and for every stroke made, a stroke returned.

The performances are variable: Welles's lovable, Father Christmas-like Falstaff and Keith Baxter's virile, lean, and hungry Prince Hal, a far remove from Olivier's matinee idol Henry V, are very good. The women fare badly: Jeanne Moreau is an absurdity as Doll Tearsheet (for all her effectively slatternly appearance), and Margaret Rutherford evokes unfortunate memories of Miss Marple and Madame Arcati in *Blithe Spirit,* blancmange jaw wobbling as Mistress Quickly.

Like so many of his films, *Chimes at Midnight* asserts Welles's emphasis on the mortality of human beings, on their essential fragility. While Falstaff carouses in the tavern with Prince Hal, we already see that ahead of them both lie two deaths: for Hal the death of his youth, killed by his assumption of power; for Falstaff the death of his friendship with Hal, and the death of his spirit — goodness crushed by high office. And the film powerfully reminds us of the horror and loneliness of power, as witnessed before in *Kane* and in the other Shakespearian adaptations: no more shattering sequence exists in Welles than the still, cold, and beautiful episodes of Henry IV's "Uneasy lies the head" speech, delivered with agonizing magnificence by John Gielgud.

This is a film that has a predominating mood of pain, of suffering, which makes it perhaps the most deeply felt of all Welles's works; a film that is the product of pain itself, of Welles coming to grips with the realities of middle age, old age, and death. If *Kane* was more dazzling and *Ambersons* more richly poetic, if *The Lady from Shanghai* emerges as a more striking *tour de force* of technique, then we must still reserve for *Chimes at Midnight* the special place in an artist's history we keep for the simple and profound, the momentary humble distillation of genius. Many of Welles's films have been showier; none has been nobler.

Against a background of spiky, bare trees, a hump of snowy hillock, two ancient figures wend their way: a grossly fat man, waddling uneasily on a stick, and a shriveled, toothless figure, seen in silhouette, dwarfed by the landscape. Thus, in the introductory sequence of *Chimes at Midnight,* we are introduced to Falstaff and

to Mr. Justice Shallow, both of them crumbling ruins, symbols of an England of carefree jollity and wassail doomed shortly to be destroyed.

After the beautiful opening in the snow, we move into a Breughelian barn or byre, mud-floored and arched with wooden beams. Falstaff and Shallow crouch before the flames which flicker over their faces. So perfectly is the scene realized that we can almost feel the ache of cold in old bones, the creaking of the wood, with outside the muffling benison of the snow. We fancy we can smell the thick perfume of leather, and the stink of feathers; each word spoken by the two old men chinks as loudly as an iron boot against a stirrup. To Welles's bass, reminiscing about the past ("We have heard the chimes at midnight"), the old judge's voice is by musical contrast a nervous, quavering piccolo ("Jesus, the days that we have seen!").

From the exquisite wintry stillness of this interior, we cut to the blazing splendor of the credits, restoring on a more modest, less immediately dazzling scale the style of the credits of *Othello,* and intermittently linking with images from *Macbeth* to indicate that Welles intends us to see this as the third part of a triptych or trilogy. The music is strongly reminiscent of Othello's as well: a gallant show of martial jollity, a blaze of brass and woodwind.

But if the images of *Othello* — similar processions winding across the skyline, battlements looming and drenched in sunlight — were essentially images of a blazing North Africa, of the Mediterranean basin, so the images here are essentially northern; and the winter trees, recurring in shot after shot, are significantly bare. A wind ruffles the robes of the passing figures, and it is not a hot wind out of Africa, but a cold wind, an English wind: a wind that forebodes the end of a whole period, much as it blows away the helmet of a soldier on a battlement or stirs the great hanged figures of the doomed on the skyline's gibbets.

Ralph Richardson's dry, calm narration, drawn from *Holingshed's Chronicles,* begins: "King Richard II was murdered. Some say at the command of the Duke Henry Bolingbroke. In Pomfret on February 14, 1400. Before this the Duke Henry had been crowned King. But the true heir to the realm was Edmund Mortimer, who was held prisoner by the Welsh rebels. The new king was not hasty to purchase his deliverance." These words are spoken against a castle intended to represent Pomfret. Then, as we move into the great stone court of Henry IV, we see the treacherous noblemen, among them Northumberland and his son Hotspur, gathered in the apses waiting their chances to thrust at the occupant of the throne.

As the noblemen argue, we are made aware of the misery of Henry, perched above them and yet threatened by them ("My blood hath been too cold and temperate./ Unapt to stir at these indignities"). Henry seems a remote, formal figure of medieval legend, his crown metallically glittering in the slanting light from a high slit window, as paternal and divorced from common reality as a saint in a stained-glass window. The camera probes in closer; and under the crown, as agonizing to its wearer as a chaplet of thorns, we see the distorted, wretched face of monarchy.

The camera tracks back in front of Henry, an embittered and angry figure hemmed in tightly and claustrophobically by courtiers on each side, the stone walls pressing in on him threateningly. Voices angrily echo and re-echo from the stone walls, planning the dissolution of his reign, the rise of Hotspur.

Meanwhile, in the cellar, deep beneath the inn where Falstaff lives, the fat knight grumbles about his pocket having been picked, and the tone becomes less poised, less grand, the camera fussing about to match the boisterous energies of less favored human beings, Mistress Quickly charging Falstaff with ingratitude for his accusations to her. Against Falstaff's generous girth and violent bursts of merriment and rapine, we learn that Prince Hal, the future Henry V and son of the somber reigning monarch, beats like an audacious gadfly, darting round Falstaff's huge shape like a merry familiar.

The conversation continues outside, against snow and bare birches. Meanwhile, Harry Hotspur is immersed deep in a hip-bath, presented, like Eugene Morgan in the early stages of *Ambersons*, as a figure of comic *gaucherie*.

Trumpets announce his plan to attack the King and Prince Hal in battle and to use his cousinhood as an excuse to seize the British throne. The intercut shots of fanfaring heralds effectively presage and summarize Hotspur's warrior ambitions against the King, ironically contrasting with his farcical lack of impressiveness as he steps clumsily from his bath, the pomp of wished-for office illustrating the extent of human folly.

While Hotspur assembles his army, the doomed friendship of Falstaff and Prince Hal continues under snow-laden trees. They and their friends, dressed as friars, plan to surprise the King's procession, and they weave in patterns among trunks, like the schoolboys in *The Stranger*, the camera smoothly moving with them, rushing along in lateral tracking shots, the music militarily at a gallop, each tree as cool and still as a pillar.

In a parody of ambush the "friars" grapple with the King's men. The camera imitates the capering, clownlike rushings to and fro of pursuers. But soon more serious business is at hand: not an amusing ambush, but the threat of war. To Henry IV comes news that while Northumberland lies sick, his son Hotspur has assembled a force. Henry expresses his anguish, not merely

at the news of the rebellion but at the fact that Hotspur, whom he admires more than his own son, should have turned against him, and that Prince Hal is a hopeless wastrel to be looked for in the taverns — a wanton and effeminate boy carousing with his probable lover, the foxy, sinister Poins, his other catamites, and his swarming doxies as well.

We have seen that Henry is not merely isolated from his court, and from what is going on in his realm, but from his bisexual dissolute son. The comic Pistol whirls round the tavern, telling Hal that Henry wants to see him; reality is beginning to intrude on the murky, cheery world of the barrel-filled carousing place. In an ingeniously cut exchange Falstaff talks about his encounter with some assailants at Kendal Green, the story of his defeat of them becoming more exaggerated at every moment; but we are all too clearly aware that this boisterous fun cannot last.

In mockery of the King, Hal and Falstaff pantomime his might, Falstaff with a cushion and a tin pan, and Hal with the same pan; they take places on a rude wooden "throne." Underlying the humor of the scene, and effec-

tively undermining it, is the feeling that everything here parodied is in effect tragic; and we do not, if we are sensitive, laugh. At the end of the scene a line almost subliminally slipped in indicates that Hal prophetically foresees he will one day banish Falstaff and destroy him.

The mockery extends to the inn doxies, and the whole happy establishment echoes to English mirth, observed indulgently by Mistress Quickly. The camera continues to dance effective atendance on these revels, as busy as it was in the Turkish bath scene in *Othello,* tracking and closing in feverishly. (This scene is perhaps unduly protracted for the sake of cinematic bravura, and it is marred by the recording.)

At court Hal has obeyed his father's behest to appear; the noblemen withdraw, leaving them together; the father's parodied speech of reproof now becomes real. In close-up, his face barred with light from the high window, Henry condemns Hal's profligate behavior. It is a face already partly withdrawn into shadow; we are made to feel that his end is not far off.

War breaks out; the atmosphere of the tavern is shat-

tered; martial preparations burst upon us in a panoply of vivid images. Pistol's fatuous farewell is only a comic overture to the tragic horror that will forge Prince Hal's greatness.

In the scenes before battle, before the great confrontation of Hotspur and Henry IV, *Macbeth*-like forests of spears bristle, while in the tavern the shrill and toothless Mr. Justice Shallow and the stammering, Holbein-like figure of Master Silence shirrup away on the brink of the vanishing of their order. This scene does not merely presage ironically but also says something new about Falstaff's character: his mocking of Silence indicates that he can assert his strength now in no other direction.

Before his army, head bare, face drawn and pale with pain and distress, King Henry gives his orders. We are in a windy, beaten expanse of rocks, the swelling contours of cumulus and the wild streaking of cirrus seen in the ocean of sky. Spears are thrust high, row upon row fencing off the heavens, Welles drawing again on the inspiration of Eisenstein.

Flags are wind whipped, as Prince Hal bravely prom-

ises to engage Hotspur in single combat; the treacherous Worcester, told to bring a possible conciliatory message from monarch to rebels, does not do it. Worcester, black and sinister and crouching, moves below the spear forests in the wind, bearing his message like some evil bird of omen.

With a great rattle of pulleys, the grotesque, hugely armored knights of England are lowered onto their horses in a vivid, ironical image of false grandeur; and at the end of this display Falstaff crashes helpless to the ground, foundering in his metal plates. Now the tremendous central sequence of the battle begins: horses advance through the white forest mists, their nostrils flaring, steaming the chilly air; Falstaff waddles along; the battle cry resounds across the great field; the musics repeats its martial theme, and the camera darts like a deer through the silver birch.

The twin armies crash with a tremendous thud of flesh and armor. The camera rushes through the horses, showing swords thwacking down on helmets and, to a superb wordless Lavagnino chorus on the sound track, great maces sending men spinning into the mud. Thrashing figures erupt in astonishing, shocking images of medieval warfare, hundreds of shots linked together in a tremendous continuity of violence: blood soaked faces, feet tangling in stirrups, horses tilting over directly into the camera, the whole accompanied by the wild screaming of the victims and the frantic whinnying of horses. Bodies writhe as spears are plunged into them over and over again. And Falstaff rushes forward, glimpsed through the horses — once in an astonishing shot that lasts only a fraction of a second, seen framed through the crook of a horse's tail.

The intensity of the violence reaches a crescendo, the sound track swamped with screams and groans. Figure after figure is hacked to pieces; and now, buried almost completely in mud, the figures of the last survivors flounder like primitive beasts. As the horses gallop off, they leave a field strewn with bodies.

Prince Hal and Hotspur are left to face each other in a final duel. Hotspur challenges Hal to combat; they clash, and Hal's sword pierces Hotspur through the

chest. Hotspur feels the death thrust and delivers a speech that is among the most moving Welles has yet interpreted: "Harry, thou hast robbed me of my youth!" As Hotspur kneels, his virility and beauty doomed, it is a moment of piercing individual pain in a sequence that has so far only offered the generalized distress of battle. Hal's noble requiem is delivered beautifully to the sounds of a single trumpet in the background. In the wake of this, Falstaff's boast that he has killed Hotspur seems pathetically vainglorious, not sickeningly absurd. Yet the peremptory justice administered by Henry IV on the treacherous Worcester ("to the death") seems to us, in this handling, stark and horrible, the figure in black shrinking off screen beyond the lines of soldiery.

The rebellion has been quelled and victory is to be celebrated; the inn fills with the carousing of Falstaff and his friends. Festive sequences these — but a moment later the Holingshed commentary strikes a more somber note. We discover the king in London, "sore vex'd with sickness," stricken and ghastly, his unhappiness expressing itself in an illness that will soon result in death. The castle glooms over him like an antique tomb, and as the dying monarch totters down a vastly looming corridor of stone, the noblemen pressing about in a near-repetition of the pattern of the opening sequence, he collapses, pushing the crown to the ground. In his vast bed, he calls for the crown, the one single thing that is solid, that he can hang on to, a possession cosseted like Kane's glass ball at the end.

He groans over his lack of sleep, standing at the win-

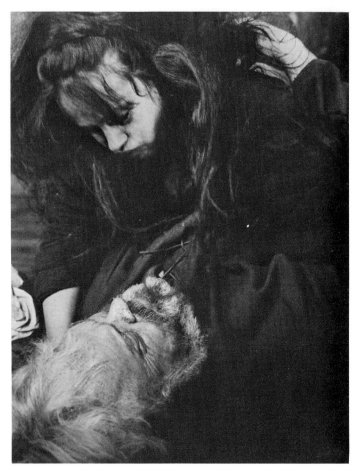

dow now, his face half-lit. Here, Gielgud's superb playing gives the speech that conveys Henry's weariness under the burden of office an almost unbearable intensity. As he speaks the last words, "Happy low, lie down! Uneasy lies the head that wears a crown!" the camera withdraws, leaving him doomstruck and alone, dwarfed again by the stone walls of his own castle.

We become aware in the following scenes that, in anticipation of his father's death, Hal is already becoming separated from his friends, that he is already preparing for kingship. And we see, too, that melancholy has settled on Falstaff, that his end is as surely due as the end of Hal's carefree youth. Even while Pistol careers round the inn with a phallic object pointed at the womenfolk, cracking bawdy jokes, the authentic jollity of the earlier scenes has drained away.

At the end of the sequence in the inn Doll Tearsheet climbs over the great mound of Falstaff's belly, while Hal and his friend Poins watch from a gallery, remarking on the way in which desire continues in the old after performance is no longer possible. Their comment is given an added touch of bitterness by its homosexual savagery.

At the castle the old king dies, his crown prematurely snatched from his pillow by his son, who, we now see, cannot wait to place it on his own head. The *Kyrie Eleison* accompanies the end of one reign and the start of another as, in a reprise of the precredits sequence, Mr. Justice Shallow and Falstaff brood on mortality before the fire. Henry IV's death occurs on a high throne against another slant of sunlight, a figure frozen into history. He dies; the old men await death by the fire at the inn; the sense of mortality — for kings and commoners alike — chills the mind.

Now comes the deathblow for Falstaff. The camera tracks slowly past the lined figures at the coronation as Falstaff rushes among them trying desperately to obtain ingress to the dim cathedral nave where Hal — solemn, statuesque, every inch as isolated, formalized, and remote as his father — moves forward to be crowned.

His voice echoing with embarrassing loudness, Falstaff stumbles into the royal procession. From below eyelevel in a magnificently powerful image we see Hal look upon him with absolute contempt, dismissing him into exile, the spears already fencing him off from his former friend, the figures of the retinue like icy robots shielding him off from the world. As Hal says "I know thee not, old man," Falstaff's face crumbles and his eyes start with astonished tears. He withdraws to the tavern, bleak and remote, to die; at his last moment, as he leaves the cathedral, he is shown as a kind of humped fat shadow vanishing under brooding eaves, stricken at the twilight hour.

The final scenes have an elegiac stillness, a dead calm: Falstaff shut in his coffin, Mistress Quickly sitting helpless on the ground delivering her speech of farewell, and at the end of the coffin trundled off on a wheeled platform to the skyline, across the rutted earth of England. The film ends with a coda as gentle as a sigh, a fitting conclusion to the simplest, most direct, most human of Welles's works.

I have indicated in the foregoing my admiration for *Chimes at Midnight,* for its qualities of warmth and simplicity — qualities that survive its sometimes flawed technique. Why, then, does the film leave one with a feeling

of inedequacy, a sense that something is missing? Chiefly, I think, because — except in the battle scene and in the greatest moments of Gielgud's appearances — it lacks the dynamism, the energy, the daemonic power that have marked Welles at his greatest. It falls short of being a masterpiece — though not far short — because of that failure of the energy which has so often marked Welles's career as an artist. There are not merely evidences here of exhaustion, but of an impatience with detail and finalization that, combined with Welles's tragic perennial lack of funds, have left the work just short of the triumph it should have been.

14. TWO TELEVISION FILMS:

THE FOUNTAIN OF YOUTH and THE IMMORTAL STORY

As early as 1939, Welles had been intrigued by television. He told William A. French of *Motion Picture Magazine* (December 1939): "The great entertainment form of tomorrow will be television shows on film. Today they are all live. But television films will combine all the best that the stage, radio and motion pictures have to offer."

While in England in the fifties, he directed many shows, none of them particularly inventive; of these, the most interesting appears to have been a documentary about the murder of the British diplomat Sir Jack Drummond and his family in the South of France (the French government was unhappy about this filming before the trial of the accused murderer). Most of these programs have now vanished. After finishing *Touch of Evil,* he was intrigued to note that early in 1958 his old stomping ground, RKO-Radio, was bought by Desilu (Lucille Ball and Desi Arnaz). Soon after, he received an offer from Arnaz, one of his greatest fans, to direct a pilot for a television series which he would narrate and sometimes direct, based on various short stories.

It was a great opportunity, but Welles's methods were impossible in a tightly organized studio like Desilu. He horrified Arnaz by taking almost a month over the pilot, based on a story called "The Fountain of Youth," by John Collier, originally published in 1952 as "Youth from Vienna" in a collection called *Fancies and Goodnights.* The pilot was considered uncommercial, and was never used. It was finally shown in a graveyard of unused pilots presented as specials on Colgate Theatre, on Sep-

tember 16, 1958. It was typical of Welles's career that, after all that, *Fountain of Youth* won a Peabody Award.

Welles adapted for the pilot many techniques used by him in theatrical productions and by Laszlo Benedek in *Death of a Salesman* (1951). Cutting from scene to scene was eliminated; when a character was to be seen in a different situation, the background faded, leaving him isolated in darkness; then the light increased again, and a different set or back projection and materialized. Significant objects were highlighted dramatically, while shifts of time were indicated as the background beyond the object changed in shifting light.[1] In an extension of the "flickering" images of *Too Much Johnson,* Welles used — with comic effect — rapid juxtapositions of stills showing the characters framed in successive attitudes, rather than providing the usual fluid images. The effect was like looking through a funnel at an ancient zoetrope.

The result as seen today is an extremely economical, clean, precise technique that reflects Welles's seldom-commented-on fondness for a kind of visual shorthand, the direct antithesis of his baroque methods elsewhere. One's only regret is that the camerawork by Sid Hickox is no more than functional, and downright flat in the dialogue scenes, which are rather uninterestingly handled by the director as well. There is a quite monotonous series of two- and three-shots, and the film is largely in medium shot; the surface is very plain and unvarnished. To be blunt, for all its brilliance, the pilot looks physically rather cheap, and one may understand the exasper-

[1] A direct parallel with Leland's hospital scene in *Kane.*

ation of the network chiefs on being confronted with such a massive budget. If Welles's determination to get to the Carnival in Rio helped wreck his career at RKO and *Touch of Evil's* failure destroyed his Hollywood film career, then the extravagance of *The Fountain of Youth* wrote *finis* to the possibility of a Hollywood television career.

The story of *The Fountain of Youth* is *echt* Collier, about a rather seedy endocrinologist who has distilled an essence (contained in the obligatory phial) that can enable a person to live for two hundred years in the condition he was in when he swallowed it. Welles's adaptation is faithful, energetically recapturing Collier's bitter, whimsical wit, which is closely related to his own: half fey, half deadly. At the very outset, Welles makes a sly dig at commercials; commercially excusable in the case of a Hitchcock, but hardly so here — referring to the properties of the youth potion, he says that he is not "plugging some cosmetic." One sees here, too, though it is hidden in a joke, the essential ambiguity of his attitude to commerce.

The opening of the film is accompanied by honky-tonk music, very much as *Too Much Johnson's* was intended to be: we are in 1922. As Welles, the narrator, describes the career of the endocrinologist Dr. Humphrey Baxter, Baxter is seen frozen against a bookcase while Caroline Coates, stage and screen star, is seen on a poster advertising a production called *Destiny's Tot* (the name of a story in that psychiatric *vade mecum, The Jet-Propelled Couch*). She seems to be based on Rita Hayworth, and Welles's comment may be reminiscently unkind: "She was more than an actress . . . she stands for something greater than talent." With equal cynicism we are introduced to a poster of tennis star Alan Brodie, with a tennis racket jauntily brandished. Welles moves in front of these figures as they appear, weaving in and out of his own visual and aural narrative with effortless insouciance.

We observe Humphrey introducing himself to Caroline, for whom he has set his cap; "You can imagine the effect of this gaunt man lecturing a popular idol of twenty-three on the ductless glands." Caroline "falls head over heels in love" with Humphrey, and their affair is as ironically and swiftly charted as Eugene Morgan's wooing of Isabel Amberson. There follows a narration on the fountain of youth, again strongly reminiscent of *The Magnificent Ambersons* and spoken against a still of an ornamental water-jet:

There are all sorts of fountains . . . some are beautiful, some are purely mythological, some are silly fountains . . . The silliest of all is the fountain of youth . . . old Ponce de Leon thought that one was somewhere down in Florida, three centuries before the invention of Miami Beach. He aged a whole lot looking for it!

It was only human. Most all of us wish we were a little younger than we are. Ladies quite late in their seventies can be addressing each other as girls. Very rich old ladies, even rich old gents, have squandered fortunes on monkey glands and I don't know what all.

Here we can see a cynical revision of Welles's obsessive central theme: age, and the passage of time.

Caroline jilts Humphrey for the tennis player, preferring looks to wisdom — a fatal choice, as it turns out. The scene shifts, without cuts or dissolves, from an excited gossip columnist announcing the change of marriage plans, to Humphrey discovering the pair in a New York restaurant, to a party celebrating her new engagement — all achieved with simple changes of lights. Billy House (the inane shopkeeper Potter in *The Stranger*) is introduced as Morgan, an editor preparing a science magazine article on the endocrinologist. Morgan and the gossip columnist jointly announce the discovery of VB282, the miracle potion. "It controls the aging of the tissues!" the columnist gurgles. "Girls! Just imagine what that means!"

Here we have a really brilliant device. As Welles repeats the dialogue of the characters in the narration, his words are matched in with the lip movements of Humphrey and Caroline — particularly amusing as Welles's *basso* flees the girl's pretty lips. Caroline is being shown a kitten by Humphrey; as she coos exaggeratingly over it, Humphrey tells her: "The kitten had a birthday last week. It was five years old." (A subtle "black" touch here: since he doesn't refer to the creature by name, it is

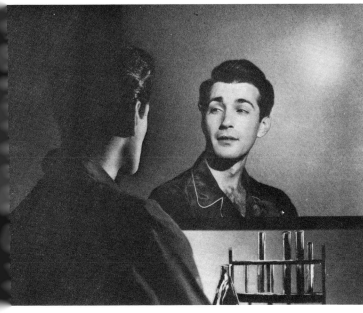

clearly an experimental object rather than a pet.) She drops the animal with a hilariously timed scream of horror. At this moment Humphrey describes his secret to Caroline: there is one dose left.

Sinisterly, Humphrey presents the happy couple with his wedding present: the remaining dose, knowing well what they will do with it. As he describes the violent endocrine disorders that would accompany a half dose, Welles brilliantly uses the (musically simulated) slow and awful ticking of a clock, thus paralleling the ticking of the bomb in *Touch of Evil* and the jigsaw puzzle scene in *Kane*, as well as commenting on the inexorable nature of time. (There is another reminiscent musical passage: the return of Alan and Caroline home from the doctor's apartment is accompanied by Latin American themes adapted directly from the Acapulco music of *The Lady from Shanghai*.)

As the phial is placed on the couple's mantelpiece in the place of honor, Welles expertly adapts the poison-bottle scene in *Citizen Kane*: the phial is given every ounce of light while the background fades, reflected in the mirror above the fireplace, and the couple are seen in silhouette, the phial glowing with an unearthly brightness; as time passes, we see her gradually brighter, then his face in silhouette again; gradually he moves forward into the light. By slow degrees, the full set comes into view. A moment later there is a superb silhouette shot of the couple leaning statuesquely on either side of a table. As we see them more clearly, we know that they are reflected in the mirror again, and that they are — because of their awareness of the potion's possibilities — becoming acutely aware of their own (and each other's) aging. "She watched him in the mirror," Welles says, "and he saw her watching him." She says that most men would think they were in heaven if she looked at them; he tells her that all she is looking for is wrinkles. As a tennis match follows, expertly managed in a series of stills of the various ritualistic actions of the game, we are aware that Alan is conscious, during the playing, of his own increasing age. At midnight that night, he takes the potion, lacing the phial with cocktail bitters and water, so that Caroline will think the dose is still intact.

After this, the most remarkable sequence in this remarkable work occurs. As Caroline watches her reflection in the mirror, we see her profile change into ugly old age, then into a pathologist's abstract head threaded with X-rayed veins, then into a skull, as the accompanying words, heavy with foreboding, are delivered by Welles: "She could feel and almost hear the remorseless erasures of time. Moment after moment particles of skin wore away, hair follicles broke, splintered, all the little tubes and lines and threadlike chains of the inner organs were silted up like doomed rivers . . . the glands, the all-important glands were choking, . . . clogging." And she too drinks the contents of the phial, refilling it with medicinal quinine.

"So (each), secure in imperishable youth . . . saw in the other as through a magnifying glass more of the hastening signs of decay," Welles says, as Caroline goes to Humphrey and confesses her guilt. Humphrey discloses to her that he never put the youth serum in the phial he gave them; that he knew each would cheat the other, and wanted to see them suffer. At the end of this bitter trifle, as Humphrey's face fades on a sneer, the music becomes jazzy, and Welles's final title (after the cast is reviewed in early talkie poses, as in *Mr. Arkadin*) is characteristically grand: "Screenplay, musical arrangement, production designed and directed by Orson Welles." And the tone of pride is justified, for this — with its theme of the erosions of time, its brilliant adaptation of theatrical lighting techniques — is among the most personal works of the master.

• • •

So, too, is *The Immortal Story*, shot in color in France ten years after *The Fountain of Youth*, and based on the novella by Isak Dinesen (Karen, Baroness Blixen). Produced for French television in 1968, *The Immortal Story* is the most still and calm of all Welles's films, perfectly beautiful and composed; it is precisely accurate in reflecting Isak Dinesen's world while conveying, in the simplest terms, the full force of Welles's own talent. From the very first moments, when we see Welles as the millionaire Mr. Clay sitting in a *Kane*-like chair against a background of mirrors, we see the reflection not only of himself but of the poet that at his best he is: here again and welcome is the Welles of Kane's corridor walk after Susan's departure, Mistress Quickly's speech, Kindler's false reminiscence of the drowning, the nostalgic passages in *Ambersons,* all echoing and re-echoing harmoniously.

This new film is a miniature, a distillation of Welles's knowledge and experience in a tiny frame. A few notes of Satie, subtly elegant and wistful on the sound track, introduce us to an abstract evocation of Macao in a single image: a curving white sail against ruined houses. This could also be taken as a symbol of the innocent sailor who figures in the chronicle, contrasted with the hopeless wreck that the millionaire, who is the central figure, has become.

We see the millionaire Mr. Clay (the merchant's name is itself a reminder of frail mortality) in a mansion in Macao some time in the last century. We are made aware, in images desolate and stark, of Clay's isolation in his great house, surrounded by mirrors, with only a quiet, subdued clerk for company. Like Kane, he is cut off by his very wealth and power: "The idea of friendliness had never entered his scheme of life." Crickets chirp in the background as the clerk, dressed in somber black, brings in ledgers. The compositions are plain and straightforward, the director cutting from millionaire to servant and back again without any particular touch of invention. Yet one is aware all the time of the brooding silence of the house, the cold gleam of a Chinese lantern, the separating and excluding bars and cross-struts of the metal fittings that shut out the world.

The clerk reads to the sad, ancient figure of his master a passage from Isaiah — a passage of the prophet promising relief to the old, water to the desert of their despair: Clay asks if this relief ever occurred or is occurring, and the clerk bitterly answers, "No." Clay tells him that he is interested only in what has happened, not in what might happen; and he recalls the legendary story of a rich old man who picked up a sailor on the waterfront and took him to his house. There the young man made love to the

old man's young wife, and for a moment the impotent old man, aware of what was happening, relived his virile youth. The clerk says that he, too, has heard the story, and he continues with it, taking it up to the very point at which Clay left it — before the description of the encounter in the bedroom. The two men face each other under awnings and arches, trapped in the empty recollection of a dream. But Clay wants to release himself from mere fantasies: he wants the legend to be made real. As the servant goes out to help make this possible, the iron doors close, cutting Clay off more firmly from the world. And we see that the servant, too, is isolated — for, as

Welles's narrating voice says, he is like some insect only waiting to scuttle for cover, a sexless monastic creature. His own room, which is as stark, as cheerless and cold, in its poverty as Clay's house is in its opulence, closes in on him before our eyes like a coffin. ("The clerk had only one passion: the craving to be left alone.")

The clerk's first goal is the woman in the play: Virginie (Jeanne Moreau), sister of a fellow clerk, whose father died bankrupt, losing the mansion where Clay now lives. The clerk's offer to her to take part in his master's plan is conducted in slow, elegant sequences set against crumbling arches and squares and awnings, in cool afternoon light, sunbeams throwing a complex of shadows: we are once again suspended in a dream, almost as though we are in an Antonioni film. Yet the effect is not static; rather it is one of slow motion, of sleepwalking in the heat.

Virginie looks at the Macao Xanadu her father had left, gazing through iron *Kane*-like railings as she talks forlornly about all she lost. She speaks of her dream of returning there, but adds that she will never go back as a figure in a sexual charade. Her white parasol, the birds chirping in the trees, the cool soft light, help to form a composition as magical as any Welles has given us, a pastoral picture suffused in a Seurat-like elegant coolness.

On a balcony, dealing Tarot cards on a table covered with a shawl, while tiny black-clad Chinese children dart across a square far below, Virginie continues to discuss Clay's plan with his eager advocate. Sometimes there is one silent, solitary black figure down below, sometimes groups of figures, and here the composition has all the apparent informality yet the closely worked, subtle classic harmony of a Breughel, placing his people darkly against snow.

In her little room the conversation continues, based in part on the subject of a picture of Empress Eugenie on Virginie's cupboard. Virginie talks wistfully of the stories her father had told her of the empress: how Eugenie would wear a pair of satin shoes only once. The motto on Virginie's family coat-of-arms is *Pourquoi pas?* So with a kind of shrug, Virginie decides — but for a higher fee — to agree to Clay's proposal.

A sailor is Clay's next objective. As the huge old merchant, like King Lear (the make-up is almost identical with that used in Welles's stage portrait of Lear), broods in his carriage, he catches a glimpse of a golden-haired boy sitting half asleep in rags against an alley

wall. The first shots of the sailor (Norman Eshley) are deliberately lyrical, suggesting the appearance of a creature of legend: Welles conveys a sense of torpid heat, shadows of leaves spraying across an amber-colored wall; a single tree divides the composition down the middle, with the boy at the right, sunbeams falling with almost shocking intensity on his fair hair. As the camera tracks with him, he runs with the carriage, following his new captor on foot; we are reminded of that other powerful figure of the Orient, Elsa Bannister, picking up the sailor in Central Park.

The conversation between merchant and sailor in which Clay gradually makes known his plans has an authoritative strength; each composition is beautifully tight and harmonious. While Clay sits sadly in another of his vast chairs, the sailor is at the other end of a long table, dumbfounded by the luxury surrounding him, half assuming some homosexual purpose in the old tycoon. The table divides them as inexorably as a knife, a continent of wood dividing two worlds: wealth and poverty, youth and age.

The slow, ritual quality of the story is conveyed in formal arrangements of lamps and screens, the deliberate movement of the servants as master and latest acquisition discuss their mutual concerns — Clay elaborating on his fantastic wealth, the boy half bored, half uncertain whether he can go through with whatever the old man wants. Then Clays makes clear that there is an underlying motive in his desire for the boy's sexual performance in the bedroom next door: he wants to leave his fortune to a child that he himself has caused to be conceived.

The sequence in which Virginie is finally possessed is among the most magical Welles has given us. Once more the legendary quality is preserved in slow, drifting, formalized movements as spare and austerely composed as the body patterns in a Kabuki play. Virginie's bed — this was once her father's room — is surrounded by drifting mosquito-net veils, pale gray or white according to the light. She gazes into mirrors under a forest of lamps in red shades, a bristle of candelabras, while beyond her the room glistens with comfort and erotic promise.

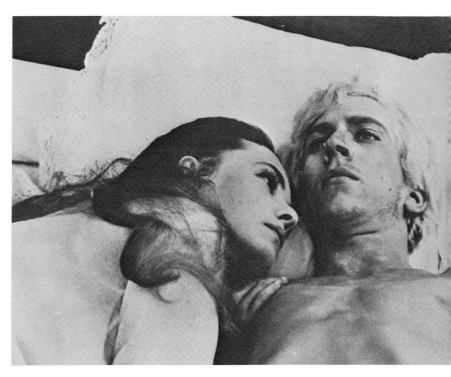

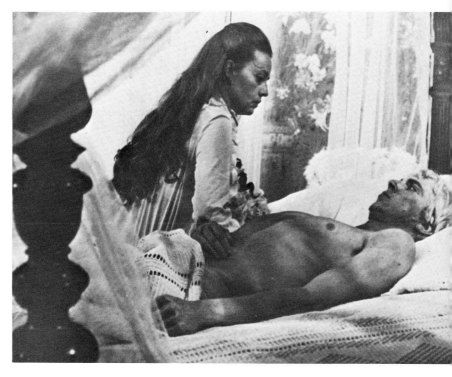

At first Virginie is afraid of the experience to come; she distracts herself with soliloquized memories of her father in the house, and the recollection that the sum the merchant is paying her may help recoup her family fortunes. She lies down on the bed naked, cupping her breasts in her hands, closing her eyes, like Desdemona in the last sequence of Welles's *Othello*. Around her the veils, stirred faintly in the breeze, give an illusion of purity. As she prepares, she has told the clerk that she hopes the erotic show will forever destroy the merchant who took over her father's estate, that he will die of locomotor ataxia.

Crickets chirp loudly; the door opens, and Virginie surreptitiously looks up. We see, through the veils, a series of candles blown out and the curtains drifting in elegantly mirrored reflections. Clay is watching; and slowly, as though walking on a path strewn with broken glass, the sailor approaches, still cut off from us by the floating, translucent white bed canopy. He removes his clothes, and lies beside Virginie quietly; he asks her age,

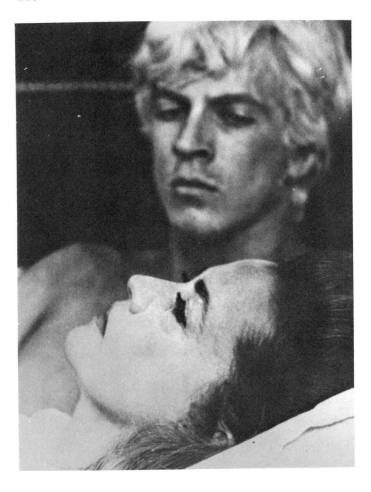

and she pretends she is young; in a kind of sadness, he accepts the myth. It is a drug he will need to help him make love to her because, as he confesses in a whisper, he has never been naked in the arms of a woman before.

The erotic intensity of this sequence is remarkably sustained; we are totally involved as the cool light of the room shines with startling vividness on the couple's flesh, veils giving way with sharp immediacy to the reality of soft or muscled arms, of her heavy-lidded dark eyes and his startling blue ones, while outside in the gloom of the corridor the watching ancient millionaire thinks of mortality, of his endless pain and distress. Inside the room there glistens the golden mythical light of a Renaissance painting; outside, there glows sadly a

Gothic study in stillness. The juxtaposition of the shots could not be more charged with meaning.

At the end of the sequence, after the youth makes his confession of virginity, his body rises to make the sexual thrust; and the two bodies shine still more beautifully with health and vitality as curtains once again close about them like a tent. A shimmering grayish whiteness of silk fills the whole frame, the bodies move with sensual ease, and the noise of the crickets increases to a sharper and sharper intensity. Outside, Clay talks of their young lust and health with grim realization of his own dryness.

The last scene of the film sets the seal on a triumph. Daylight has a drab tropical patina as the couple awake in bed, to a chorus of birdsong; and on the veranda Clay sits dying, talking to his servant as though unraveling his own elegy. The boy gives Virginie one of those imagistic fragments — the story of the Fortaleza sharks is another example — that figure repeatedly in Welles, poetic and isolated from the main narrative: "As I was keeping the middle watch, and the night was cold, three swans flew across the moon, over her round face of gold . . . the sky is brown and the sea yawns three thousand fathoms down, and the tide runs downward like a whale." He discloses that, like Virginie, he is an orphan; her father was ruined, his was drowned at sea. And we see that all of the film's main characters are in fact derelicts, castaways of life. Soon there are only two: for in the final moments, a shot from behind his chair indicates that Clay is dead.

The Immortal Story does not break any new ground technically — some critics have found it dull and unenterprising — yet its very lack of mannered camera angles and elaborate compositions is the film's most attractive feature. Welles's style is pared here to a romantic essence, stripped of all needless decoration.

If *The Fountain of Youth* excites with its verve and inventiveness, *The Immortal Story* moves us more deeply, for here we are made aware of how much of the elegiac flavor of *Ambersons* has survived. Cool and poised as the exquisite Satie piano works which run through it like a refreshing stream, *The Immortal Story* points to the late reflowering of this incomparable artist.

15. ENVOI

Like Thompson in *Kane* or Van Stratten in *Arkadin,* my purpose has been to pursue a minotaur in its labyrinth, to explore a multitude of facts in the hope that they will disclose a real creature at the center of the maze. Thompson missed the clue to Kane's central concern: his anguish at the loss of the irrecoverable joy of childhood. Van Stratten discovered at last that the agony which haunted Arkadin was his fear that his daughter would discover the truth about his nefarious past. My own search, hardly less harrowing, has led me to the conclusion that Welles has spent his entire lifetime creating, like El Greco in *The Burial of Count Orgaz,* multitudinous images of himself, while still remaining the most private of screen artists, trapped in contemplation of his own bizarre image, preoccupied with time and loss.

I have only seen Welles in person once: in the theater of the County Museum of Art in Los Angeles, where he was directing a magic show — recreating his celebrated stage performance of the past thirty years for a television spectacular. In one unforgettable hour he emerged in all his colors. He was grotesque as he forced an unhappy duck over and over again into a brass bowl for a trick, saying jokingly to a notably unsettled handmaiden, "I had 2,000 pigeons with me in the South Pacific in World War II and not one of them died." He was tragic as he brooded alone, pushing back his assistants, his face knotted in grief and despair, lost, totally isolated, upset by their slowness. He was terrifying in his anger at the incompetence of his young assistant magicians; a thunderous oppressive force seemed about to break from him and destroy all concerned. He would laugh bravely in the face of destiny as he guffawed over his own jokes through a Churchillian cigar. He would be momentarily affectionate and understanding to a confused girl. Yet, especially in brief moments of pause, I sensed the face of a man at once anguished by all that had been lost and afraid that beyond the gargantuan meals and wine-bibbing, the anecdotes and the backslapping, the raucous laughter and the assembly of famous friends, there would only be silence and loneliness and invalid rugs: the cold truth of dissolution.

Thompson talked to Kane's wife, his butler, his manager, his best friend. Van Stratten, too, narrowed down the focus of his investigation to a few close to the master. My own pursuit took me to Norman Foster, whom Welles discovered after years in the wilderness of *Mr. Moto* and *Charlie Chan* films; to Stanley Cortez, whom he also rescued from the B-picture world; to Joseph Cotten, who knew him perhaps more intimately than anyone, and who occupied in Welles's life a role not entirely unlike that of Jedediah Leland; to Richard Wilson, perhaps a lighter-hearted and certainly a far more brilliant Bernstein; to Agnes Moorehead, the actress on whom he placed the greatest burdens in *Ambersons,* and who triumphantly bore them; to Brainerd Duffield, who worked closely with him on *Macbeth* and *The Lady from Shanghai;* to Russell Metty; and to Jeanette Nolan McIntire, who courageously tried to give him the Lady Macbeth he wanted, in the face of insurmountable obstacles. From these people, and many other colleagues and friends, an immediate enthusiasm and warmth — a laugh at some remembered, eccentric joke — came when the name of Orson Welles was mentioned, followed by an odd, persistent reluctance to discuss him. Then as the interviews went on, as natural guardedness vanished and the feeling that a mystery must remain inviolate no longer held good, the darker strains in Welles's character emerged. Above all I sensed a feeling, not directly expressed by the people I spoke to, but nevertheless omnipresent, that Welles hated to see a film finished, that all his blame of others for wrecking his work is an unconscious alibi for his own genuine fear of completion. The accounts of these friends of Welles's have been woven together in the warp and woof of my story to form the portrait of an artist seen through the mirrors of his films.

Interviews with Welles in print have seldom been helpful in teasing out clues to the real nature of Welles's creative life; and, like all of us, he has a memory colored by his own need to enhance reality and to tell a good story. We cannot, I think it is fair to say, rely on every detail of his conversations with the press, intellectual or not; I recall — as one example of his memory — that he told Dilys Powell Hollywood had never heard of the samba in March 1942, when it was all the rage there. Like other directors, he can genially allow even the most gifted interviewers to make fools of themselves — as, for instance, when he let Kenneth Tynan, in an interview some years ago, commit the uncharacteristic folly of discussing with him the nonexistence of Kane's father. Especially in certain *Cahiers du Cinéma* interviews he has clearly, like Hitchcock, rejoiced in leading his pretentious interrogators into a fen of meaningless verbiage or muddled fact. He wrote to *The New Statesman* in 1958 to say that *Touch of Evil* was ruined by the producer, and in 1960 he told Derick Grigs in *Sight and Sound* that it was released close to the form which he intended. His scattered accounts of abandoned projects, particularly of *It's All True,* have been notably unhelpful and vague. If some of the facts in this book are at odds with his published statements over the years, it is not because I was unaware of those statements.

And, almost as though his gift for obscuring the past were contagious, the memories of his colleagues have often contradicted each other, *Rashomon*-like, during my talks to them in my journey through the labyrinth. Agnes Moorehead swore there was no Mercury radio version of *The Magnificent Ambersons,* while Richard Wilson correctly remembered one. Joseph Cotten recalled only one test of *Kane* being included in the finished film, Richard Wilson recalled several. Herman Mankiewicz's relatives and John Houseman all claim Mankiewicz's as the main contribution to the script of *Kane;* most of the Mercury people give equal, or greater, credit to Welles. The story of *It's All True* varied so radically from one person to another — I have interviewed almost every man still living who was concerned with it — that at one stage I thought it should have been called *It's All Lies.* Most published articles or books on Welles have fallen foul of constantly repeated inaccuracies, legends, and half-truth, forcing me to a staggering amount of cross-checking. It is as though the minotaur, shying and bucking, has created behind him a dust screen that no one, least of all his interviewers, has been able to penetrate.

And now at last, though other eyes may see him differently, I think I see the minotaur clearly, bellowing in his lair, his eyes full of distress. Like so many novelists discussed in Leslie Fiedler's brilliant *Love and Death in the American Novel,* Welles is an utterly American figure in his obsession with death, his inability to portray a wholly rounded heterosexual relationship, his childish and dilettantish humor, his honesty, realism, and ferociously splendid native energy.

Welles not only converts other artists' works in his own image — from Shakespeare and Kafka all the way down to Tarkington and Dinesen — but he is among those great nonrepresentational artists who totally creates his own world. His places — Florida, Chicago, Atlantic City, New York, Indianapolis, Batum, Istanbul, Rio, Sausalito, San Francisco, Acapulco, Dunsinane, Mogador, Venice, Italy, and Venice, California, Zagreb, Paris, Portuguese Macao, and Spanish castles — are all converted into his private landscape, the landscape of his imagination. We can move from each to each with magical ease, for each is one. His act in converting the civilized world into one condensed planet in his personal possession is an act not performed as completely by any other artist of the screen. Sometimes even the voices of actors are changed for his own. No one, no place for him appears to have an independent reality of its own; at the moment of encounter everything is absorbed into a pattern where it becomes part of a dream. And that dream is one of death.

For Welles, his own films are dead, which is one reason he cannot bear to look at them again. In his works, he freezes forever images of dissolution. Bazin has referred to the fact that film harks back to the mummies of the Egyptians in its attempt to defeat death and time. Yet Welles's films remind us of our mortality constantly, capturing vigor and energy at the very moment of decay. He turns the time-binding capacity of the film back upon itself, making us feel its literal "unreeling" as the projector ceaselessly recounts and recreates time during the duration of a film. The voice-over narration that is his passion is part of this: it is his habitual use of narration that enables him to achieve this kind of double perspective, an almost physical sense of time passing and past, conveyed most sharply at such moments as Susan's forming of the jigsaw puzzles accompanied by the ticking of a clock, or Caroline in *Fountain of Youth* aware of the erasures of time. Welles may see his films as dead, but more than any other director — except in *The Trial* — he seems to me to capture the very texture and movement of time as it is consuming us from minute to minute, leading us toward death, freezing living things in the deadness of celluloid, framing a moving, pulsating, decaying world within each dividing frame of film, as though paintings could breathe and love and dance.

In his fear of time, of all that has been lost, Welles has in his films made references back to earlier days, as though unable to bear the thought of something gone forever and dead: in *Ambersons* a newspaper unfolded (*The Indianapolis Inquirer*) and a review by Jedediah Leland shown almost subliminally in the top left-hand corner; in *Touch of Evil* the words "The people of this county!" boomed by Hank Quinlan. Most touchingly of all, in the gymnasium in *The Stranger* he put up a sign reading "Harper vs. Todd," surely as nostalgic a gesture as Kane's preservation of the snowstorm paperweight, in itself an echo of Welles's small-town life in the winter snows of Wisconsin.

His masterpieces confront dissolution with shows of energy, for his is an art of vitalism. *Citizen Kane* is a great film because it is a completely self-contained and interlocking masterpiece of *structure*. It is not so much to be compared to a great novel — its content is essentially, as I hope I have demonstrated, journalistic and descriptive — as to the funerary, marmoreal perfection of a Taj Mahal, in which every tiny piece interlocks. It makes us see that the nature of Welles's art is plastic and architectural rather than literary and searching. Even his many unfinished monuments — self-portraits like those of the pharaohs — have the grandeur of the legless figure of Ozymandias, out in the great desert, king of kings.

It is the fear of death that gives Welles's films a gleam, an effulgence. Almost all the love relationships in his films are doomed: Kane and Susan, Fanny and Eugene and Isabel and Eugene, the Longstreet girl and Franz Kindler, Macbeth, Othello and Desdemona, Arkadin and his daughter Raina, Michael and Mrs. Bannister. Death or destruction follow in the wake of desire, and at the end the central figure is left grimly contemplating himself: Kane looking at the whirling snowflakes of the glass globe's tiny world or the infinite mirrors of Xanadu, Eugene walking into the once beautiful city and seeing what he has made of it, Mr. Clay on the veranda in Macao filled with sad reminders of time and death, the Bannisters seeing their own images reflected to infinity as they die in a spray of bullets, Hank Quinlan sinking into a swamp below the oil wells like a primeval beast. The happiness of youth is a frail memory: a flutter of snowflakes, a mournful train whistle, a jaunty carriage ride, a recollection of some sad Chinese port — that last memory shared by Elsa Bannister and Mr. Clay. As *The Fountain of Youth* proves, nothing comes back. All his people are Welles; all are his mirrors, grotesquely distorting mirrored faces like those which he designed so brilliantly in *The Lady from Shanghai*.

The most memorable single aspect of *Citizen Kane* is

the painful, gradual revelation of the disintegration of all the characters: Kane himself, chillingly alone in Xanadu, extinguished with only a hired nurse and a corrupt butler for company; Bernstein, sentimentally reminiscing; Leland, a nodding senile mummy in an eye-shade, crippled and isolated; Susan, an alcoholic ruin. Beyond the brass bands and the ballyhoo of the film, Welles discloses a total hopelessness which his humor, buoyant and sophomoric, cannot shut out, which his deafening laughter at last cannot repress.

In *Ambersons* all paths again lead to the grave, and with unbearable honesty we are shown one Amberson after another ruined by time, until the great house itself is humbled and becomes a lodging for the poor. In Welles's original final scene, the black comedy duologue I have referred to earlier told the story of the destruction of the city through sinister exchanges of master and servant, including at one moment a description of candles tipping from a coffin and setting fire to a house.

Pressed hard into the concluding of *Ambersons*, Welles impetuously rushed in to the disastrous Latin American adventure which, more than anything else, wrecked his American career. We may conjecture that he was not merely hurrying to get to the Rio Carnival in time — the fact is that he had no clear idea of how *It's All True* would be fully structured — and we can be forgiven for feeling that his unconscious drive was to avoid the agony of editing and scoring and finishing of *Ambersons* in 1942. With a masterpiece on his hands, it seems inconceivable that he would have left work on it to others, or allowed Robert Wise to direct certain scenes while he busied himself with a radio show; it seems impossible that he could have believed that editing the film by telegram or by interrupting *Carnival* and *Jangadeiros* scenes to work on it with Wise in Rio could produce a satsifactory result. Apart from his fierce impatience and drive, we may guess that subconsciously he was tired of *Ambersons* two thirds of the way through its making, that the slow and painstaking methods of Stanley Cortez irritated him, and that, most importantly, he could not face seeing it rounded off, dead now for him.

Ironically, incompletion was then forced upon him in the case of *It's All True*, which, started impatiently and hurriedly, with no clear idea of its conclusion, was brought to an end by the studio. No segment of this film was completed, and it is characteristic of Welles that any hopes for finishing *My Friend Bonito* were destroyed by his own action.

The Stranger was finished by Welles, but it is outside the body of his personal work, a commercial venture undertaken suddenly and polished off with little involvement. *The Lady from Shanghai* never seemed to be finished, and remains somewhat fragmentary: Welles, as we have seen, initially shot no close-ups in Mexico, failed to record sound for some scenes, confused his locations in others, and was not present during much of the cutting and dubbing. He may blame Columbia, but the fact seems to be that he was disturbed about seeing the film through and did not even supervise the first cut.

I have told the horror story of the making of *Macbeth*, for which the sound track was never properly rounded off. And the record of avoidance of last-minute polishing goes on and on through the tale to the end, so that *Don Quixote* has never been finished, and Welles has said he cannot bear to finish it.

Bucking at the approach of dissolution and the finishing of works of art, desperately impatient, the minotaur may laugh as loudly as he likes, but his eyes are pits of darkness. Welles's is the tragedy of a man who fears the conclusions tragedy reaches: that men are mortal, their works imperfect, their lives and arts doomed.

A black and driving obsession with dissolution and an addiction to the pleasures of the flesh are the two sides of the hedonism Welles has embraced. He is in love with the physical world, with the pleasures of eating and drinking, art and women, sculpture and architecture, the theater, the circus and the cinema, travel and financially dangerous living; but he is also tormented with boredom and the distress of the man who fears that the apple he has just eaten may have contained an undetectable poison. His rowdy, life-loving, heavily decorated films circle around death at their core — an elimination of the senses.

Welles is a private romantic, not a public one in the

sense that Renoir or Ford are public. He is, as I have noted in writing of *The Trial,* the most secretive and self-enclosed of artists of the cinema; and he has never understood or found a mass audience. The public, of which he called himself the "obedient servant," has not grasped the beauty or meaning of his art. He looks at himself, as I have said, in a mirror; he is forever gazing into the faces of his young, middle-aged, and older self; he sees a glass which reflects to infinity, like those which reflected Kane, the people of *The Lady from Shanghai,* and the millionaire in *The Immortal Story.* Like Arkadin, he longs to solve the puzzle for himself, just as he made us long to solve the puzzle of *Citizen Kane.*

In the intentness of his creation, Welles has often forgotten the audience, and the audience has forsaken him as a creative artist, knowing him chiefly as an actor; most moviegoers smile when his name is mentioned; they recall, vaguely, Harry Lime high in the Prater wheel over postwar Vienna, or bearded grotesques, cut-rate King Lears in endless now happily forgotten films. A few recall that Welles fled into films to pay for his stage productions, and into acting in other people's films to pay for his own; that he has not only been pursued by the specter of death and the hound of heaven, but by that equally grim figure, the debt collector.

And his is a very American predicament. Behind the rapid flow of autobiographical discourse, that central American habit of communicating by unraveling intimate accounts of one's own past, behind the dashing youthful ventures into a dozen kinds of performing art, looms the threat of the sudden emptying of the theater, in which the audience and the other players have been only parts of a dream. Life and success have gone by; and the ending of his performance, powerful and magical, can only mean the end of all dreams. So he goes on exploding the

fireworks, pulling the rabbits out of the hat; but the brow is furrowed, the ornamental candles flicker in the draft. Clay looks back at Kane, and both look at the reality of mortal clay; and all the answers are blanks. Yet Welles the artist, if not Welles the man, has beaten death: his greatest works, the best that he has achieved, are his immortal story.

APPENDIX I

PAMPERED YOUTH

David Smith's 1924 version of *The Magnificent Ambersons, Pampered Youth,* provides some fascinating comparisons with Welles's. I am deeply indebted to David Bradley for his assistance in preparing the following description.

The film opens with a title, "1870 — Midland America. In the Indiana State." We are introduced at once to Isabel Amberson, "the prettiest girl in the midland." She is watching a trotting race in which George (Eugene) Morgan is competing with another of her admirers, Wilbur Forrest (Minafer). George wins, and Isabel congratulates him. Soon after, George serenades Isabel with a drunken crony, and clumsily knocks over the bass viol, stepping into it. Isabel slams the window shutters. The handling here is very close to Welles's, but with a front instead of a reverse shot. We see the local old ladies talking about the romancing of Isabel; the sewing circle and the composition are less elaborate, but similar.

There follow a series of shots of Major Amberson's house, with horses and carriages driving up, while George and his daughter Lucy appear in the horseless carriage; the period detail, cars, clothes and trappings, are identical, probably because the art directors of both films drew from authentic period sketches and photographs. The Amberson ball to which the visitors are coming is far more conventionally handled here, and devoid of Welles's marvelous complexity of detail. After the ball, Jack (Georgie) Minafer and Lucy ride in a carriage and come across Morgan with his car broken down; the bang of the exhaust causes the carriage to run off the road and turn over. Lucy and Jack climb into the horseless carriage, and their own runaway horse draws the vehicle into the distance. In the car George seeks Isabel's hand in marriage, and Jack is visibly upset.

The next sequence is almost identical with Welles's. George arrives at the house to collect Isabel, and Jack slams the door in his face, saying "My mother is not going out with you." The playing, dialogue, even the door appear to be nearly the same. Morgan is shown in the final shot through the glass door, moving away.

Isabel primps herself to go out with George, and waits at the window, but George has already left. Cut to Lucy; she is tearing Jack's photograph into two pieces. George points out it's clear that the reason Jack was rude is that he was blinded by his mother's love. Meanwhile, we see that Jack has won: Isabel, almost in tears, says, "I have decided not to marry Mr. Morgan."

The second half of the film traces the deterioration in the Amberson fortunes following the collapse of the affairs of Jack and Lucy, George and Isabel. Jack is shown searching for jobs, with "No Help" signs; finally, he comes to a mean boardinghouse, where Isabel is now living (similar to the original ending Welles shot). Later, Jack is seen run over, and the boardinghouse catches fire (the parallel here with the story of the upset candle told by the two comedians on Fanny's record scarcely needs stressing). George rescues Isabel, and at the hospital, Jack relents and permits George to marry his mother.

Of course it would be grossly unfair to charge Welles with plagiarism, although it is possible he saw *Pampered Youth* — he was ten or eleven when it was released. Although it is possible Welles screened it when he was preparing the new adaptation, the most likely explanation for the similar handling of such scenes as George's (or Jack's) rejection of Eugene or George at the door lies in the two films' common source and in well-established conventions in handling such scenes.

APPENDIX II

CUTS AND CHANGES IN THE MAGNIFICENT AMBERSONS

This list of alterations and excisions has been made by a comparison of letter and image based on the only possible guide: the cutting continuity prepared by RKO *after* Welles had finished his rough cut before leaving for Rio. The film, it should be noted, did not follow the screenplay in every particular. A full release print has been examined, and the continuity was kindly lent by Richard Wilson. It has not been quoted from.

REEL ONE, SECTION ONE

Scenes 14-16; While Eugene walks along the streets of Indianapolis, the narrator comments on the city people's thrift.

Scenes 21-22: Bystanders discuss the Amberson mansion's "White House" pretensions.

Scenes 37-38: George in his little cart argues with laborer.

Scenes 66-75, end of reel: Portion of boy's aggressive ride. Scene in club introducing him as a young adult, in with George quarrels with the newly elected president. The suggestion is that this is a Masonic lodge.

REEL ONE, SECTION TWO

Scenes 1-7. Argument at the club, in which George discloses that he was thrown out of college.

Portion of Scene 16, Scenes 17-portion of Scene 20: Various snatches of conversation during Amberson ball.

Portion of Scenes 22-23: Discussion between Jack, Isabel, and Eugene on the faces of the young at the ball, and how time will age and destroy them. Enormous take cut to pieces.

REEL TWO, SECTION ONE

Portion of Scene 1: Conversation continues, mainly about George, among Jack, Eugene, and others. Mrs. Johnson introduced. Discussion about attitude of mothers to their children.

REEL TWO, SECTION TWO

Scene 9: Brief line of George's.

Scene 12: Final Section, Scene in stable, with horses heard in ironical counterpart to Eugene and Lucy with garaged car. They discuss George.

Scenes 72-81: Important scene as Eugene, Jack, and Isabel in the car after the scene of the winter outing ride discuss the way in which the air is already being polluted in the city. They remember the pure air and sunshine of the past. Then the others join in and discuss snobbery as well, and the Amberson power.

REEL THREE, SECTION ONE

Scenes 3-4: Shots of Amberson tombstones. Shot of George's college diploma, both following death of Wilbur.

Scene 5: Portion of sequence in which George and Fanny talk in the kitchen. Exterior scene: George and Jack leave the house in pouring rain, and find excavations suggesting that Major Amberson is preparing to build houses to extend his fortunes. George is shocked, and Jack discloses he has encouraged the Major to build apartments.

Scene 19, end of reel: Lucy and George climb on a buggy.

REEL THREE, SECTION TWO

Scene 3: End of scene of Major Amberson in carriage. He complains about the workmen excavating his lawn for the new houses. He says that death is approaching. Scene of Fanny, Isabel, and George sitting in silhouette at night on the porch. Fanny discusses the fad of motor cars, they analyze George's apparent depression, the busybody Mrs. Johnson across the street, and death.

Scenes 4-7 to end of reel: Lucy arrives on steps; the others have now gone, except George. She makes it clear she rejects her father's opinions and is siding with George.

REEL FOUR, SECTION ONE

Scene 1: Eugene and Isabel against tree in garden. Extensively recut. Transposed to follow Reel Three, Scene 38.

Scene 16: Small line of George's expressing sarcasm.

REEL FOUR, SECTION TWO

Scenes 31-32: Part of conversation between George and Jack in the bathtub, relating to Isabel's intention to marry Eugene.

REEL FOUR, SECTION FOUR

Scenes 1-2: George in mirror image puts picture of his dead father on a mantelpiece.

Scenes 14-18: Isabel talks to George after George tells Eugene Morgan he may not call on her. Isabel asks him if he needs something to eat and discusses George's explanation of the call as that of a peddlar.

REEL FIVE, SECTION ONE

Scene 1: Shot of Cotten reading letter added, with enlarged frame from previous scene of Amberson hall used as a bridge. Formerly scene showed Isabel as the words of the letter were read on the sound track, and Cotten was not shown.

Scene 2: George almost puts the letter in the fire but thinks better of it.

Scenes 8-22: Discussion between George and Isabel about letter and about her intended marriage. Completely recut, rescripted, and reshot. Effect is now of a softer, less angry scene with a warmer tone to the mother-son conflict. This appears to have been deliberately softened on studio orders.

REEL FIVE, SECTION TWO

Scene 1: After Lucy acquires the spirits of ammonia, an interpolated shot not directed by Welles shows clerk saying, "For gosh sakes, miss!" as he sees her faint.

Scene 3: Fanny and the Major on the porch at night. They discuss the rise of the city, the smoke and dust, the decline of the Amberson fortunes, Jack's headlight investment in which Fanny is doomed to lose her money, and their dangerous new interest in the machine age, an interest which itself is to destroy them far more than their former ignorance.

Scene 4 and part of Scene 5: Jack and Lucy outside mansion discuss its antique style.

Part of Scene 7: Hall of mansion, Major asks nurse if he can see the sick Isabel. Major, Jack, Fanny, and George discuss the dying woman.

REEL SIX, SECTION ONE

Scene 1: Discussion of Isabel between Fanny and Eugene completely reconstructed and partially reshot.

Parts of Scenes 7 and 8: Further conversation surrounding death of Isabel. Part of narrative about Major Amberson's thoughts, and voices of Jack and Fanny off screen talking about the house deeds.

Scene 8: Major Amberson's speech about the sun and the earth reconstructed (possibly due to trouble of actor in memorizing lines).

REEL SIX, SECTION TWO

Scene 1: Opening of scene between George and Jack at the railroad station.

Scene 2: Long sequence of George walking through the growing city, showing the scenes of his youth while the narrator recalls the innocent past. Only the first and last portions of this are retained, and the sequence has been transposed to Reel Seven.

Scene 3: Scene of George by his mother's bed. Narration cut, and only one line, "Mother forgive me," retained.

REEL SEVEN, SECTION ONE

Opening of scene by the boiler reconstructed and partly redirected.

Scene 2: Discussion between Lucy and Eugene in the garden moved back to follow railroad station scene.

REEL SEVEN, SECTION TWO

Scene 2: Accident to George cut: conversion between young man bystander and policemen reduced.

REEL SEVEN, SECTION THREE

Scene 1: Eugene at table. Scene added, not by Welles. Lucy exits right in theatrical fashion. Music by Roy Webb, not Bernard Herrmann. Scene added here in hospital corridor, again with Webb score.

REEL SEVEN, SECTION FOUR

Entire last portion removed. Eugene asks to be driven to the city hospital. Now time has passed. Eugene visits with Fanny in the boardinghouse. They discuss George and his accident. A phonograph record plays in the background: a comedy duet about the loss of a city. Fanny and Eugene discuss the almost certain wedding of Lucy and George, and the change in George. As Eugene leaves the boardinghouse the various people there are seen in mirrors. He goes out and gets into his car. Above him he sees, as he looks back, Fanny in the doorway, and the skyline of the great city. End.

FILMOGRAPHY

COMPLETED FILMS DIRECTED BY ORSON WELLES

CITIZEN KANE. RKO-Radio Pictures, 1940-1941. Screenplay by Herman J. Mankiewicz and Orson Welles. Photographed by Gregg Toland. Art Direction by Van Nest Polglase and Perry Ferguson. Décors by Darrell Silvera. Gowns by Edward Stevenson. Special Effects by Vernon L. Walker. Sound Recording by Bailey Fesler and James G. Stewart. Music by Bernard Herrmann. Edited by Robert Wise and Mark Robson (uncredited). Cast: Orson Welles as Charles Foster Kane, Dorothy Comingore as Susan Alexander Kane, Joseph Cotten as Jedediah Leland, Everett Sloane as Mr. Bernstein, George Coulouris as Walter Parks Thatcher, Ray Collins as James W. Gettys, Ruth Warrick as Emily Norton Kane, Erskine Sanford as Carter, William Alland as Thompson and the Newsreel Narrator (uncredited), Agnes Moorehead as Mrs. Kane, Richard Baer as Hillman, Paul Stewart as Raymond, Fortunio Bonanova as Matiste, Joan Blair as Georgia, Buddy Swann as Kane at eight, Harry Shannon as Kane Sr., Sonny Bupp as Kane III, with Charles Bennett, Edith Evanson, Richard Wilson, Georgia Backus, Alan Ladd (bits). 119 minutes.

THE MAGNIFICENT AMBERSONS. RKO-Radio Pictures, 1942. Screenplay by Orson Welles, based upon the novel by Booth Tarkington. Photographed by Stanley Cortez (and Harry J. Wild and Russell Metty, uncredited). Additional scenes directed by committee and/or Robert Wise (uncredited). Art Direction by Mark-Lee Kirk. Gowns by Edward Stevenson. Special Effects by Vernon L. Walker. Sound Recording by Bailey Fesler and James G. Stewart. Music by Bernard Herrmann (and Roy Webb — uncredited). Edited by Robert Wise and Mark Robson. Cast: Joseph Cotten as Eugene Morgan, Dolores Costello as Isabel, Anne Baxter as Lucy, Tim Holt as George Minafer, Agnes Moorehead as Fanny, Ray Collins as Jack, Richard Bennett as Major Amberson, Erskine Sanford as Benson, J. Louis Johnson as Sam, Don Dillaway as Wilbur Minafer, Charles Phipps as Uncle John. Georgia Backus and Gus Schilling (bits). About 53 minutes of cut material has apparently vanished in the complex disposition of RKO's assets (see Appendix I). The original running time was 131 minutes; the present version is only 88 minutes.

JOURNEY INTO FEAR. RKO-Radio Pictures, 1942-1943 (1943 version with narration added and last reel recut). Directed by Norman Foster and Orson Welles (uncredited). Screenplay by Joseph Cotten. Photographed by Karl Struss. Art Direction by Albert S. D'Agostino and Mark-Lee Kirk. Set Decorations by Darrell Silvera and Ross Dowd. Gowns by Edward Stevenson. Special Effects by Vernon L. Walker. Sound Recording by Bailey Fesler and James G. Stewart. Music by Roy Webb. Edited by Mark Robson. Cast: Joseph Cotten as Howard Graham, Dolores del Rio as Josette Martel, Ruth Warrick as Stephanie Graham, Agnes Moorehead as Mrs. Mathis (pronounced Matthews in parts of the film), Jack Durant as Gobo, Everett Sloane as Kopeikin (pronounced Kopenkin in parts of the film), Eustace Wyatt as Dr. Haller, Frank Readick as Mathis (or Matthews), Edgar Barrier as Kuvetli, Jack Moss as Peter Banat, Stefan Schnabel as The Purser, Hans Conreid as The Magician at Le Jockey, Richard Bennett as The Captain, Shifra Haran as Mrs. Haller. Robert Meltzer, Herbert Drake, and Bill Roberts (bits). 82 minutes.

THE STRANGER. International Production for RKO release, 1946. Produced by Sam Spiegel. Screenplay by Anthony Veiller (pseudonym of Anthony Veiller and John Huston), with Orson Welles (uncredited). Based on an original story by Victor Trivas. Photographed by

Russell Metty. Art Direction by Perry Ferguson. Gowns by Michael Woulfe. Assistant Director, Jack Voglin. Music by Bronislaw (later Bronislau) Kaper. Edited by Ernest Nims. Cast: Orson Welles as Franz Kindler/Charles Rankin, Loretta Young as Mary Longstreet Rankin, Philip Merivale as Judge Longstreet, Edward G. Robinson as Wilson, Byron Keith as Dr. Lawrence, Richard Long as Noah Longstreet, Billy House as Potter, Martha Wentworth as Sarah, Konstantin Shayne as Konrad Meinike, Theodore Gottlieb as Farbright, Pietro Sosso as Mr. Peabody. 95 minutes.

THE LADY FROM SHANGHAI. Columbia Pictures, 1947. Screenplay by Orson Welles, based on the Inner Sanctum mystery, *If I Die Before I Wake*, by (Raymond) Sherwood King. Associate Producers, Richard Wilson and William Castle. Photographed by Charles Lawton, Jr. Art Direction by Stephen Goosson and Sturges Carne. Set Decorations by Wilbur Menefee and Herman Schoenbrun. Gowns by Jean Louis. Assistant Director, Sam Nelson. Sound Recording by Lodge Cunningham. Song, "Please Don't Kiss Me," by Allan Roberts and Doris Fisher. Music by Heinz Roemheld. Special Effects for the mirror maze (uncredited) by Lawrence Butler. Edited by Viola Lawrence. Cast: Rita Hayworth as Elsa Bannister, Orson Welles as Michael O'Hara, Everett Sloane as Arthur Bannister, Glenn Anders as George Grisby, Ted De Corsia as Sidney Broome, Erskine Sanford as The Judge, Gus Schilling as Goldie, Carl Frank as The District Attorney, Louis Merrill as Jake, Evelyn Ellis as Bessie, Harry Shannon as The Cab Driver, Wong Show Ching as Li, Sam Nelson as The Yacht Captain. Richard Wilson appeared as an assistant to the District Attorney. 86 minutes.

MACBETH. Charles K. Feldman for Republic Pictures, 1948. A Mercury Production. From the play by William Shakespeare. Associate Producer, Richard Wilson. Photographed by John L. Russell. Art Direction by Fred Ritter. Set Decorations by John McCarthy, Jr., and James Redd. Gowns by Adele Palmer. Men's Costumes by Orson Welles. Dialogue Director, William Alland. Assistant Director, Jack Lacey. Sound Recording by John Stransky, Jr., and Garry Harris. Music by Jacques Ibert, Conducted by Efrem Kurtz. Special Effects by Howard and Theodore Lydecker. Make-up by Bob Mark. Edited by Louis Lindsay. Cast: Orson Welles as Macbeth, Jeanette Nolan as Lady Macbeth, Dan O'Herlihy as Macduff, Roddy McDowall as Malcolm, Edgar Barrier as Banquo, Alan Napier as A Holy Father, Erskine Sanford as Duncan, John Dierkes as Ross, Kenne Curtis as Lennox, Peggy Webber as Lady Macduff, Lionel Braham as Siward, Archie Heugly as Young Siward, Jerry Farber as Fleance, Christopher Welles as Macduff child, Morgan Farley as Doctor, Lurene Tuttle as Gentlewoman, Brainerd Duffield as The First Murderer, William Alland as The Second Murderer, George Chirello as Seyton, Gus Schilling as Porter, Brainerd Duffield and two Goldwyn girls as The Three Witches, voices dubbed by Peggy Webber, Lurene Tuttle, and Mr. Duffield. 86 minutes.

OTHELLO. Mercury Films, 1952. Photographed by Anchise Brizzi, George Fanto, and Troini Fusi. Art Direction by Alexandre Trauner. Gowns by Maria de Mateis. Music by Francesco Lavagnino and Alberto Barberis. Assistant Director Michael Washinsky. Edited by Jean Sacha and John Shepridge. Cast: Orson Welles as Othello, Suzanne Cloutier as Desdemona, Micheál MacLiammoir as Iago, Robert Coote as Roderigo, Hilton Edwards as Brabantio, Fay Compton as Emilia, Nicholas Bruce as Ludovico, Doris Dowling as Bianca, Joan Davis as Montana, Michael Laurence as Cassio. 91 minutes.

MR ARKADIN or CONFIDENTIAL REPORT. Filmorsa, 1955. Produced by Louis Dolivet. Distributed by Warner Brothers. Photographed by Jean Bourgoin. Art Direction by Orson Welles. Costumes by Orson Welles. Music by Paul Misraki. Assistant Directors, José Mario Ocha, De la Serna, Ferri. Sound Recording by Jacques Lebreton and Jacques Carrere. Edited by Renzo Lucidi. Cast: Orson Welles as Gregori Arkadin, Paola Mori as Raina, Robert Arden as Guy Van Stratten, Michael

Redgrave as Bergomil Trebitsch, Patricia Medina as Mily, Akim Tamiroff as Jacob Zouk, Mischa Auer as The Professor, Katina Paxinou as Sophie, Jack Watling as The Marquis of Rutleigh, Grégoire Aslan as Bracco, Peter Van Eyck as Thadeus, Suzanne Flon as The Baroness Nagel, O'Brady as Oskar, Tamara Shane as The Blonde. 99 minutes.

TOUCH OF EVIL. Universal Pictures, 1957. Produced by Alfred Zugsmith. Script by Orson Welles, based upon the novel *Badge of Evil*, by Whit Masterson. Photographed by Russell Metty. Art Direction by Alexander Golitzen and Robert Clatworthy. Gowns by Bill Thomas. Assistant Directors, Phil Bowles and Terry Nelson. Music by Henry Mancini. Sound Recording by Leslie I. Carey and Frank Wilkinson. Edited by Virgil W. Vogel and Aaron Stell. Additional scenes directed by Harry Keller (uncredited). Cast: Charlton Heston as Mike Vargas, Janet Leigh as Susan Vargas, Orson Welles as Hank Quinlan, Joseph Calleia as Pete Menzies, Akim Tamiroff as "Uncle" Joe Grandi, Joanna Moore as Marcia Linnekar, Ray Collins as Adair, Dennis Weaver as The Motel Manager, Victor Millan as Manelo Sanchez, Lalo Rios as Risto, Michael Sargent as The Boy, Marlene Dietrich as Tanya. Zsa Zsa Gabor, Keenan Wynn, Mercedes McCambridge, and Joseph Cotten (bits). 93 minutes.

THE TRIAL (or LE PROCES). A Mercury Production by Orson Welles, for Paris/Europa, FI-C-IT and HISA-Films, 1962. Script by Orson Welles, based upon the novel by Franz Kafka. Produced by Alexander and Michael Salkind. Photographed by Edmond Richard. Art Direction, Jean Mandaroux. Costumes by Helene Tri-bault. Sound by Julien Coutellier and Guy Villette. Music by Jean Ledrut. Edited by Yvonne Martin, Denise Baby, and Fritz Mueller. Pin-Screen by Alexander Alexeieff, Claire Parker. Cast: Anthony Perkins as Joseph K., Jeanne Moreau as Fraulein Bürstner, Madeleine Robinson as Mme Grubach, Elsa Martinelli as Hilda, Romy Schneider as Leni, Suzanne Flon as Miss Pitti, Orson Welles as The Advocate, Arnoldo Foa as The Inspector, Fernand Ledoux as Clerk of the Court, Maurice Teynac as The Assistant Bank Director, Billy Kearns as a Police Officer, Thomas Holtzman as The Student, Paola Mori as The Woman, Naydra Shore as Ermie, Max Haufler as Uncle Max, Michael Lonsdale as The Priest. 120 minutes.

CHIMES AT MIDNIGHT. International Films Espanola, 1965-66. Screenplay by Orson Welles, Adapted from *Richard II, Henry IV,* Parts I and II, Henry V, and *The Merry Wives of Windsor.* Photographed by Edmond Richard. Art Direction by José Antonio de la Guerra and Mariano Erdorza. Sound Recording by Peter Parasheles. Music by Francesco Lavagnino, Directed by Carlo Franci. Edited by Fritz Mueller. Cast: Orson Welles as Falstaff, John Gielgud as King Henry IV, Margaret Rutherford as Mistress Quickly, Jeanne Moreau as Doll Tearsheet, Norman Rodway as Henry Percy, Marina Vlady as Kate Percy, Alan Webb as Justice Shallow, Tony Beckley as Poins, Fernando Rey as Worcester, Walter Chiari as Silence, Michael Aldridge as Pistol, Beatrice Welles as The Child, Andrew Faulds as Westmoreland, José Nieto as Northumberland, with Jeremy Rowe, Paddy Bedford, Julio Pena, Fernando Hilbert, Andres Mejuto, Keith Pyott, Charles Farrell (bits). 92 minutes.

TELEVISION FILMS

THE FOUNTAIN OF YOUTH. Pilot for ABC, 1958; shown on Colgate Half Hour, September 1958. Produced, Directed, Written by Orson Welles, from the story "Youth from Vienna," by John Collier. Photographed by Sid Hickox. Production Management by Argyle Nelson. Art Direction by Claudio Guzman. Editorial Supervision by Dan Cowan. Edited by Bud Molin. Assistant Director, Marvin Stuart. Music Supervision by Julian Davidson. Musical Arrangements by Orson Welles. Re-recording Editor/Supervisor, Robert Reeve. Cast: Dan Tobin as Humphrey Baxter, Joi Lansing as Caroline Coates, Rick Jason as Alan Brodie, Marjorie Bennett as The Columnist, Billy House as Morgan, with Nancy Culp (bit role). 30 minutes.

HISTOIRE IMMORTELLE (THE IMMORTAL STORY). ORTF—Albina Films, 1968. Distributed by Omnia. Produced, Directed, and Adapted by Orson Welles, from the novella by Isak Dinesen. Photographed by Willy Kurant. Assistant Cameramen: Jean Orjollet, Jacques Assuerds. Edited by Yolande Maurette, Marcelle Pluet, Françoise Garnault, Claude Farney. Assistant Directors: Olivier Gerard, Tony Fuentes, Patrice Turok. Production Manager: Marc Moret. Miss Moreau's Wardrobe by Pierre Cardin. Music by Erik Satie, Performed by Aldo Ciccolini and Jean-Jol Barbier. Cast: Jeanne Moreau as Virginie, Orson Welles as Mr. Clay, Roger Coggio as The Clerk, Norman Eshley as Paul. 58 minutes.

UNFINISHED FILMS

IT'S ALL TRUE, RKO 1941-1942

THE STORY OF JAZZ. Color tests shot with various jazz bands. Screenplay by Elliot Paul and David Stuart. Based on Louis Armstrong's life story.

MY FRIEND BONITO. Produced by Orson Welles. Directed by Norman Foster. Screenplay by Norman Foster and John Fante. Photographed by Al Gilks and Floyd Crosby. Assistant Cameraman: Harold Wellman. Additional Cameraman: Alex Phillips. One reel edited by Joe Noriega. Nine reels of takes, including one brief cut sequence of picadors, in the possession of Paramount as of May 1969. Cast: Domingo Soler as Don Luis, Jesùs Vasquez ("Hamlett") as Chico.

THE STORY OF SAMBA, THE SAMBA STORY, or CARNIVAL. Produced and Directed by Orson Welles. Screenplay by Orson Welles (improvised on location —treatment in the possession of Richard Wilson). Photographed by W. Howard Greene, Harry J. Wild, Eddie Pyle, and Joseph Biroc. Additional Camerawork by Harold Wellman and Alex Phillips. Music (not recorded) by Paul Misraki. Partly Edited by Joseph Noriega. Cast: Grande Otelo (Sebastiâo Prata) and the people of Rio.

JANGADEIROS. Produced and Directed by Orson Welles. Screenplay by Orson Welles (improvised on location). Photographed by W. Howard Greene, Harry J. Wild, Eddie Pyle, and Joseph Biroc. Additional Camerawork by S. Harold Wellman and Alex Phillips. Sequences at Fortaleza Photographed by George Fanto. Partly Edited by Joseph Noriega. Cast: José Olimpio Meira ("Jacaré") and the members of the Jangadeiros raft expedition, with the people of Rio and Fortaleza.

DON QUIXOTE. Produced, Directed, and Adapted by Orson Welles. Photographed by Jack Draper. From the novel by Cervantes. Cast: Francisco Rieguera as Don Quixote, Akim Tamiroff as Sancho Panza. Unfinished as of May 1970.

DEAD RECKONING. Produced and Directed by Orson Welles. With Orson Welles, Jeanne Moreau, and Laurence Harvey. A multimillionaire and his wife (Welles and Moreau) are alone on a yacht at sea; a psychotic, the only survivor of a liner holocaust (Harvey) climbs aboard. Like *Knife in the Water,* the film explores the tensions among the three. At the time of writing, no further credits are available. The title has reportedly been changed to *The Deep*.

Welles is currently shooting *The Other Side of the Wind,* a film about a temperamental director, with a cast headed by Robert Aitken, Marlene Dietrich, Paul Mazursky, and Curtis Harrington. Personally financed; locations in Los Angeles, Utah, Arizona, and Europe.

NOTE: Welles also shot filmed sequences for stage productions including *The Green Goddess, The Unthinking Lobster, Around the World,* and the aforementioned *Too Much Johnson.*

Another unknown Welles film has come to light at press time. Costarring Virginia Nicholson, *The Hearts of Age* was shot at Todd School, apparently in 1934. Lasting about a reel, it shows grotesque figures in masks (representing extreme old age) capering about Todd buildings; these were all pupils, some of them disguised as women. The images are intercut with death knells tolling, thin white hands crawling around a gravestone, a glass ball (precursor of the Kane crystal ball) revolving, and skulls decaying. Strongly influenced by Jean Epstein, and *Nosferatu,* with a climax of Welles in mask distorted with a combination of humor and anger banging furiously at a piano as the images of time and loss crumble about him, it is typical in its combination of facetiousness, prankish high spirits, and an obsessive fascination with images of mortality — half-humorously, half-sinisterly observing bones, withering fingers, and consuming flames. (I am grateful to the American Film Institute, David Shepard, and David Bradley for arranging a screening of this film.)

Welles is also said to have returned to Todd after making *Citizen Kane,* and supervised or aided a Todd production, on film, of *Twelfth Night.* In 1967 he made a three-minute silent film in San Francisco, involving an encounter between a director and two men on the Bay Bridge. Welles is also known to have made numerous home movies on 16mm over the years.

SELECT BIBLIOGRAPHY

Note: The most exhaustive interview with Welles to date was written by Juan Cobos, Miguel Rubio, and José Antonio Pruneda; it appeared in *Cahiers du Cinéma,* April 1965, and was reprinted (marred by some gross misprints) in *Cahiers du Cinéma in English,* No. 5, 1966. Most other interviews contain unreliable material and have been omitted.

Bazin, André. *Orson Welles* (Preface by Jean Cocteau). Paris: Editions Chavanne, 1950.

Bentley, Eric. Othello on Film. *New Republic,* October 3, 1955.

Beranger, Jean. Citizen Welles. *Kosmorama,* October-December 1962.

Bessy, Maurice. *Orson Welles.* Paris: Editions Seghers, 1963.

Billard, Pierre. Chimes at Midnight. *Sight and Sound,* Spring 1965.

Biographical articles. *Current Biography,* 1941, 1965.

Bourgeois, Jacques, and Doniol-Valcroze, Jacques. Orson Welles Enchainé. *La Révue de Cinéma,* Autumn 1947.

Castello, G. C. The Magnificent Orson W. *Bianco e Nero,* January 1949.

Cocteau, Jean. Profile of Welles. *Cinémonde,* March 1960.

Cowie, Peter. Orson Welles. *Films and Filming,* April 1961.

Cutts, John. Citizen Kane. *Films and Filming,* December 1963.

Drake, Herbert. Citizen (Orson Welles) Kane. *California Arts and Architecture,* July 1941.

Downer, A. S. Orson and the Carpenters. *Sewanee Review,* January 1944.

Fowler, Roy. *Orson Welles: A First Biography.* London: Pendulum Publications, 1946.

Giametteo, Fernaldo de. Macbeth. *Bianco e Nero,* July 1948.

Grigs, Derick. Conversation at Oxford. *Sight and Sound,* Spring 1960.

Johnson, William. Of Time and Loss. *Film Quarterly,* Fall 1967.

Kael, Pauline. "Raising Kane," in *The Citizen Kane Book* [includes script]. Boston: Atlantic, Little Brown, 1970 (in press).

Kurnitz, Harry. Antic Arts. *Holiday,* January 1956.

Lean, Tangye. Citizen Kane. *Horizon,* November 1941.

MacLiammoir, Micheál. Welles. *Sight and Sound,* Summer 1952.

Morgenstern, J., and Sokolov, R. Falstaff as Orson Welles. *Newsweek,* March 27, 1967.

Noble, Peter. *The Fabulous Orson Welles.* London: Hutchinson, 1956.

Pechter, William S. Trials. *Sight and Sound,* Winter 1963/1964.

Sarris, Andrew. Citizen Kane: The American Baroque. *Film Culture,* 1956.

Sartre, Jean-Paul. Citizen Kane. *L'Ecran Français,* August 1945.

Toland, Gregg. Motion Picture Cameraman. *Theatre Arts*, September 1941.

Truffaut, Francois. Citizen Kane. *L'Express,* November 26, 1959.

[Whitebait, William?] Winged Gorilla. *New Statesman and Nation,* January 21, 1956.

Files of *The New York Times, The New York Herald Tribune, The New Republic, The Nation, Commonweal, Film Quarterly, The American Cinematographer, Life, Time, Newsweek, Theatre Arts, The Sydney Morning Herald* (on *Othello*).

INDEX

A

Abe Lincoln in Illinois, 15
Acoma, the Sky City, 84
Alexander, Ben, 48
Alexeieff, Alexandre, 162
Alland, William, 18
Alstock, Francis, 93
Ambler, Eric, 167; *Journey into Fear,* 72, 74, 75
American, 10. See also *Citizen Kane*
Anders, Glenn, 111, 114
Antonioni, Michelangelo, 161, 185
Archer, Eugene, quoted 159
Arden, Robert, 145
Armstrong, Louis, 84
Arnaz, Desi, 178
Around the World in 80 Days, 136
Atlas Corporation, 92
Aubry, Cecile, 136
Auer, Mischa, 145, 148
Aural effects, 1, 3-4. *See also* sound tracks under individual films

B

Ball, Lucille, 10, 178
Bankhead, Tallulah, 127
Barnes, George, 11
Barrett, Charles, 15
Barrier, Edgar: in *Too Much Johnson,* 7-8; in *Journey into Fear,* 75, 79, 83; in *Macbeth,* 134
Baxter, Keith, 170
Benedek, Laszlo, 178
Bergman, Ingrid, 11
Bernstein, Maurice, 5
Bitzer, Billy, 12
Black Cat, The, 48
Black Rose, The, 136
Blair, Betsy, 136
Blake, Nicholas (C. Day Lewis), *The Smiler with the Knife,* 10
Blitzstein, Marc, 7; *The Cradle Will Rock,* 6
Boettiger, John, 24n

B (continued)

Bonito, the Bull, 84. See also *My Friend Bonito*
Bradley, David, 194, 202
Brave One, The, 94
Breen, Joseph I., 48, 91-92
Brisbane, Arthur, 22, 23
Brook, Peter, 145
Brooks, Louise, 114
Brulatour, Jules, 18
Butler, Lawrence, 112

C

Calhoun, Alice, 48
Calleia, Joseph, 154
Camerawork, 1, 3-4, 9, 10, 11. *See also* individual films
Cameron, Shirley, 169
Capra, Frank, 11, 39
Captain's Chair, The, 84
Carnet de Bal, 84
Carnival. See *It's All True; Samba Story, The*
Caught, 21n
Castle, William, 111
Carnival in Rio, 94
Chaplin, Charles, 18, 20, 85
Chappell, William, quoted, 159
Characterization, 2-3, 189, 191-193; in *Lady from Shanghai,* 2-3, 114-115; in *Touch of Evil,* 3, 153-155; in *Citizen Kane,* 18, 45-46; in *The Magnificent Ambersons,* 57; in *Journey into Fear,* 75; in *The Stranger,* 108-110; in *Macbeth,* 133-134; in *Othello,* 138; in *Mr. Arkadin,* 145, 148; in *The Trial,* 161, 163, 165-166; in *Chimes at Midnight,* 170; in *Fountain of Youth,* 179; in *Immortal Story,* 183, 185. *See also* Grotesque
Chicago Opera Company, 6
Chimes at Midnight: evaluation, 1, 125, 135, 177; themes, 2, 170; camerawork and editing, 43, 168-169; sound track, 169, 173; screen-

C (continued)

play, 169, outlined, 170-177; imagery, 170; use of Holingshed, 170, 175; filmography, 200
Churchill, Douglas, 18
Citizen Kane, 6, 54, 85, 100, 115, 127, 156, 189; evaluation, 1, 45-47, 191; themes, 2, 4, 46-47, 48, 125, 191-192, 193; camerawork and editing, 3, 11-13, 17, described, 34-45; screenplay, 10-11, 17, 21-24, 190, outlined, 24-34; sets, 13-14, 46; newsreel, 14-15, 17; sound track, 14-17, 169 *(see also* Herrmann); cast and characterization, 18, 45-46; Hearst controversy over, 18-20, 21-24; reception, 20-21, 72; filmography, 198
Clair, René, 11
Cloutier, Suzanne, 136, 140, 142
Cohn, Harry, 111, 112, 113
Colbert, Claudette, 100
Collier, John, "Youth from Vienna," 178
Collins, Anthony, 14, 15
Collins, Ray, 9, 17, 57
Comingore, Dorothy, 17, 18, 46
Compton, Fay, 138
Confidential Report. See *Mr. Arkadin*
Conrad, Joseph, *Heart of Darkness,* 9
Conreid, Hans, 82
Coote, Robert, 140
Co-ordinator of Inter-American Affairs (CIAA), 85, 93, 94. *See also* Rockefeller, Nelson
Corbos, Juan, 165n
Cornell, Katharine, 6
Cortez, Stanley, camerawork on *The Magnificent Ambersons,* 3, 48-52, 54-56, 62, 64, 67, 68, 189, 192
Costello, Dolores, 57
Cotten, Joseph, 6, 145, 190; in *Too Much Johnson,* 7-8; in *Citizen Kane,* 18; in *The Magnificent Ambersons,* 52, 53, 56, 57, 66; in *Journey into Fear,* 72, 74, 75, 77; in *Touch of Evil,* 155